D0097788

Makers, Users, and Masters

ARTHUR F. BENTLEY
1870–1957

Makers, Users, and Masters

Arthur F. Bentley

EDITED WITH AN INTRODUCTION
BY SIDNEY RATNER

Assisted by Peter Asch

SYRACUSE UNIVERSITY PRESS

Copyright © 1969 by Syracuse University Press

Syracuse, New York

All Rights Reserved

FIRST EDITION

Library of Congress card catalog number: 69-12458

Manufactured in the United States of America

330.973
B47

Baker + Taylor

7.88

10 Feb 70

To
WALT WHITMAN
The Livest American

34254

ARTHUR F. BENTLEY, Ph.D., 1870–1957. Author, *The Process of Government; Relativity in Man and Society; Linguistic Analysis of Mathematics; Behavior, Knowledge, Fact; Inquiry Into Inquiries: Essays in Social Theory;* with John Dewey, *Knowing and the Known.*

SIDNEY RATNER, Ph.D., Professor of History, Rutgers University. Author, *Taxation and Democracy in America;* editor, *Inquiry Into Inquiries: Essays in Social Theory;* co-editor, John Dewey and Arthur F. Bentley, *A Philosophical Correspondence, 1932–1951.*

Editor's Foreword

The publication of this book grew out of my interest in the writings of Arthur F. Bentley, dating back some forty years, and from a personal association with Bentley which began in 1939–40. The friendship that gradually developed between Bentley and myself in the 1940's and 1950's inspired me to study his life and works in relation to the wider American intellectual scene and then to edit and write introductions to a volume of his essays, *Inquiry Into Inquiries* (1954) and (with Jules Altman and James Wheeler) John Dewey's and Bentley's, *A Philosophical Correspondence, 1932–1951* (1964).

In 1949 Bentley told me about his unpublished full-length book, entitled *Makers, Users, and Masters;* five years later I read this manuscript and suggested to Bentley that this book deserved publication. He gave me permission to edit it with such modifications as I deemed proper. But other obligations intervened until the spring of 1966 when I lectured at Syracuse University on Bentley's life work, with special emphasis on *Makers, Users, and Masters,* in a seminar directed by Professor Bertram Gross. He suggested that I edit Bentley's manuscript and proposed the Syracuse University Press as the publisher.

Mrs. Arthur F. Bentley kindly gave me her permission to edit the manuscript and to arrange for its publication. The Arthur F. Bentley Publication Fund, established by Mrs. Bentley, underwrote the costs of editorial assistance, typing, and photoduplication. Dr. Peter Asch, Assistant Professor of Economics at Rutgers University and a specialist in the economics of antitrust, verified Bentley's citations of primary sources and secondary authorities. But I alone am responsible for editorial decisions on additions to and deletions from the text. I am indebted to him for his scholarly help and critical suggestions. Mrs. Carolyn Kappes typed with great skill the corrected and emended manuscript of this book. The librarians at the Indiana University Library Manuscript Division, Rutgers University, Princeton University, and the New York Public Library have been most kind and cooperative.

Few changes have been made in the major part of Bentley's text except to correct some minor errors in spelling, grammar, and punctuation. Some very long paragraphs have been broken up, and some very short paragraphs have been merged into larger units. A mass of statistical material, useful to readers in the early 1920's, has been discarded, but the high points of the statistical analyses have been retained in the text, and references have been given to relevant statistical sources. Two of Bentley's chapters in their original form have been omitted because they seemed to offer excessive detailed evidence on one industry that is not as central to most people's concerns today as it was in 1920. The highlights of a compact government report on the meat-packing industry, however, have been substituted in Chapter VIII for Bentley's fifty-page discussion, and a one-page editorial précis of Bentley's views on collusion, advertising, and profiteering in the meat-packing industry is given in Chapter IX in place of his original extensive treatment of the subject.

Where I found it necessary to change parts of Bentley's text, square brackets are used to indicate the editorial substitutions. Editorial ellipses indicate the places where material has been omitted. Bentley's endnotes are numbered consecutively in each chapter. The editor's footnotes are indicated by various typographical signs, and in certain cases the editor has inserted relevant material that has become available since Dr. Bentley finished this manuscript. The titles and numbers of the chapters are Bentley's. No bibliography has been compiled for this volume, as it was Bentley's practice to give all bibliographical data in the footnotes. Miss Roberta Blaché deserves credit for the fine index.

Rutgers University
July 8, 1968   S.R.

Editor's Introduction

If a scholar can achieve distinction in one field during his life-time, he is fortunate; Arthur F. Bentley won recognition as an originative thinker in four areas: political science, sociology, psychology, and the theory of scientific inquiry. Now the publication of *Makers, Users, and Masters* adds another dimension to his career, and another area of accomplishment: welfare economics and political reform.

During the first six decades of his life Bentley failed to get the widespread academic recognition he merited. Until the mid-1930's, he endured a neglect comparable to that suffered by C. S. Peirce in philosophy and Thorstein Veblen in economics. In 1957 distin-guished figures in diverse fields, among them P. W. Bridgman in physics, Adelbert Ames, Jr. in psychology, and Sidney Hook in philosophy, paid Bentley tribute in an impressive volume entitled *Life, Language, Law.*[1] A decade later Syracuse University honored Bentley's work by sponsoring a Bentley Seminar in which eleven eminent scholars evaluated the domestic and foreign aspects of President Johnson's Great Society program.[2]

Arthur F. Bentley was born in Freeport, Illinois, October 16, 1870, the son of Charles Frederick and Angeline Alice (Fisher) Bentley. His father was a man of unusual candor and intellectual ability. Arthur Bentley obtained his early education in the public schools of Freeport, Illinois, and Grand Island, Nebraska. After studying briefly at York College in Nebraska and at the University

[1] Richard W. Taylor, ed. (Yellow Springs, Ohio: Antioch Press, 1957).
[2] Bertram Gross, ed., *A Great Society?* (New York: Basic Books, 1968).

of Denver, he withdrew to work for some three years in his father's bank. In 1890, at the age of twenty, he entered Johns Hopkins University in order to pursue as his main interest the economics of labor and social welfare as expounded by Richard Ely. After two years Bentley was awarded an A.B. with high honors. Although Ely left for Wisconsin after Bentley's first year, two noted economists, John Bates Clark, then at Smith College, and Simon Nelson Patten of the University of Pennsylvania came down to lecture at Hopkins and undoubtedly made some impact on Bentley. He demonstrated his ability to do original research in a scholarly essay, "The Condition of the Western Farmer as Illustrated by the History of a Western Nebraska Town." This appeared in 1893 in the *Johns Hopkins University Studies in Historical and Political Science* and is still cited for its incisive, objective analysis.

The next three years he devoted to graduate work in economics and sociology: two at Hopkins and one at the Universities of Berlin and Freiburg im Breisgau. At Berlin he gained some insights from Adolf Wagner and Gustav Schmoller on the desirability of social and economic reform through governmental legislation. Georg Simmel stimulated Bentley to analyze on his own the complex interactions of individuals and social groups. At Hopkins Bentley explored with J. B. Clark and others a wide range of subjects ranging from the economics of competition and monopoly to the history of economic thought. In June, 1895 Bentley received his Ph.D. degree for a thesis called "The Units of Investigation in the Social Sciences," which was published in *The Annals of the American Academy of Political and Social Science* in May, 1895.

During the academic year 1895–96, he taught sociology as a lecturer at the University of Chicago, where he came to know John Dewey, with whom he later worked as a collaborator. But Bentley decided that his gifts were not in college teaching, and he spent the next fourteen years in the newspaper world, first as a reporter, later as an editorial writer for the *Chicago Times-Herald* and *Record-Herald*.

As a newspaper man in Chicago, Bentley encountered the hard facts of life as revealed in the economic, political, and social activities of that turbulent industrial and transportation center with all its contrasts in wealth and poverty, virtue and iniquity. During the years 1896 to 1908 he did the research, thinking and writing that resulted in the publication of his first great work, *The Process of Government*.[3] In this classic work Bentley laid a firm basis for the whole development of the study of "pressure groups" or "group pressures" that has flourished in America from 1908 to the present. But Bentley's own approach was more subtle than that of Charles Beard, whose *An Economic Interpretation of the Constitution of the United States* (1913) became the model for many political scientists during the next few decades. After a thirty-year period of being unappreciated, however, Bentley was able to witness an upsurge of intense appreciation of *The Process of Government*. From the late 1930's on, some of the most perceptive political scientists, e.g., Bertram Gross, Charles Hagan, Earl Latham, and David Truman, began to rediscover and apply Bentley's insights. Bentley's unusual combination of tough-mindedness and open-mindedness enabled him to be the most devastating political realist of his time and yet to escape the limitations and dogmatism of a Beard, on the one hand, or of a Pareto, on the other. Bentley's candor in pointing out the ways in which all forms of government, including the despotic, respond to the pressures of different social groups and hence in some degree are representative of the "lower orders" over which the "elite" groups rule, exposed him to the charge of being an extreme relativist and one who might condone various forms of dictatorship or absolutism. These critics, e.g., Robert MacIver, missed the unique position that Bentley upheld in American political science. He insisted on portraying the "whole truth" about political behavior, yet he joined to this unflinching realism a genuine idealism and concern for improving the welfare of all exploited or underprivileged groups. In *The Process of Government* Bentley chose deliberately not to advance any reform program of his own. Instead he regarded this book as an attempt to fashion a tool for viewing political phenomena from the perspective of objective sociological method.

Three years after the publication of *The Process of Government*,

---

[3] Chicago: University of Chicago Press, 1908. The latest reprint is edited by Peter H. Odegard (Cambridge, Mass.: Belknap Press of Harvard University Press, 1967).

Bentley decided to quit Chicago and the newspaper world for a rural retreat in Paoli, Indiana, to manage his private business affairs, including the running of an apple orchard for many years, and to put his major energies into his scientific researches and writing. During World War I he helped to organize the State of Indiana for the American Red Cross. With the return of peace, Bentley became greatly interested in the cooperative work of the Non-Partisan League in North Dakota and made an intensive investigation of their activity. Then he wrote a book on the American business and political scene, entitled *Makers, Users, and Masters*. Unfortunately, the volume was turned down by several publishers, probably because it was too heavily statistical and technical for the general public, and not sufficiently focused on one subject to be a technical monograph for a professional economics audience.[4] The result was that Bentley allowed the manuscript to remain unpublished. The book, however, is valuable because it reveals Bentley's social philosophy and his reform program at this time.

During the early 1920's, Bentley concentrated on a reformulation of his ideas about a science of society. In 1926 he published *Relativity in Man and Society* which argued that sociologists should adopt Einstein's method of viewing space and time as dimensions or integral phases of the events they describe. They needed also to introduce their own observational position in space-time and society as an essential factor in their reports on social events.[5]

After 1926 Bentley devoted himself to working out the foundations for a philosophy of scientific inquiry. In 1932 Bentley published *Linguistic Analysis of Mathematics,*[6] a challenging study of the nature of meaning and postulate in mathematics and the other sciences. He tried to solve various problems in the philosophy of mathematics by clarifying the relations of "ordinary language" to mathematical signs and symbols. Three years later his views on

[4] Horace Liveright to A. F. Bentley, March 5, 1920, Bentley to Liveright, March 15, 1920; Liveright to Bentley, March 19, and March 29, 1920. Manuscript Division, Lilly Library, Indiana University, Bloomington, Indiana.

[5] New York: Putnam's, 1926. The latest reprint has an introduction by Sidney Ratner, New York: Octagon Books, 1968.

[6] Bloomington, Indiana: Principia Press, 1932.

the proper methods for studying human behavior were presented in a probing work, *Behavior, Knowledge, Fact*.[7] Bentley rejected the traditional dichotomies: mind and body, mind and object, man and society, the organism and its environment. He also stressed the need for constructing a relativistic "behavioral space-time" that social scientists could use in adequately describing or analyzing an entire social situation. These two philosophically iconoclastic volumes were appreciated only by a small group of readers, but among this choice number was John Dewey, who found these volumes helped to clarify his ideas on some important problems as he was completing his great work, *Logic: The Theory of Inquiry*.[8]

Dewey's interest in Bentley's later writings led to their collaborating in the writing of *Knowing and the Known*.[9] This volume was a notable exposition and extension of naturalism and pragmatism. One important innovation was their emphasis on the central importance of viewing persons and objects against the perspective of the transactions or processes of change and action within society and physical nature. This transactional approach was welcomed and applied by various research workers in biology, physics, political science, psychology, and sociology.

After the critical praise received by *Knowing and the Known*, Bentley settled down to round out his ideas on language, logic, and scientific inquiry. Five years later these essays and other papers of Bentley's were published in *Inquiry Into Inquiries*.[10] On May 21, 1957, at the age of 86, Bentley died at his home in Paoli, Indiana. Seven years later the Rutgers University Press published the philosophical dialogues of John Dewey and Arthur F. Bentley: *A Philosophical Correspondence 1932–51*.[11] This volume is notable for its keen analyses of major problems in the behavioral sciences and the philosophy of science, but is important also for revealing the human side of John Dewey, one of America's greatest philosophers, and Arthur Bentley, its greatest political theorist. The publication

7 Bloomington, Indiana: Principia Press, 1935.
8 New York: Holt, 1938.
9 Boston: Beacon Press, 1949.
10 Sidney Ratner, ed., Boston: Beacon Press, 1954.
11 Sidney Ratner and Jules Altman, eds., with James E. Wheeler, associate editor, New Brunswick, N.J.: Rutgers University Press, 1964.

in 1968 of the Syracuse University Seminar volume, *A Great Society?* and of the present volume, *Makers, Users, and Masters* testifies to the continuing vitality of Bentley's ideas.

In reading *Makers, Users, and Masters* today, one must remember that Bentley undertook the research for this book in 1918 and completed it by the spring of 1920. This was the time when Woodrow Wilson was trying to reconstruct Europe and to prevent future world wars through creating the League of Nations. War-weariness and disillusionment with Wilsonian idealism, coupled with Big Business fear of radicalism, socialism, and bolshevism, led to the Senate's rejection of the Versailles Peace Treaty and the League of Nations, to the persecution of radicals, and to the presidential election of Warren G. Harding. His victory over the Democratic and Socialist Party candidates, James M. Cox and Eugene V. Debs, ended the hope for either the postwar restoration of Wilson's "New Freedom" or the inauguration of a more radical program.[12]

Before Congress declared war on Germany in April, 1917, President Wilson had told close friends:

Every reform we have won will be lost if we go into this war. We have been making a fight on special privilege. . . . War means plutocracy. . . . for we shall be dependent upon steel, oil and financial magnates. They will run the nation.

Industry will be so demoralized, profiteering run rampant, . . . and prices will soar so high . . . it will require a generation to restore normal conditions.[13]

This statement of Wilson's turned out to be more pessimistic than the actual facts warranted. Although big business and high finance secured important positions in various executive war agencies, enough Wilsonian supporters, like William G. McAdoo, Bernard Baruch, and Herbert Hoover played key economic roles to minimize harm to the common man. Moreover, a larger volume of heavy income and corporate taxation was passed during World War I than in any previous period in American history. The result

[12] Sidney Ratner, *Taxation and Democracy in America* (New York: John Wiley, 1967), pp. 400–402.
[13] *Ibid.*, p. 369.

was that although a large new class of millionaires appeared by the end of the war, the degree of inequality in the distribution of the income throughout the United States was, perhaps, less than it had been before 1913.

Yet the increase in the cost of living undoubtedly created hardships for the working man, and the profiteering that went on during the war made big business and high finance unpopular with many. These facts aroused Bentley and other champions of the small businessman, the farmer, and the worker, and made them fear for the future of democracy. At the same time, Bentley was concerned about the repression of honest opposition to the war effort by the passage of the Espionage Act in June 1917 and the Sedition Act in May 1918. The harsh enforcement of these laws and persecution of radical economic opinion militated against the democratic ideals that Wilson had proclaimed during the war.[14]

Against this background, *Makers, Users and Masters* stands as a penetrating contemporary analysis of the power exerted by the captains of business and finance in America at the time of World War I. Bentley wrote with detailed knowledge comparable to that of established economists like Richard Ely and John R. Commons. At the same time Bentley shared the viewpoint of social critics like Louis Brandeis, Lincoln Steffens, Ida Tarbell, and Thorstein Veblen. Bentley's book warns the American people that they are facing a crisis created by the excessive claims of the business elite against the future national income.[15] Beside the democratic political government of the United States, he claims, there had evolved after the Civil War an autocratic industrial government based upon the closely concentrated holdings of a small group in industry, trade, and finance. In Chapter II, entitled "Wealth and Industry: Ownership and Control," Bentley gives a statistical analysis of the unequal distribution of wealth in land, industry, trade, transportation, communications, and banking. He also presents an original formulation of a national balance sheet as a summary statement of all the country's resources and liabilities. Here he was forty years ahead of his time.

[14] *Ibid.*, pp. 362–402.
[15] Cf., Alpheus T. Mason, *Brandeis and the Modern State* (Washington, D.C.:

Bentley's indictment of oligopoly and monopoly and the economic theory expounded in his book rest on the view that the reign of big business enterprise in the United States was due to a system of economic and political power that enabled the captains of business and finance to dominate the small businessmen, the farmers, and the workers. He accepted the right to private property as basic to the welfare of both the middle classes and the working class, but he objected to "appropriation," the ethically unjustified claim to property based on the power to obtain wealth or income without investment of either labor or capital. Examples of such appropriative power are the exercise of oligopoly or monopoly power by such trusts as Standard Oil or giant concerns like the United States Steel Corporation that got control of markets, not just through superior efficiency but through various corporate and financial devices for eliminating competitors outside the usual "rules of the game." One of the main evils he objected to was overcapitalization of corporations by fixing the value of the stocks far above the original cost of tangible property and of current improvements.[16] Here Bentley stands with Justice Brandeis and Thorstein Veblen as an opponent of the great trust builders and bank-promoters of giant corporations like Rockefeller and J. P. Morgan.

On the subject of profits and profiteering, Bentley differs from Veblen in accepting profits in its customary sense "as that part of the product which a man gets for special ability, skill, or luck in managing his enterprise . . . modified by a tendency to wipe it out by the free spread of knowledge and training, except as the profit-maker continually keeps ahead of the procession." He objects, however, not only to the wartime super-normal profits of big business, but the permanent peacetime opportunities for big business to make exceptionally high profits above the level that most small and medium-sized business enterprises approach, where the bigger enterprise wins this high profit not through the production of a product of exceptional quality or low price, such as the Ford Motor

National Home Library Foundation, 1936), pp. 190–202; James C. Bonbright, "Valuation," R. A. Seligman, ed., *Encyclopaedia of the Social Sciences,* Vol. 15 (New York: Macmillan, 1937), pp. 212–18.

[16] Fritz Machlup, *The Economics of Sellers' Competition* (Baltimore: Johns Hopkins Press, 1952), pp. 17–18, 347ff.

Company, but where the enterprise has oligopoly or monopoly power, such as the meat packers.[17]

Fundamental to Bentley's evaluation of the American economy in 1920 is the theory of waste he enunciated in Chapter VI, "Waste and Welfare." He regarded as waste the cost to the American people, primarily as consumers, of the products and services they might have obtained if they had used alternate methods of production and distribution than were prevalent under oligopoly and monopoly capitalism in 1920. Here Bentley anticipated Frank Knight's theory of "opportunity costs." Most of the wastes that Bentley found in the American economy came, in his judgment, from the "exploitative" activities of the giant business enterprises which were concerned about oligopoly or monopoly profits. Although we cannot go into a detailed discussion of the theoretical issues and factual evidence on the various questions that Bentley raises, we shall mention a few of the main social problems for which he urged reform.

Advertising, in Bentley's eyes as in Veblen's, was an outstanding waste of scarce resources. The money expended on advertising resulted, as he saw it, usually in profits to the advertiser at the expense of higher prices being charged the consumer, and in many, although not all cases, a smaller quantity of goods. This "waste" of advertising he associated also with the waste arising from "absurd multiplication of types" of products created purposely to entice the consuming public by packaging or styling variations. These devices Edward H. Chamberlin later called "product differentiation," as one form of substitution for price competition by firms engaged in what he designated as "monopolistic" competition. Bentley urged either the elimination of advertising or drastic reduction to purely objective informational statements, and the standardization of production that would result in a drastic cut in the number of closely similar products. These strictures of his on advertising and "excessive" duplication or variation of product types have been supported by other critics of capitalism from Thorstein Veblen to John K. Galbraith.

[17] Lewis H. Haney, "Profiteering," *Encyclopaedia Britannica*, 12th ed., Vol. XXXII (London-New York, 1922), pp. 166–67.

But many economists in the United States, at least, such as Edward Chamberlin and Fritz Machlup, regard advertising, when controlled against fraud and misrepresentation and excessive expenditures designed to prevent free entry into a field by new concerns, as performing a useful function in the market. They also consider product differentiation as satisfying, through variations in quality and styling, the wide range of consumer differences in taste, and hence as not falling automatically under the category of "waste." Some standardization, undoubtedly, is useful and conducive to conservation of scarce resources, but excessive standardization may bring about a reduction of production costs at the expense of the "sovereignty of the consumer." Therefore, each standardization case has to be judged on the specific evidence for the particular product under review.[18]

Among other types of wastes in the American economy that Bentley criticized were the paralleling of railroads and the duplication of factories, public-service plants, and stores. Here he anticipated the kind of analysis of allocation of resources that operations research and linear programming have developed in the past few decades, but he probably assumed that centralized planning would be able to create these facilities more efficiently than private enterprise. This central planning might possibly work out in certain cases, but the experiences of Soviet Russia and other planned economies have shown, since 1920, that there are wastes in centralized planning as well as in competitive private enterprise. I might also point out that large-scale firms, either of the oligopoly or monopoly type, have often in the past effected consolidation of competing plants and the elimination of the less efficient plants or other facilities. This practice proved beneficial to the consumer in those cases where reductions in costs were passed on in lower sale prices.

Sophisticated economists realize that Bentley's criteria of economic welfare cannot be based purely on objective economic criteria, independent of ethical notions about the desirability of the distribution of wealth and income. As Paul Samuelson recently

18 Edward H. Chamberlin, "Product Heterogeneity and Public Policy," *American Economic Review*, Vol. XL, No. 2 (May, 1950), pp. 85–92; Fritz Machlup, *The Political Economy of Monopoly* (Baltimore: Johns Hopkins Press, 1952), pp. 124–26, 158–77.

wrote, "Without norms, normative statements are impossible. At some point economics must introduce ethical welfare functions from outside of economics. This should dispel the notion that by a social welfare function is meant some one, unique, and privileged set of ends."[19]

One other factor that the reader of Bentley's critique of oligopoly and monopoly capitalism should keep in mind is that his standards of economic welfare are derived from a static competition model. If one shifts to economic dynamics and follows the teachings of Joseph A. Schumpeter and John K. Galbraith, then one may argue that the large-scale business enterprise accompanying oligopoly and monopoly have brought about increased efficiency through large-scale operations that would not otherwise be possible, and have led to the acquisition of the funds needed for expensive research and experimentation in technology. These have become the basis for innovations in business enterprise, and have led to economic progress in terms of increased per capita income. But this subject is a highly controversial area in which there are two opposing schools: on the one side, the University of Chicago School headed by Frank Knight, Milton Friedman and George Stigler, and on the other side, the Harvard and MIT School, led by Schumpeter, Chamberlin, Galbraith, and Samuelson. Despite extended logical analysis and empirical research, there are still differences that an honest scholar must say have not been resolved. Hence, it is possible for some economists and citizens to differ with Bentley's conclusions on these matters.[20]

Having laid down his criteria of economic welfare, Bentley proceeded to present detailed evidence on how exceptionally high gains in wealth and income had been obtained by giant firms and trusts such as Standard Oil and the United States Steel Corporation. With audacity and skill, the promoters and controllers of these huge business enterprises had seized strategic positions between the

[19] Paul Samuelson, *Collected Scientific Papers*, Joseph E. Stiglitz, ed., 2 vols. (Cambridge, Mass.: Massachusetts Institute of Technology Press, 1966), Vol. II, p. 1103.

[20] Cf., Edwin Mansfield, ed., *Monopoly Power and Economic Performance* (New York: W. W. Norton, 1964), pp. 3–64; Edward H. Chamberlin, ed., *Monopoly and Competition and Their Regulation* (London: Macmillan, 1954); William L. Baldwin, *Antitrust and the Changing Corporation* (Durham: Duke University Press, 1961), pp. 77–117.

makers and users (workers and consumers) in industry, wholesale and retail trade, banking and credit, agricultural mining and urban land, transportation, and technology. As a result, in Bentley's judgment, there had been exorbitant gains obtained through restricted production, avoidable waste, and high prices for the benefit of those entrepreneurs and capitalists. The quantitative magnitude of these gains he attempted to disclose in a statistical chapter on the distribution of wealth and income as well as on the concentration and control of industry and finance in the period 1910 to 1920. Although he used monographs like W. I. King, *The Wealth and Income of the People of the United States*,[21] Bentley drew upon a huge mass of statistical material that he dug out from many hitherto unexploited statistical reports of varied government agencies. The research he carried through on his own almost equalled that in the publications of the National Bureau of Economic Research, just then getting under way under the leadership of Wesley C. Mitchell.

Bentley's indictment of the malpractices of big business and high finance in the period 1900–20 is in accord with the findings of such noted "muckrakers" as Louis Brandeis, Lincoln Steffens, and Ida Tarbell. Yet more recent researchers in business history, such as Thomas Cochran, Alfred D. Chandler, Jr., N. B. S. Gras, Henrietta Larson, and Edward C. Kirkland differ from Bentley in being less harsh on many of the past big business entrepreneurs. They argue that some of the misdeeds were exaggerated, that various achievements in consolidation of business with accompanying increases in efficiency have not been given due weight, and that the standard of living of the consumer was increased to a larger extent than the critics of big business have usually admitted. These defenders of big business also argue that during the past few decades the ethical standards of big business have advanced greatly over those of the "muckraking era."[22]

Challenging as the first half of this volume is in its economic analysis, the second half is even more rewarding for the light it throws

21 New York, Macmillan, 1915.

22 Cf., Thomas C. Cochran, *The American Business System: A Historical Perspective 1900–1955* (New York & Evanston: Harper & Row, 1962); Stanley Coben and Forest G. Hill, eds., *American Economic History: Essays in Interpretation* (Philadelphia & New York: Lippincott, 1966), pp. 362ff.; N. B. S. Gras and Hen-

on the social and political strains and problems of the American people at the end of World War I. Bentley sensed that the economic strains of World War I and the success of the Bolshevik Revolution in Russia had created a new critical situation for the established order in America and Europe. During World War I, the tremendous profits of big business, the great government war debt, and the severe inroads on civil liberties in Europe and America had imposed burdens upon the working classes that made some consider revolution against industrial and financial capitalism the only solution. In the United States the autocratic behavior of big business had produced the conditions for revolution in the ranks of dissatisfied wage-earners, especially among the members of the IWW, the "Wobblies." Bentley thought that a convulsive proletarian revolution in this country would result in radical destructiveness, a revolution of nihilism, rather than in the construction of a viable new social order. He anticipated that big business might react to the prospect of a workers' revolution by abandoning political democracy and establishing a right-wing dictatorship, as big business did in Fascist Italy a few years later with Mussolini as its leader.

The middle classes in America, Bentley believed, had to avoid being made a supporter or a victim of either the workers' or the big businessmen's revolution. The first task of the middle classes was to realize that big business had put through a revolution in the post-Civil War period when it destroyed laissez-faire competition and systematically replaced it with oligopoly or monopoly, wherever possible. In so doing, the business and banker oligarchy had also, at critical depression periods, been responsible for driving labor toward revolution.

Consequently, the middle classes should, in Bentley's judgment, set in motion a "counter-revolution" that would be directed at abolishing the "profiteering" system, but not the private property or profit system in their legitimate senses. Bentley urged the government to go beyond antitrust activities by systematically encouraging and financing the formation of more small business and farm enterprises. Forty-five years before President Johnson's Anti-Poverty Program, Bentley made the remarkable proposal that the

rietta M. Larson, eds., *A Case Book in American Business History* (New York: Crofts, 1939).

government should establish a minimum income for all workers; what is now called "a guaranteed income." Another major objective of the middle classes should be to promote the general welfare through extensive increases in the public sector of the economy, such as public buildings and parks, and the widest expansion of public education. Here Bentley anticipated John K. Galbraith's plea in *The Affluent Society*.[23]

In this expansion of the public sector of the economy, Bentley saw the need for nationalization of certain public utilities, such as the railroads. He also wished to promote producers' and consumers' cooperatives and to have the government use its credit facilities for helping small producers enter agriculture and business. The powers of big business he wished to curb through dismantling the trusts and other corporate power-devices, e.g., holding companies. He also favored extensive use of inheritance and income taxation to reduce the inequalities in the distribution of wealth and income. But he was not rigid in his proposals, and suggested that as the middle classes gained power, they should develop new plans to meet the changing situation. In the area of labor, he was radical enough to urge worker-participation in the control and management of business enterprises.

Although the two major parties represented different regional and occupational group interests, during and after World War I they had acted to a large extent as the northern and southern sections of one political agency for big business. Hence, Bentley proposed that the middle classes rely on non-partisan pressure groups as foundation stones for a National Property Rights Party, and thereby bring about the consolidation of the Democratic and Republican Parties as their opponents. In other words, he was for a sharp differentiation between the big business interests on the one hand and the small-business, farm, and worker groups on the other. Evidently he felt that most of the working classes would join forces with this new middle class party.

After World War I there were some terribly bitter struggles between Labor and Capital in America, especially in the coal-mining and steel industries. In 1919 over 4,000,000 workers were

---

[23] Boston: Houghton Mifflin, 1958.

involved in strikes, as compared to 1,250,000 workers the year before. But no workers' revolution emerged in the United States then or later. Nor did Bentley realize his hope that the two major parties might merge and one of them be replaced by a new party. In 1924 Bentley became a member of the National Progressive Party committee and was chairman of the Indiana state committee in charge of the campaign for Robert La Follette as President. With the victory of Calvin Coolidge, the newly founded Progressive Party went into eclipse.

After the October, 1929, stock crash and the ensuing Great Depression, the Democratic Party under Franklin D. Roosevelt became rejuvenated through new ideas of welfare capitalism which in part were borrowed from the Socialist Party, in part from the old Progressive Party. The New Deal averted the possibility of any seizure of power either by big business or labor. Nevertheless, the coup d'état by Mussolini in 1922, and by Hitler in the spring of 1933, can be regarded as confirming Bentley's earlier uneasy forecast of deep trouble ahead in Europe and America.

Various parts of Bentley's reform program were realized in varying degrees, first by F.D.R.'s "New Deal" and Truman's "Fair Deal," then by Kennedy's "New Frontier" and Johnson's "Great Society" program. Bentley's proposal for the organization of small businessmen, farmers, and workers into cooperating pressure groups became realized on a large scale during the New Deal. As a consequence, our political and economic system has developed into a "system of countervailing power."[24] Big business was not cut down in size, but it became counterbalanced by the big trade unions and the great agricultural bloc. Unfortunately, many unskilled or low-skilled industrial workers, tenant farmers, and agricultural laborers were either not organized at all or not enough to get equal recognition by the other power groups. This is one reasons why there was a Poor People's March on Washington in June, 1968, as well as why riots in the slum areas of the big cities broke out during the past few years.

Bentley undoubtedly favored a vigorous antitrust program and large-scale government aid for small business. He would have sym-

[24] John K. Galbraith, *American Capitalism* (Boston: Houghton Mifflin, 1952).

pathized with those who advocate decentralization of government and utilization of people on a local level for initiating or administering the national welfare programs. His heart would also have gone out to those who foster producers' and consumers' cooperatives. Here there has been some success, but not the widespread movement that Bentley had hoped for in 1920, perhaps because the chain stores and supermarkets have been so successful in the last few decades.

Bentley's preference for the smaller groups would have been based on his theory that they stood a better chance than very large groups to develop communal feelings. He was conscious of the possibility of alienation of individuals and underprivileged from "the society" around them. Yet he realized that a powerful central government was needed to free oppressed ethnic groups or exploited workers and farmers from the powerful vested local and state interests, in the South and elsewhere. He probably would have proposed that the civil rights movement be broadened and strengthened by full employment and minimum income guarantee programs for Negroes and whites. Although Bentley wrote little on the international problems, his personal correspondence justifies the belief that he would have approved the American government's resistance to totalitarian aggression, whether left-wing or right-wing, support for the United Nations, and aid to the under-developed areas of the world.

The significance of *Makers, Users, and Masters* to political and social scientists, stems in part from its disclosure of Bentley as a person who demonstrated that he could be both a rigorous social scientist and a committed reformer. As a citizen, he articulated his values and worked out an action program for the middle-class and working groups with which he identified himself.

This volume is also important because Bentley called attention to important areas where the welfare of the American people was not adequately safeguarded. The social problems he perceived, and his proposed solutions, are still relevant in current efforts to improve our society. As we grapple with these problems, we are carrying on the great tradition that Bentley exemplifies: the fusion of science, values, and social action.

To historians, *Makers, Users, and Masters* will be a significant addition to the outstanding works written by leaders in the Progressive Movement. To students of American social literature, this volume will be notable as an example of incisive, lucid analysis of important public issues. To champions of civil liberties and civil rights, Bentley's criticisms of the suppression of these rights stand out as beautiful and passionate utterances in a great cause, worthy of comparison with the writings of a Justice Holmes.

Contents

xxviii   MAKERS, USERS, AND MASTERS

Makers, Users, and Masters

I

Introduction

Perhaps no more radical change in habits of thought ever came to a people than when in the early days of the war [World War I] we were forced to consider national income and economy in terms of actual commodities. For decades the dollar signs of commodities had answered most of our practical purposes, both individually and nationally. Suddenly we found ourselves where dollar language did not suffice. Bushels of wheat, pounds of fat, and spoonfuls of sugar were what actually counted. The nation was forced to economize [to set priorities and to allocate scarce resources] in these physical necessities, and the individual citizen was called upon to ration himself to do it. Economies in dollars had become of lesser importance. Economies in usable goods had become the condition of national existence.

The war is over, but the need for thought in terms of commodities is not over. The need is greater now and wider than it was before. A relapse into dependence upon dollars, prices, and capitalizations, as the satisfying terms for the discussion of national welfare in its economic phases, will mean blindness where there is vital need for light. It is not merely that the grains and the fats are still [in 1919–20] in deficient supply, and that for a few years more we may require commissions or other agencies to deal with them directly till world food needs and world food production become better adjusted. We must go wider afield than that.

Not Germany alone, but almost every European victor nation is now substantially bankrupt. One fifth of all the wealth of Europe, as wealth is usually measured, has been destroyed.

The war debts are so enormous that we can no longer success-

1

fully think of them as merely incidental charges upon future national incomes. They bite into the very heart of each nation's industrial life. They condition the system of organization for industry. They condition and may even require some legal restatement of property rights themselves. None know this better than the statesmen who are now beginning to face the problems of amortization.

With this goes the revolutionary trend the world over. Bolshevism is discussed as in part an outgrowth of [Russian] famine. But the Bolshevist program and many programs of industrial revolution are similarly involved in certain conditions of undernourishment among large proportions of our population in peace times. They are involved as possibilities, I believe also, in certain excessive wastes and powers in our general industrial organization.

Just as in war we were forced down to the underlying facts of the actual food supply, so in the solution of these problems of the future we shall be forced to the underlying facts of other phases of our economic life: of wages and incomes, of property and profits, of health, efficiency, and enjoyment. We shall find the dollar interpretation of all of these things, the discussion in terms of present costs and prices, a delusion, full of elements of danger when action is finally forced upon us.

If this is so, then certainly the earlier and the more frankly we face these underlying facts, the easier and the simpler the ultimate solution will be for us all. If labor, to take an illustration, has in its own way already peered behind the dollar, and if it has from its own special point of view already worked out programs of reorganization, socialisms of one sort and another, which some other elements of the population fear and abhor, that fact should not deter those other elements from themselves seeking the deeper truths in their own way: rather it should drive them to deeper truths on their own account and in their own defense.

This volume is to concern itself with the facts of wealth and power in the United States in this second decade of the twentieth century. It does not purport to have value beyond that restriction of place and time. Its main reliance is upon facts that can be quantitatively stated. These available facts are for the greatest part pre-war facts, but to some extent they are supplemented by knowledge secured under war conditions. So far as it is possible, they will be stated objectively, not with reference to current theories, not with blind reliance on the symbols which must be used in stating them, but instead in terms of groups, of their interests as related to one another, of their viewpoints as developed out of those interests or as latent in them, and of the probabilities of their political or extra-political action in accordance with those interests.

No observer or student of such facts can hope to occupy a position outside of them from which he can judge them. We may as well all of us be frank about it. Whoever we are, whatever we say or do, we express some special phase of the process. We are not supermen. No more are we absolutely individual men. We are representatives, chosen not by popular ballot, but constituted as such by the requirements of thought and expression. The content of our thought is the people and the interests of the people as manifested in the various groups with which we are more or less identified, and to which we are in varying ways and degrees opposed.

The greatest difficulty in getting to the meat of any book, or indeed of any argument or discussion on industry or government, lies in identifying the interests or group relationships represented by its writer. The greatest difficulty in reaching agreements with others lies, not in handling the facts or arguments, but in dovetailing the underlying points of view, and in getting mutual recognition of these factors for what they are. Indeed it is harder for a writer or debater to define his standpoint clearly and successfully than it is for him to develop his theme. To obscure this standpoint is insincerity. To ignore it is only too often self-delusion. To reveal it honestly is at least a proffer of sincerity.

It is therefore without apology either for the intrusion of his personality or for the imperfection of his statement, that the writer attempts to define at the outset his personal standpoint and his presuppositions.

The writer likes to work: he likes opportunities to work, and even compulsions to work: he appreciates leadership in his work and recognizes the value that efficient leadership can give to his work: he has no prejudice against, above all no contempt for, the kind of working ability that needs leadership: of course he prefers to win to leadership himself where he can.

At the same time he enjoys income without work and the security that it gives; he has a reasonable expectation of finishing his days with such enjoyment and under such security. He confesses to very little sympathy for suffering, to very little ethical indignation where suffering exists, and to very little utopianism in this respect. Life has such a universal technique of pain, that he is compelled to accept it as it is. Nevertheless he feels a strong hostility towards all advantages or enjoyments gained by procedures that result in pain to others, whether the possessor of the advantage is active in pain-giving or tacitly permits it, whether he obscures the effects from himself as much as he can, or by mere lethargy lets them seem obscured.

In especial he dislikes bartering and trafficking where they are pursued deliberately and persistently, not as an incident to productive work, but as an occupation; where "more to me and less to you" is the measure of successful employment. He will admit that this feeling goes so far with him as perhaps to be a prejudice.

He appreciates the spirit of initiative and of adventure, and the struggle of strength and wit, in all industry and business, but he believes that these have limitless fields in which to develop themselves where loss and pain to others are comparatively negligent results. He cannot conceive of an organized society without focuses of power and authority, but he finds himself chronically opposed to all those systems of power which show an especially marked tendency to increasing absorption of benefits to themselves, particularly where they are accompanied by persistent efforts to decrease the benefits that go to the subjects of the power. That is to say, he is always ready to fight against whatever abuses of power seem worst at any moment.

He is well-disposed towards a standard which aims to let "every man count [as] one" in the enjoyment of life and in the regulation of social organization, wherever there is any practical question of working towards the realization of such a standard. He [the author] does not necessarily consider the present advantage or type of advantage of any one man or class of men as a final test of all law and order, of all advantage. And in that connection he is more than a little inclined to laugh at the regalia of superiority, whether they be crowns on heads, multiplicity of little-used estates, extravagantly priced trifles of dress, or display expenditures in daily living; and he is fully open to argue the question of their permissible extent, not tested ethically as individual matters, but tested nationally as gross expenditures of the peoples' income.

And for a final prejudice, if prejudice it be, he admits a deep-seated and seemingly indestructible desire for civil liberty, for freedom of thought, of speech and of belief. He cannot bring himself to be afraid of what anybody in the society he lives in believes or says. He cannot give magical power to the word of mouth that issues from some one man's head. He cannot conceive of one man's brain breeding a word-germ that will destroy all men. He is willing to trust to the sunlight of all men's brains and words to work a cure, if cure be needed. He cannot fear a philosophy of burglary or piracy, much less a philosophy of profiteering or anarchy or bolshevism, turned loose into a world of common sense. He demands for himself his unrestricted constitutional rights to think and believe and talk, whether he thinks crooked or straight, whether he represents in his mental processes much or little of the social world around him. He holds the threat of a prison cell for thinkers and talkers who stand in the open to be the last word in stupidity and tyranny. He holds the [national government's] censorship in times of peace and the administrative exercise of authority under the so-called espionage laws [Espionage Act of June, 1917, and Sedition Act of May, 1918] to be the worst of all destructive tendencies under any government. He cannot conceive of himself or of his fellow citizens submitting to such mutilation of themselves for any length of time.

From the above it is clear that the writer is not specifically representative of the interests of any one of the great groups of wage-earners, manufacturing enterprise, promotion and investment banking, or commerce. He is more specifically representative of the interests of farmers and of investors. Even more characteristically, he would seem representative of the interests of consumers—those vital and broad interests, vaguely formulated, subordinated by most people to their more clearly defined interests as producers, and triumphed over with great display by the few whose power of dollar expenditure is extraordinary. This specific interest as consumer is probably the occasion for the writer's admitted personal antagonism to the extreme forms of trafficking occupations [advertising, for example].

Taken in political, rather than in economic, terms, there would probably be no hesitation in characterizing him as typically middle-class in his interests. His prejudices in behalf of civil liberty and free speech and his attitude towards the use of power in government are indeed, historically, the very essence of the middle class. If his viewpoint as herein developed could hardly be regarded as the typical middle-class viewpoint at the present hour, that fact has no bearing on the character of his interests. The viewpoints change with the changing interests, not vice versa. We have a thousand illustrations in the discussions of the last two decades—witness the words "protection," "municipal ownership," "monopoly," "competition," and the content given to them and the stress laid on them with the changing years.

The very problem of this book is that of the present middle-class interest and the probable changes in middle-class viewpoint and programs. It would perhaps not be stretching matters to find a very considerable identity in all cases between the consumers' interest and the middle-class interest, and to interpret the middle-class power as the power which appears when a common consumers' interest subordinates various producers' oppositions and unites them for a common political purpose. The suggestion is given for what it is worth and dropped forthwith, for it belongs in a study ranging far outside of our present prescribed limits—the United States in this decade.

Let us now generalize these personal attitudes or prejudices, such as they are, and these group relationships into a set of presuppositions for this study.

Our subject matter, to start with, is men; and the aspect of men which we study is their acquirement, possession, and use of income. Men without income, in the sense of commodities which they use for maintaining and enjoying life, are impossible: and wealth and income . . . [if] considered apart from men receiving them, are equally impossible. All men in society must be regarded as "self-justified" as procurers and enjoyers of income.

These men present themselves to us in various classes and groups with respect to the acquirement, possession, and use of their incomes . . . [from] wages and property. All of our economic, and most, if indeed we do not say all, of our political theories and programs must be understood in terms of the varying interests of these groups with respect to one another.

It is not our place [objective] to treat any program or institution as superior to this organization of society, or as capable of determining the fate of society, but to understand all of them alike in terms of the, or any [group], interests affected.

It is not our place to take the point of view of workers under the wage system or to take the point of view of property-owning men, either in general or in the special form of owners of capital goods, but to get the points of view of both of these groups and of all similar groups, and to get them so far as possible in such terms as will most readily permit comparison.

We shall have to study not merely their points of view as expressed in their theories or programs, but also their interests underlying these points of view, the probable development of those interests, the consequent possibilities of change in programs, and the methods of harmonizing them that we may see working themselves out.

This will require a maximum coldness [objectivity] in examining and stating the facts, as free as possible from prejudice arising from any special class relationship or from any standard of sympathy or ethics.

It will require full recognition of whatever intelligence, boldness, initiative or information exists among the several groups.

It will require a dispassionate consideration of the tools of power that now exist at the service of the several groups, including such tools as the ballot, argument, press, strike, constabulary, secret service [and] "direct action" revolution.

It will require a summing-up, not in terms of what we ourselves would like or what we ourselves think ought to be, but of what probably will come to pass, given the existence of the various factors of production, income, knowledge, and force.

Whether the writer has succeeded in his desire to make his examination cold-blooded is not for him to say. He feels, however, that he has made considerable progress toward it, except in the one matter of civil liberty, with regard to which he is frank to admit he "sees red," first, last, and all the time.

It is by considering the various interests at stake in terms of income rather than of wealth that the best basis is found for comparing them in a way which will give the arguments used by opposing sides approximately identical meanings for all parties.

In the current [1919–20] discussions between labor and capital we find hopeless arguments, largely unintelligible the one side to the other. In the current discussions of property as something of another realm from wage-labor, we find even worse difficulties. Working back from income into questions of labor and capital, wealth and power, we have a better track.

Of property in the sense of material goods, held in private title as a source of enjoyment and of productive income this at least may be said here; that no greater incentive to industry, that no better security for old age, . . . ill-health, and the nurture of a family has ever been developed among men.

Its alternative, the minimum wage and pension system, now appearing [*circa* 1920] in many lands for protective purposes, and seemingly an absolutely necessary device as industrial organization now stands, may or may not prove superior to property ownership. It presents itself to us, however, as a system of the day and of the hour, and of the special condition of society in which it arises.

With property—not as possession and means of enjoyment, but as a source of [oligopoly or monopoly] power, a kernel upon which a great structure of masterful organization arises much as credit builds itself upon its kernel of gold reserve—the case stands very differently.

Here we have not property-enjoyment, but, potentially, the destruction of property-enjoyment. Here we have the institution, because of the very aggressiveness of which, the protective system of the minimum wage and the industrial pension has been called into being.

The victory in the long struggle between these systems—one foreshadowing itself as a system of great [corporate, organizational] power with rigid defensive bulwarks, the other as a community of income earners, enjoying the fruits of their efforts and the fruits of the property which results from their efforts and which offers protection to their future—may not be for this decade or this generation to see. We are involved in one phase of the struggle, a phase which before it is ended may indeed point towards the probable outcome; a phase which is as of vital importance to the passing interests of every citizen today, as it will be to the interests of their descendants.

II

Wealth and Industry:
Ownership and Control

Certain essential facts about our national life should be kept in mind, or at least readily at reference, when one attempts to weigh carefully his position towards our coming industrial and political problems. Such are the facts as to the employment of land; as to the main branches of industry, occupations, and types of employment; as to wealth, income and financial power; as to price and wage changes; and as to capitalizations. Too often they come to us with emotional coloring which leads to over- or under-emphasis. Yet as facts, established and attested by the various bureaus of government and considered apart from emotional coloring, they furnish the solid substance of our problems; not to be dodged, glorified, or reviled, but to be coldly reckoned with.

The ordinary comfortable citizen who expects to live twenty or thirty years longer, makes a serious mistake, perhaps even a fatal one, if he thinks the existence of any considerable proportion of the population with incomes below a decent standard of comfort is a more vital matter to the immediate sufferers than it is to him. Just as much is he in error if he thinks that the existence of any large number of corporations with "good will" (a present-day euphemism for power of income-seizure) three or four times their material assets, is any more important as a fact to them than it is to him. And it is just as true that the "proletariat" or "plutocracy" makes a mistake if it disregards the welfare of the average [person]. In one boat, sailing to a common fate, much that seems most vital today would melt out of mind, should shipwreck perhaps put us on a barren island.

To assemble such facts, supplementing the results of government investigations in part by the work of private foundations, and making supplementary estimates where necessary[1] can hardly be a grateful task. Nevertheless, we shall strive to bring them together in this chapter, stating them directly and without mutilation, for examination together and for reference later.

Most of the information necessarily relates to the years immediately preceding the [First World] War. Occupation statistics are for 1910, wealth statistics for 1912, and income statistics for 1916, while the facts as to wages and family budgets cover roughly a decade. For later conditions, we must rely in the main on the various government index numbers showing rates of change. The necessity of getting figures from several different years will not interfere with their interpretation, since we are concerned not so much with [absolute] positive quantities as with proportions. If the ratios are worked out with due care within each class of facts, we cannot go far wrong in bringing them together for further comparison.

Studying the opposing campaigns of rival [economic] forces within our society, we are somewhat in the position of an army strategist who gets all the facts he possibly can but is compelled to eke them out with guesses, and whose success (impossible without such guessing) is dependent on the care with which he judges. The assembling of the essential facts in this one place may perhaps be some protection against the danger of their misuse.

Occupations and Wealth, The Employment of the Land: The land area of the continental United States is 1.9 billion acres. Our [main] utilization of it [*circa* 1910–16, in millions of acres], as well as can be . . . [estimated was as follows: farm lands, 879 (347 in cropland, 191 in woodland, 284 in grassland pasture);* city and town sites, 20; reservations, 294 (national forests, 153; Indian, 71; coal, 44; phosphate, oil, power, 18; national parks, 8; unappropriated and unreserved, 231; not ascertained, 166)].†

* Census Bureau, *Historical Statistics of the United States Colonial Times to 1957* (Washington, D.C.: Government Printing Office, 1960), p. 239, Series J49–64.

† Bentley's estimates based on *Abstract of Census 1910 of the United States* (Washington, D.C.: Government Printing Office, 1913) and *Reports of the Department of Interior for . . . 1917*, 2 vols. (Washington, D.C.: Government Printing Office, 1918), Vol. I, pp. 139–42.

Working Personnel and Wealth Employed: The [gainfully] occupied population in 1910 (the men, women, and children employed in all branches of industry, business, and public service),
numbered 38 millions; and the total wealth of the country according
to the census of 1912 [in *Wealth, Debt, and Taxation, 1913*] (land
and buildings, machinery, tools, and equipment, stocks of merchandise in stores, and goods in hands of consumers) was valued at
$187.7 billion.

[The chief components of national wealth are structures—residential and non-residential; producer-durables or equipment, inventories, consumer-durables, and land. On the basis of the 1912
census figures, land and buildings of all types, taxed and tax-
exempt, accounted for more than half the estimated national wealth
in 1912. Productive equipment of all enterprises, agricultural and
non-agricultural, including the public utilities, approximated 20
per cent of the total wealth. The remaining wealth, some 30 per
per cent, consisted of goods in the hands of consumers or in the
process of passing from producer to consumer. Gold and silver
coin represented slightly more than 1 per cent of the global total.*

[Out of some 37 million gainfully employed persons in the
United States in 1910, somewhat more than one-third were engaged in agriculture and forestry; about one-third in manufacture,
mining, and construction; roughly one-twentieth in transportation
and public utilities; about one-eighth in trade, commerce, and
finance; one-seventh in the professions, domestic and personal
services, and government. According to the statistics in the 1912
Census of Wealth about one-fourth of the national wealth was
invested in agriculture (land, buildings, equipment, and products in
stock), about one-tenth in manufacturing, mining, and construction, about one-seventh in transportation and public utilities, about
one-ninth in trade (farm, industrial, mineral, and imported products); and about one-fifteenth in public and other tax-exempt
institutions.

[On the basis of these estimates of (1) the number of personnel
gainfully engaged in the major occupations, and (2) the billions
of dollars actually invested in these sectors of the economy, one

---

* Cf., *Statistical Abstract of the United States 1920* (Washington, D.C.: Government Printing Office, 1921), p. 716.

might venture to assert that the largest amounts of capital per person engaged were invested in transportation, public utilities, trade, and commerce; the next largest amounts in agriculture and forestry; the smallest amounts in the construction trades.]*

A National Balance Sheet: Balance sheets are the summary statements of resources [assets] and liabilities which we use to enable us to grasp quickly and easily the condition of our affairs. If we look upon the national business as one huge enterprise of the whole nation at work, we can frame a balance sheet for it to give us similar assistance. We must not, indeed, interpret such a national balance sheet as indicating solvency or insolvency. The liabilities (the claims) may not be enforceable. Like private liabilities, it is one of their characteristics that they shrink or expand under market estimations, and adjust themselves in that way instead of through bankruptcy courts. But taking them for what they are, such a balance sheet is . . . illuminating.

[In such a national balance sheet the tangible assets would embrace residential and non-residential structures and land, producers' and consumers' durable goods, inventories, livestock, gold, and other monetary metals. The intangible assets would include currency, commercial bank deposits, life insurance receivables from business enterprises and households, farm and non-farm mortgages, corporate bonds, preferred and common stock, and the equity in unincorporated business.

[On the other side of the ledger, we have as liabilities public and corporate bonds and notes, mortgages and rentals on both producers' and consumers' property, accounts payable to banks and other business enterprises, deposits at commercial banks and other financial institutions, life insurance reserves, currency, and borrowing on securities.]†

The National Savings: National savings in terms of mounting [corporate] capitalizations [based in part on watered stock] are one

---

* *Ibid.*, pp. 276ff., 716, 764. Cf., *Historical Statistics of the United States*, pp. 599–602; Colin Clark, *Conditions of Economic Progress* (London: Macmillan, 1940), p. 389.

† Dr. Bentley anticipated by thirty years some important modern ideas; but it seems wisest to use here the formulations of Raymond W. Goldsmith et al., *A Study of Savings in the United States*, 3 vols. (Princeton, N.J.: Princeton University Press, 1956), Vol. III, pp. 44–45.

thing; and national savings in terms of physical goods produced and kept unconsumed for use in further production are another and very different thing. Our figures here deal only with the latter; the realities of national wealth. Professor Willford I. King, in his *Wealth and Income of the People of the United States*[2] has estimated that the nation saved, in the decade 1900 to 1910, about $2 billions a year out of an income of $30.5 billions, or about 6.6 per cent of what it produced. [Recently, however, Professor Simon Kuznets in his *Capital in the American Economy** has presented us with more reliable and higher estimates of national saving, defined as percentages of gross and net capital formation. His findings on the percentage shares of net capital formation in the Gross National Product, based on volume in current prices, are 12.4 [per cent] for the period 1899–1908; 10.6 [per cent] for the period 1909–18. The corresponding percentages for gross capital formation are 22.8 per cent and 22.1 per cent.]

Distribution of the National Wealth: We have no satisfactory statistics [as of 1919–20] as to the distribution of the national wealth, but a number of interesting [but questionable] estimates have been made, by persons with varying points of view, using different methods and different material. No such estimates can have a solid basis, however, until we obtain a much better understanding than we have today of the relations between real wealth [tangible assets] and capitalized claims to the future income of the nation. Some time [in the future] we may hope to have that and to have statistical material gathered with clear reference to the distinction. In times of optimism, capitalization figures run far beyond [estimates of tangible] wealth. In times of depression they may run close together, or capitalizations may even fall behind.

[If one may generalize from the estimates on wealth distribution in Massachusetts and Wisconsin made by Professor Willford I. King during the period 1860–1900, the richest 2 per cent of the population held 60 per cent of the total wealth in the United States while the poorest 65 per cent of the American people owned about 5 to 6 per cent of the wealth.]†

---

* Princeton, N.J.: Princeton University Press, 1961) p. 95, Table 9.
† W. I. King, *Wealth and Income*, pp. 64–86. Cf., C. L. Merwin, Jr., "American Studies of the Distribution of Wealth and Income by Size," Conference on Research in National Income and Wealth, *Studies on Income and Wealth Volume Three* (New York: National Bureau of Economic Research, 1939), pp. 4–84.

Distribution of the National Income: The distribution of the income of the people of the nation can be shown much more exactly than the distribution of the national wealth. This is fortunate, since income, not wealth, in the last analysis, is the real object of everyone's interest.[3]

[In 1916] over 400,000 families . . . had incomes of $3,000 a year apiece or more. [Those with annual incomes over $150,000 received 24 per cent of the total income of this group of taxpayers; those receiving $40,000 to $150,000 a year, over 21 per cent; those receiving $3,000 to $40,000, 55 per cent.] It will be observed that seven-eighths of one per cent (0.869 per cent, to be exact) of the families represented in this table received almost a [third] of the total income included.[4]

The surplus earnings of corporations are true income to the holders of the common stock, even though left in the corporation treasury and not paid out as dividends. The stockholder is the beneficiary just as much as though the earnings had been paid to him, and he had invested them elsewhere. Allowing for such surplus increments, as shown by the corporation tax reports, . . . we get the following showing for persons with incomes over $3,000. [Those with annual income over $150,000 received 30 per cent of the total income; those with incomes $40,000 to $150,000 got 24.1 per cent; those with $3,000 to $40,000 obtained 42.9 per cent.]* This raises the incomes of seven-eighths of one per cent of the income-tax payers to [at least] 30 per cent of what they all receive. . . .

The next step is to estimate the incomes of persons receiving less than $3,000 a year and therefore not included in the income-tax returns for 1916. For this purpose we shall take . . . the figures put out by the Bankers Trust Company of New York during the Third Liberty Loan campaign as a guide to Liberty Loan subscribers. Roughly . . . [these speculative statistics] show us a third of the national income going to a middle group of the population with annual incomes of $1,200 to $3,000), comprising about one-third of the people. [Below them is] another group with annual incomes of $800 to $1,200 comprising . . . [another third] of the people, [receiving about one-fifth] of the [national] income. [On the bottom is the poorest] group [with annual incomes below $800,

* Estimates by Bentley based on unpublished Table VIII and Appendix F attached to manuscript of Chapter II.

about one-fourth of the population and receiving almost one-tenth of the national income.*]

Nor have we yet introduced all the facts showing income concentration. We have considered wage and book incomes of all kinds, but we have not considered the increment of value in farms and city real estate, which was so strikingly shown by the [1912] Wealth census, in comparison with that of 1904. Nor have we considered the increment of "franchise values, monopoly rights, and good will and other vendible competitive advantages." These latter words are quoted from Professor A. A. Young, former president of the American Statistical Association,[5] who has estimated them, together with real estate increments, to amount to from $5 to $7 billion a year. Corporations allow for them in reappraisements and inventories, usually without passing them through profit accounts. Private holders realize [capital gains] on them when they sell the property. While not part of the national income in terms of commodities, they are parts of the national "distribuendum," as Professor Young calls it—values that are distributed among individuals; and as such, they belong in income as we are here considering it.

Taking the minimum figure above of $5 billion, we may apportion it pro rata among all incomes of $1,800 a year or more, dropping to this level to include increments of values going to farm owners. [Our final judgment is] that about two-thirds of the people get one-third of the [national] income, that another third of [this] income goes to less than one-third of the people, and that the remaining third of the income goes to a group . . . less than 2 per cent of the population. [Of this top 2 per cent] some 3,700 families, representing certainly not over 15,000 persons, receive [about] one-tenth of all the product and benefit and value of the nation at work.†

[Between 1896 and 1916] the growth of [income] concentration

---

* Cf., Wesley C. Mitchell *et al.*, *Income in the United States: Its Amount and Distribution 1909–1919* (New York: Harcourt, Brace, 1921), Vol. I, pp. 108–16.
† Wesley C. Mitchell *et al.*, *Income in the United States . . . 1909–19*, Vol. I, p. 147, concluded "that in 1918, the year with the best available data, the most prosperous 1 per cent of the income-receivers had nearly 14 per cent of the total income, the most prosperous 5 per cent of the income-receivers had nearly 26 per cent of the total, the most prosperous 10 per cent had nearly 35 per cent of the total, and the most prosperous 20 per cent had about 47 per cent of the total income." In short, the poorest 80 per cent of income-receivers had only 53 per cent of the total income.

is striking. [According to W. I. King, the 1.6 per cent of the richest families in the United States received 10.8 per cent of the national income in 1890 and 19 per cent in 1910.][6]

A graph showing the curve of income concentration is usually in order in connection with such [statistics as we have given]. Graphs are useful in comparing the results of one investigation with those of others, but how can a set of lines within the limits of a printed page adequately visualize for us such a curve of concentration as the facts show in the distribution of the people's income? Let us try to get the picture before us instead in terms of a small area of land, circular in form, with the poorer incomes distributed around the circumference and the greater ones at the center towering up mountainously. Let us take a radius of one mile for our circle, and let us figure the normal income sufficient to support a family's life in health and decency (say $800 a year for conditions of 1916) as equivalent to a foot of soil.

What then will be the geographical aspect of our incomes? For a quarter of a mile or so, as we pass along the radius from the circumference to the center, we shall be in the swampy ground of incomes below the decent standard of life. For the next third of a mile and more the soil will average 1.25 feet deep, rising at the inner part to 1.5 feet. [For] another third of a mile the average will be less than 2 feet deep, with the inner limit some 3.75 feet. We are within 85 feet of the center, and now suddenly comes the change. A sharp mountain pinnacle shoots up, precipitous beyond any parallel in geography, sharper than the sheerest cathedral spire. In 80 feet we climb 500. In 4.5 feet more we climb to 2,000 feet. In the next 6 inches we must reach an altitude of 12,500 feet, and more (how much more we do not know, for there are ten incomes of $5,000,000 or more on the 1916 list; they average above $10,000,000), and 12,500 feet in our picture is only the height of the average one of them above the herd on the plain below. . . . And yet, as a bit of still life, this picture is easier to contemplate with equanimity than it is in terms of action or of power.

The picture should not be one of landscape only. It should be one of vortex, of tornado. This pinnacle rising thousands of feet on a half-foot base is not the flimsy thing to fall at a breath that it would be in still life. It is the very essence of force. It rings when struck . . . It sucks up into itself [elements] from the entire area, from the entire population. It shoots ever higher and ever higher, and (until its limit be reached, and where that is we do not know today) it is ever stronger as it rises.

It remains now to change our point of view with regard to income; to consider it, not as pure spending power at the free disposal of the recipients, but as the [necessary] condition of the maintenance [subsistence] of the population. As such, we must set aside the costs of this maintenance before we get the net income which remains freely in the hands of the recipients; either for their comforts, luxuries, and pleasures, or as their source of savings in provision for the contingencies of sickness and old age, as well as for future well-being. We take here the national point of view about the population and its income, rather than [that of] the individual; and just as a firm or corporation deducts all its going expenses, including, for example, the maintenance of employees when traveling on its service, so we may make similar deductions of necessary living expenses for all the population as costs of maintenance.

Such an estimate must be made not as a matter of emotion or sympathy, not as a basis for drawing conclusions, or strengthening conclusions otherwise arrived at, but directly as a matter of national business fact, with such value under any given application as the situation may warrant.

Taking again $800 as the minimum necessary to keep a family in good working health, we may make larger allowances for the maintenance of families with greater incomes. If we set $800 for [each of the 7.3 million families receiving annual money incomes below $800 in 1916, we find that each family requires an increase, or supplement, of about 25 per cent of its income in order to reach a minimum living standard. Similarly, each of the 9.8 million families receiving annual money incomes from $800 to $1,200 require a supplement of 3 per cent. The families with annual money incomes of $40,000 to $150,000 are able to keep an estimated 29 per cent for enjoyment and savings. Families receiving annual money income over $150,000 are estimated to have 71 per cent of their net income for enjoyment and savings].*

* These estimates were made by Bentley on the basis of *Statistics of Income for 1916*, and Bankers Trust Company figures for income below 3,000 in 1916, *Twenty-Four Billion* (New York: Bankers' Trust Company, 1918), in manuscript

The Control of Industry: We have next to review the essential facts as to the control of industry, both as regards the relative positions of individuals in the system, and as regards the degree of [corporate] concentration in the organization itself.

Independent Businessmen, Salaried Officers, Wage-Earners and Clerks: Classification is relatively easy in one branch of industry taken by itself. It becomes much less definite when all branches are considered together. Nevertheless, with due allowance for the tests used in classification, we may group the facts by percentages in two . . . [groups]; one representing those branches of industry in which relations are most definite, the other those branches in which relations are vaguer. Together they will cover the 38 million occupied persons.

The first group is that marked by the necessary use of [considerable] capital in organized ways in connection with the employment [of white- and blue-collar workers in manufacturing, mining, transport, public utilities, trade, and agriculture. Their percentage of the total number employed in each branch ranged from 51 per cent in agriculture to 95 per cent in manufacturing and 97 per cent in mining. The remainder in each branch consisted of superintendents, managers, salaried officers, and private business heads. The percentage of the business heads varied from a low of 0.01 per cent in transport and public utilities to 34 per cent in trade and 48 per cent in agriculture, tenant farmers being included under this head.].

The second group is marked by comparatively slight use of direct capital (except in large construction companies), and the [extensive employment of hand-laborers, clerks, and teachers. Their percentage of the total occupied in each branch of industry rises from a low of about 8 per cent in the professions to 90 per cent or higher in public service, domestic and personal service, the building and hand trades].*

A freer grouping of the occupied population may be made in

Tables IX, X, and XI and Appendixes F and G, attached to this chapter, but not published here. Cf. Goldsmith et al., *A Study of Savings*, Vol. I, p. 162; Vol. III, p. 168; Bureau of the Census, *Historical Statistics*, p. 167, Series G 131–146; Robert J. Lampman, *The Share of Top Wealth-Holders in National Wealth 1922–1956* (Princeton, N.J.: Princeton University Press, 1962), pp. 234–37, 262.
* Cf., Bureau of the Census, *Historical Statistics*, pp. 76–78, Series D 123–572. Bentley's estimates, based on the *Census of 1910*, were worked out in an unpublished Appendix G to this chapter.

round numbers . . . (by the use of several estimates for purposes of subdivision) . . . somewhat as follows:* [0.5 million industrial managers; 1.2 million independent or salaried-professional type; 5.7 million small-business heads (farm-owners, tradesmen, et al.); 3.5 million artisan-business type, including tenant-farmers; 4.1 million clerks, salespeople, and public school teachers; 10 million factory-type wage-earners, including mining, transport, public utilities and construction; and 13 million other types of labor— farm, trade, public service, et al.].

The Concentration of the Control of Industry: This [concentration] can be measured by the proportion of our output which comes from large establishments, by the proportion which comes from corporations, by the extent to which single branches of industry are under the control (direct or indirect) of one corporation, and by the extent to which the greatest industries are knit together under a community of financial interest.

The evidence in the first two respects comes from the census. In manufactures [for example] one-eighth of the factories employ three-quarters of the workers and turn out five-sixths of the products. In mining one-twelfth of the establishments employ four-fifths of the wage-earners, and one-fourteenth of them turn out five-sixths of the product.†

In manufactures, corporations employ four-fifths of the workers and turn out five-sixths of the products.‡ In mining, corporations employ nine-tenths of the workers and produce nine-tenths of the products.§ The railroads are 100 per cent under corporation ownership, and the same is substantially true of the public utility enterprises. For trade and commerce, we may estimate that 60 per cent is handled by corporations, though we have no satisfactory figures.

Concerning the extent to which special branches of industry are under the control of individual corporations, the [United States]

* Estimates by Bentley given in unpublished Appendixes A and G of this chapter.
† *Abstract of the Census of Manufactures, 1914* (Washington, D.C.: Government Printing Office, 1917), p. 390.
‡ *Statistical Abstract of the United States 1920* (Washington, D.C.: Government Printing Office, 1921), p. 190.
§ *Abstract of the Fourteenth Census of the United States 1920* (Washington, D.C.: Government Printing Office, 1923), p. 1278.

Commission [on Industrial Relations] of 1916 says: "With few exceptions each of the great basic industries of the country is dominated by a single large corporation, and where this is not true the control of the industry through stock ownership in supposedly independent corporations and through credit is almost, if not quite, as potent."[7] As illustrations, one may cite the United States Steel Corporation, handling just about half of the steel trade of the country;[8] the American Telephone and Telegraph Company, handling 70 per cent of the telephone business;[9] and the "Big Five" packers, doing about four-fifths of the interstate meat trade of the country, and handling at least that proportion of all of our leather supplies. As for the anthracite coal industry, Senator Vardaman, chairman of the [United States] Senate Committee on Manufactures, has reported to the Senate that eight companies, producing 72 per cent of the country's anthracite, have "made it impossible for independent operators to compete with them on a fair basis."[10]

Through subsidiary corporations and interlocking directorates under the administration of the investment and promotion bankers, these concentrated organizations in separate branches of industry are knit into a single system, the unity of which, in its financial aspects [and] its control of output and prices, will be fully discussed later.[11] The Commission on Industrial Relations found that six financial groups controlled 2,651,684 wage-earners, and that these . . . comprised 28 per cent of all wage-earners in the basic industries which were investigated by the Commission. The capitalization of these six groups was $19,875,200,000.[12]

The Pujo Congressional Committee showed that three financial groups—namely, those headed by J. P. Morgan and Company, The First National Bank of New York, and the National City Bank of New York (commonly called the Morgan, Baker, and Stillman interests),* all closely related—controlled through 341 directorships in 112 corporations having [aggregate resources or capitalization of] $22,245,000,000 . . . . This list excluded all corporations with less than $5 million capital, and it also excluded many over that size in which only one of the three interests was openly in control.[13]

---

* J. P. Morgan, George F. Baker, and James Stillman.

Supreme Court Justice Brandeis adds for consideration 56 corporations with over $5 millions capital each and a total capital of $1,350,000,000 which have Morgan men on their boards, and 38 smaller corporations with a total capital of $79,000,000 in which two or all of the three interests are represented on the boards. In addition to these, if the full extent of the community of financial administration were to be shown, there would still [have] to be add[ed] 120 smaller corporations for which figures are not available, all corporations with "dummy" directors representing two or more of the three investment banking houses, and all subsidiary corporations, some of which are themselves huge concerns even for modern conditions. The total that all these combined would reach can only be guessed at.*

Turning from industry to the ownership of the land, concentration here must be considered separately for agricultural land and for other holdings such as timber and railroad properties. One-fifth of our farm lands (that is, all farms of a thousand acres or larger) is owned by 1 per cent of the owners, but the value of these holdings is only 8 per cent of the total farm land value.† So great is the concentration of other land-holdings, however, that 733 holders literally possess more than one-twentieth of the entire land area of the United States—and in timber properties alone, 1,694 holders have almost one-twentieth.‡

The Ownership of Corporations: Many corporations have large numbers of shareholders, sometimes of common stock, but more often of preferred stock. Many corporations encourage their employees to buy preferred shares and offer them especially favorable terms. *The Annalist,* January 1, 1917, printed statistics showing how widely distributed such holdings are. For 29 railroads, 10 mining corporations, and 56 industrials . . . with combined stock issues of $6 billion, it showed 684,168 shareholders in 1916; a

* Brandeis, *Other People's Money,* pp. 33–35.
† *Thirteenth Census of the United States . . . 1910,* Vol. V (Washington, D.C.: Government Printing Office, 1913), pp. 257, 259. The tendency here in the last census decade was not towards concentration but the reverse, the proportion of the large farms falling from 23.6 per cent in 1900 to 19 per cent in 1910. The proportion of farms operated by tenants increased, however, from 35.3 per cent to 37 per cent.
‡ United States, Bureau of Corporations, *The Lumber Industry,* 3 vols. (Washington, D.C.: Government Printing Office, 1913–14), Vol. III, pp. 177–82.

drop of 11,735 from the preceding year. As a rule, however, such holdings are continually increasing. These figures are the total number of names on all the 95 compan[ies'] books, without deduction for duplication.

What is important is not, however, how many names get on the books with one- or five- or ten-share holdings, but where the [corporate] control lies. The following analysis of the share-holdings in 1911 of the United States Steel Corporation (which has always made special endeavors for wide distribution) is illuminating. The company had 35,230 shareholders . . . [of this number almost 66 per cent owned from 1 to 25 shares of stock, about 30 per cent owned from 26 to 1,000 shares, and 3 per cent owned over 1,000 shares. This last group held 70.5 per cent of the total shares].[14]

The United States Commission on Industrial Relations states that 1.5 per cent of the United States Steel Corporation shareholders held 57 per cent of the stock and that the final control rested with a single private banking house.[15] In the American Tobacco Company, before its dissolution, ten men held 60 per cent of the stock. The entire stock of Armour and Company, except [for] a small amount of recently issued preferred shares, is held by eight or ten members of the Armour family. The Swift family does not hold a majority of the shares of Swift and Company, but in combination with two or three associates it has a heavy preponderance of control, although the company has 25,000 stockholders, 8,000 being employees.[16]

The railroads in 1917 had 627,930 shareholders, and of these 8,301, or 1.3 per cent, held 52 per cent of the stock.[17] These 8,301 consisted, however, of the total of the twenty largest stockholders of each road, and consequently the same name frequently appeared twice or more on the list. Furthermore, in many cases these "twenty largest" [stockholders] of a road consisted of two or three holders with all the stock, and eight or ten more who held one share apiece, just enough to qualify them for sitting on the directorate. A surface inspection of the detail of the figures as published would justify reducing the number of persons holding the majority of the stock to 7,500, and if duplications could be eliminated we should probably reach a much lower figure than this. The average holding of shareholders not in this group was 75 shares. For the preceding year 1916, B. M. Manly found that the [50 largest railroad stock-holders held more than 20 per cent of all the railroad stock in the country].[18]

Corporation Profits in War Years: An analysis of the 1916, 1917, and 1918 net earnings of 82 corporations, all [those] for which figures were available, has been made by Basil M. Manly, Joint-Chairman of the National War Labor Board, and these figures have been compared by him with prewar average earnings of the same corporations. They show practically tripled earnings in the war years after deduction of all interest charges and all taxes, including corporation-income and excess-profits taxes.

Mr. Manly points out that the volume of sales did not increase at all in proportion to the profits. He also points out that, especially in the last two years, extremely heavy depreciation charges were made by the corporations, and large reserve funds were built up by them, for the purpose of keeping down their showing of profits. Many of these reserve funds were entirely without justification from ordinary business practice. He believes that if normal treatment had been given to the 1918 earnings from an accounting standpoint, [these earnings] would show as high as the 1916 and 1917 earnings.[19]

Wage-earners Incomes and Necessary Expenses, Labor's Share in the National Income: The most reliable estimate of the proportion of the national product which goes to labor as compared with that which goes to property has been made by Professor King. His figures include, however, salaries of all kinds including executive management, along with wages. They cover each decade since 1850. These figures show an increasing share [of the national income] to wages and salaries from 1850 to 1890, and a [moderate] decline [from 1890 to 1910. Recent researches, however, have shown that instead of a decline there was an increase in real wages from 1890 to 1910.]*

Wages, Unemployment, and the Labor Turnover: The National Catholic War Council states: "A considerable majority of the wage earners of the United States, both men and women,

* W. I. King, *Wealth and Income,* 158–60; Albert Rees, *Real Wages in Manufacturing 1890–1914* (Princeton, N.J.: Princeton University Press, 1961), pp. 12–17, 120–27.

were not receiving living wages when prices began to rise in 1915."[20]

[In recent years, *circa* 1910–1915, between 20 per cent and 33 per cent of the male workers 18 years of age and over had weekly earnings under $10; between 66 per cent and 75 per cent had earnings under $15; and about 10 per cent had earnings over $20.[21] In this period, 25 per cent of the male adult heads of families (working in the principal industries and trades) earned less than $400 a year; 50 per cent, less than $600; 80 per cent, less than $800; and only less than 10 per cent earned as much as $1,000 a year. Approximately one-fourth of women workers in the main manufacturing industries earned less than $200 a year, and two-thirds earned less than $400.][22]

Total family income . . . often include more than the earnings of the head of the family, [such as the] earnings of wives and children, and receipts from roomers and boarders. [In the period between 1900 and 1915, the average annual income of typical workingmen's families employed in the principal industries was estimated to be between $700 and $800.[23] Important studies were made by the Immigration Commission on the annual family incomes of 15,726 wage-earners' families in 1908–1909. These showed that 7.6 per cent of the families studied had a total annual income under $300; 31.3 per cent were under $500; 64 per cent under $750; 82.6 per cent under $1,000; and 95 per cent under $1,500.

[There were marked differences between (1) the native-born and older immigrants, and (2) the newer immigrants, with the advantage going to the first group. Considerable differences in family income were also due to geographical divisions such as North and South, and varying conditions in heavy and light industry as well as in mining.][24]

Unemployment, meaning by that lack of jobs for workers [and] not unwillingness of workers to take jobs, cuts annual pay under conditions such as we have had in the last two decades [1900–20] below what daily and weekly rates would indicate. The general situation as to unemployment is summed up by [W. Jett] Lauck and [Edgar] Sydenstricker as follows: "The average male worker in the basic and more regularly operated industries loses in years of ordinary industrial activity from one-sixth to one-third of his working time."[25]

Another important factor in industrial conditions is the labor turnover; the shifting of men from factory to factory, their rehiring and retraining because of discharges or because of quitting jobs, with all [the] attendant wastes. This has been made the subject of a volume by a recent investigator, whose statistics [mainly for 1912–1914] for 105 establishments employing an average of 226,038 employees, showed the total number of terminations of employment for a calendar year to be 225,942. The average rate was thus [almost] 100 per cent of the labor force. The variation [among] different establishments was from 8 to 342 per cent. In 61 out of the 105 plants it ranged from 60 to 200 per cent.[26]

Necessary Family Expenses: Many studies of the amount necessary to keep a family of five in good working health have been made, both from the physiological and statistical points of view; some by government agencies, some by institutions, some by private investigators, and some in connection with arbitration hearings on demands for wage increases. These [provide the basis for two authorities, Lauck and Sydenstricker, presenting their conclusion [that] for a period in general prior to 1916 . . . $800 [annual income] is the minimum which for a family of two adults and three children will, with ordinary frugality, "allow provisions for separate and decent existence, health, and a modicum of reasonable comfort in the usual industrial locality and at prices which have prevailed during the last few years."[27] Below that amount the death rate of infants increases rapidly, and malnutrition can be shown by physiological tests.

Surveys [made in 1915] of the standard of living . . . to determine the amount of income necessary for a family of five . . . [concluded that such a family needed a minimum of $766 in Washington, D.C.; $772 in Buffalo, N.Y., and $840 to $876 in New York City. The Chicago Street Railway Employees felt their minimum to be $1,210.].[28]

[After World War I] the Bureau of Municipal Research in Philadelphia in December, 1919, decided that, at that time, $1,200 a year was "decidedly the minimum for a family of two adults and three children." Its allowances included only $27 a year for care of health, $15 for recreation, and $11 for education and reading. In the Seattle street railway arbitration in 1917, $1,505.60 was declared a necessary budget for the workingman's family, and the award of wages was made on that basis.[29]

The Federal Children's Bureau in a recent report has shown that there is a close connection between [the] amount of wages and child mortality. With the father earning $450 or less annually, the child mortality is 167 in the thousand. With the father earning $1,250 or more annually, the mortality drops to 59 in the thousand.[30]

Changes in Price and Wage Levels: If statistics of prices are collected for two [or more] years, and the averages for the two [or more] are compared in percentages, these percentages give us an index to the rate of change. It is usual to take the average for some one year as 100 per cent and compare with it on that basis a series of other years. The same kind of index numbers can be determined for wages. A convenient year to take as a basis with reference to problems of the present time is 1913, just before the [First] World War started.

The [wholesale price index] figures compiled by the United States Department of Labor, [taking the year 1913 as a base of 100, shows that the wholesale price index for some 294 commodities rose from 91 in 1908 to 101 in 1912, sank to 99 in 1914, and then rose steadily from 100 in 1915 to 123 in 1916, 175 in 1917, and 196 in 1918. Meanwhile, the full-time union rate of weekly wages rose steadily but slowly, at a drastically lower rate; from an index of 93 in 1908 to 102 in 1914 and 1915, 106 in 1916, 112 in 1917, and 130 in 1918.]*

The prices for 1907 were about 25 per cent above the averages for the decade 1891-1910. Retail food prices in 1907 were about 25 per cent above the averages for the decade 1890-1899. . . . Wholesale food prices increased faster than retail prices from 1907 to 1909; retail prices increased faster from [1909] to 1913, when wholesale prices again took the lead until 1917. Since 1917, retail

* *Monthly Labor Review*, Vol. VIII, No. 3 (March, 1919), pp. 116, 119 and No. 6 (June, 1919), p. 97. For a more recent statistical analysis, see John M. Clark, *The Costs of the World War to the American People* (New Haven, Yale University Press, 1931), pp. 130ff., 158ff. His conclusion, *op. cit.*, p. 282, was: "The purchasing power of salaries shrank by billions, inflicting on this class the most pinching economic burdens borne by any major group . . . wage rates . . . failed to keep pace with rising costs of living, but annual earnings per worker showed some gains, because workers were more fully employed."

prices have been gaining the more rapidly, and the tendency shows itself in that way in the monthly figures for [the spring of 1919].*

Notes

1. Such estimates do not have any great range of error when held closely in touch with the material from which they are taken . . . the writer believes that not only in this chapter, but [also] in Chapter VI on Waste, where estimates are of necessity much more freely used, he has kept all of his conclusions of a nature derogatory to the existing industrial system on a conservative basis, using estimates perhaps in every instance more moderate than those of specialists in the various fields.

2. (New York: Macmillan, 1915), p. 132. [For a critique of W. I. King, see Simon Kuznets, ed. *Income and Wealth of the United States, International Association for Research in Income and Wealth, Series II* (Cambridge, England: Bowes and Bowes, 1952), pp. 239–41.]

3. [Our] investigation is for 1916. To start with, we have the federal income tax returns of that year for [personal] incomes above $3,000, supplemented by the corporation tax returns which show surplus earnings of corporations, not distributed as dividends, but, nevertheless, a real portion of the income of the common-stock holders of the corporations. For incomes below $3,000 we must rely on estimates, and of these there are two available, both conservatively made, to guide us. . . . After our tables have been thus supplemented, we have still to make allowance for annual increments from appreciation of land and franchise values. . . .

We may, however, next shift our point of view so as to consider incomes, not as the total cash the individual has to spend on himself and his family, but as what he has left over after he has paid for the absolute essentials of life-maintenance, without which he could not continue as an income-earner. His income here will be his fund available for comforts, pleasures, and savings; and a table constructed on this basis will throw an interesting sidelight on the present status of our national efforts to measure the livings of all of the people. The figures will all be in terms of families, except for the addition of a group of unmarried or widowed wage-earners, with or without dependents. In 1916, at 4.5 persons to the family (the 1910 ratio) and with the population raised to the government estimate for 1916, we had 22,640,000 families, and the estimated additions as above will make the number of total income-receiving units about 20 per cent greater than this number.

4. Commissioner of Internal Revenue, *Statistics of Income for 1916*, House Doc. 1169, 65th Cong., 2d sess. (Washington, D.C.: Government Printing Office, 1918), p. 9.

5. "Do the Statistics of the Concentration of Wealth in the United States Mean What They Are Commonly Assumed to Mean?" *American Statistical Association Publication*, Vol. XV (March, 1917), pp. 471–84, esp. p. 481. [Cf., A. A. Young, *Economic Problems New and Old* (Boston: Houghton Mifflin, 1927), pp. 95–107.]

6. W. I. King, *Wealth and Income*, pp. 230–31. As for changes since 1916,

* *Monthly Labor Review*, Vol. VIII, No. 3 (March, 1919), p. 116, and No. 6 (June, 1919), p. 97.

an address by Congressman Henry T. Rainey in the House [of Representatives], February 8, 1919 may be referred to. In discussing our taxation system he had previously spoken of our having 25,000 millionaires. He now stated that he had secured further information and that the number should be placed at 30,000. The number of incomes of $50,000 or more in 1916, with salaries excluded, was about 13,500, a figure which will serve to indicate the rapidity of increase. Mr. Rainey's own estimate was that 22,000 millionaires had been created since 1914. [Cf., *New York Times*, February 9, 1919. Despite the increase in millionaires, the degree of inequality in the distribution of income declined somewhat during World War I because of the new federal income taxes after 1913. Cf., Wesley C. Mitchell, et al., *Income in the United States: Its Amount and Distribution 1909–1919* (New York: Harcourt, Brace, 1921), pp. 1, 115–16, 146; Sidney Ratner, *Taxation and Democracy in America* (New York: Wiley, 1967), pp. 307ff.]

7. Commission on Industrial Relations, *Final Report* (Washington, D.C.: Government Printing Office, 1916), p. 80.

8. See Arundel Cotter, *The Authentic History of the United States Steel Corporation* (New York: Moody Magazine and Book Company, 1916), p. 224, for proportions in detail for various lines of output.

9. *Final Report*, p. 75.

10. *New York Times*, March 4, 1919.

11. Interlocking directorates are now technically forbidden by the Clayton Act, but the substance remains, though the detail in expression of power is changed.

12. *Final Report*, p. 80.

13. *Report of the Committee . . . to investigate the concentration and control of money and credit*, House Report 1593, 62nd Cong., 3d Sess. (Washington, D.C.: Government Printing Office, 1913), p. 89; Louis D. Brandeis, *Other People's Money, and How the Bankers Use It* (New York: Frederick A. Stokes, 1914), p. 33. The capitalization figures are larger here than in the Industrial Commission statement, because the latter was confined to industrial corporations while the Pujo Report covered financial institutions also.

14. Basil M. Manly, "Labor's Share of the Social Product," *Annals of the American Academy of Political and Social Science*, Vol. LXIX (January, 1917), pp. 128–32.

15. *Final Report*, p. 80.

16. *Ibid.*, p. 80. Federal Trade Commission, *Summary of Report on the Meat Packing Industry* House Doc. 1297, 65th Cong., 2d Sess. (Washington, D.C.: Government Printing Office, 1918), p. 14; House Committee on Interstate Commerce, *Hearings on Government Control of the Meat Packing Industry*, 65th Cong., 3d Sess. (Washington, D.C.: Government Printing Office, 1919), pp. 712, 813, 835.

17. Interstate Commerce Commission, Bureau of Statistics, Bulletin, *Distribution of Security Holdings of Steam Roads* (Washington, D.C., March 25, 1919). The figures apply to Class I roads and their non-operating subsidiaries, having together 97 per cent of all railroad shareholders.

18. *American Labor Year Book 1917–18* (New York: Rand School of Social Science, 1918), p. 169.

19. Basil M. Manly, "America's Industrial Unrest," *Nation, Vol.* CVIII, No. 2815 (June 14, 1919), pp. 933–35. The earnings of the Standard Oil Company of New Jersey averaged $43,260,000 for four prewar years and $69,614,000 for the three war years, after payment of taxes.

20. . . . This . . . reconstruction program of the Council [is reprinted in John A. Ryan, *Social Reconstruction* (New York: Macmillan, 1920), pp. 217–38; the quotation in the text is on p. 227].

21. W. Jett Lauck and Edgar Sydenstricker, *Conditions of Labor in American Industries* (New York: Funk and Wagnalls, 1917), p. 29.

22. *Ibid.*, p. 61.

23. *Ibid.*, pp. 246–47.

24. *Ibid.*, pp. 249–50.

25. *Ibid.*, p. 360. The Commission on Industrial Relations estimates that one-fifth of the working time is lost. *Final Report*, p. 36.

26. Sumner H. Slichter, *The Turnover of Factory Labor* (New York: Appleton, 1919), pp. 20–22.

27. Lauck and Sydenstricker, *op. cit.*, p. 368.

28. *Ibid.*, pp. 373–74.

29. W. Jett Lauck, *The Cost of Living and the War* (Cleveland: Doyle and Waltz, 1920), p. 31.

30. U.S. Department of Labor, Childrens' Bureau, *Standards of Child Welfare*, Conference Series No. 1, Bureau Publication No. 60 (Washington, 1919), pp. 31ff. and *Save the Youngest*, Bureau Publication No. 61 (n.p., n.d.), pp. 14–15.

III

Political Government
and Industrial Government

The preceding chapter has shown, as exactly as statistical and other available facts will permit, to what [an] extent our wealth is concentrated in [a] few hands and to how much greater [an] extent the control over our industry has become centralized. The huge fortunes of the few [e.g., Andrew Carnegie, J. P. Morgan, John D. Rockefeller] are spectacular, but the dictatorial power of . . . the few is more spectacular. The fortunes have grown great, but the power [based upon these fortunes] has grown greater and more rapidly [than the fortunes]. Not the ownership of wealth, but the control of [tremendous economic] power is what makes this generation [of capitalists] most radically different from the last. Today, indeed, wealth is not really the basis of power; rather it is its [power's] plaything. Today, wealth is not so much substantial property to use and enjoy, as it is the powerful assertion of claims [by an elite] upon the future income of the people. Today, "good will," which is a commercial euphemism for [economic] might, is more the basis of capitalizations than is material wealth. Within such statements lie a nest of puzzles, and in the solving of these puzzles lies the fate of the nation.

To approach them, one must first of all become exact in his understanding of the organization of this power in its relation to political government. Political government is organized power, whether in an absolutism or in a democracy.* Industrial power in

* Cf., Arthur F. Bentley, *The Process of Government* (Chicago: University of Chicago Press, 1908), pp. 258 ff.

31

some of its greediest forms is commonly thought of as privately and wickedly interfering with government. Anarchist or socialist may think of it as usurping government, and perhaps he may believe that to defeat it, he must first wreck [the] government. What we need is a detached view of the two structures, the political and the industrial, noting and comparing the extent and ramifications of their organization: the foundations of their power, the nature of their relations and rivalries. We need a picture that is objective; one that differs from [the] ordinary catch-phrase description as much as the photograph taken by the military aviator or by the astronomer differs from the every-day interpretations of his [own eyes].

Such a picture will show the industrial organization we now have to be a true government itself, existing in its capacity of industrial government alongside the political government—a great compelling organization of the relations of men; of the relations not merely of some men with other men, but of all men who live in its territory with each other. An organization from which no man can break away any more than he can from the political government; an organization which has grown up alongside the political government, and splits through the middle the allegiances of the people of the common territory.

The man whose thought of government is that of the old civil government textbook will resist this view. For him, government will mean only the political organization, crowned with sovereignty, authenticated by the written constitution, and existing in all that rigid fixity which textbook language implies. For him, corporations and super-corporations in all their activities will be simply individuals, "artificial persons" under the law, subject to discipline if they misbehave, and with no rights and powers beyond what the law formally gives them. This is a bias, a convention of speech, and it must be cleared away just as much as the bias of hatred felt by some other man who, over-tense with [feeling about the] class-struggle, sees in political government only an external force, a crusher of liberties, an evil to be rooted out.

In attempting to understand our complexly organized industrial power, it is the quantities involved and the range of organization that counts. These facts of quantity and organization must be spread out before us, and studied, if [possible], to scale, so that they can be compared with the facts of political government in just measure for what they are. The political government furnishes a type [or model]: the other may be understood in terms of that type.

Looking at our industrial organization, treating it as a picture spread out before us, the first thing that we observe is that it is an organization; not merely of stock- and bond-holders, presidents, general managers, chairmen of boards of directors and affiliated directorates, but of all the population; including those men who labor in it for wages and those who, by payment of price, receive and consume its products. Without workers and consumers the organization simply would not be there. Leave them out, and it is inconceivable. Photograph it, and they will inevitably register their presence. Without men to work, without men to consume, we would have none of the special values that industrial life gives rise to. Talk abstractly as we may about systems of rights and titles or records of accounting, they are but symbols pointing at the living, moving organization of work and workers; with investors, managers, financial overseers, wage-earners and consumers, all comprised within it—either that, or nothing at all.*

Here must be the starting point for comparing industrial organization with political government. Political government likewise is an affair, not merely of elective and appointive officers, constitutions, and statutes. It is the whole political life of all people who constitute it. "We, the people of the United States," to use the opening words of our Constitution, are all involved in it. In both fields we must be all-inclusive in our facts. This initial similarity, of course, proves nothing. It does not prove that we actually have a developed industrial organization comparable to the developed political organization, differing only in kind[s] of activities involved. It merely indicates the full field in which proof must be sought.

The political government is a great positive system of organization, specializing its powers and vigorously assertive of them, both externally towards other nations, and internally towards its own citizens. But in industrial matters, in the great business of "getting

* Cf., *ibid.*, pp. 189–191.

a living" from its simplest to its most elaborate aspects, the political government is not assertive and positive, but . . . permissive and regulative; and even in the regulation field, apart from early prohibitions of murders, robberies, and the crudest frauds, it has but reluctantly advanced to its present degree of control.[1]

Now, while the political government has been thus negative towards industry, great forces have been at work in the industrial field of a nature similar to those that created the political government. The pressure of the population in its working environment of land and forces of nature has built up a huge industrial organization trending rapidly towards ever greater centralization of control. And since this organization has not been free to perfect itself directly inside of the political structure, it has perfected itself outside of it. It has produced the industrial government, existing among the same people, at the same time, and on the same territory as the political government; interacting with the political government, limiting the latter and being limited by it, but, nevertheless, in its great positive functions separate and distinct from it. This industrial government is a government itself, not some lesser form of organization, by the very tests that all of the people are involved in its workings; that the ramifications of its organization are very wide; that its control is highly centralized; and that the limitations it puts upon individual action, direct and indirect, are very great. It is important to look carefully into the truth of these assertions, not merely as a matter of description, but for the practical assistance that a comprehensive statement of the facts will give us in dealing with the great problems of industry, government, and revolution that confront us.

This industrial government involves, as has been said, the whole land and its resources, and the whole population as it is engaged in getting the livings of all of its members and in the great adventures attendant thereupon. It involves all of the wealth of the country held in private titles, and it involves that wealth not merely as a matter of private titles, but as the working equipment of the nation. We must consider it positively as a fact of observation that the whole nation contains or possesses this huge wealth, and we must take the system of private titles with its existing concentration of holdings as the form of organization in which this wealth is possessed. A man may own stocks in a big "industrial" and not even know where its factories are located. A multimillionaire may own a whole industrial enterprise without ever having laid a hand on a single piece of its physical property. Yet these properties may be the beehives for the activities of many thousands of men.

It is not forcing terms to use "government" in this way. "Self-government" means the individual's central control of his own conflicting tendencies or personalities. A governor or governess in a family is an appointive person to whom is delegated certain of the parental powers of family government. Consider the Governor of the Bank of England, the boards of governors of many institutions, and that wide field of study, ecclesiastical government. The Papacy was at one time such a strong system of government that it could rival political governments and even war with them: no one would deny the reality of its present government of its clergy and its loyal adherents. But far greater and more typical than any of these as an organized system of government is the industrial organization of the United States today. It alone has characteristics which make it possible to match it point by point with the political government.

Moreover, the conception of an industrial government is evident in the air around us. We have not only the Soviets, [who] aim to replace political government entirely by a special type of hoped-for industrial government, but we have the vaguely used term "industrial democracy," drawing a metaphor from political government. These, of course, are fighting terms, apart from our purpose, which is to attain the most comprehensive statement of fact. The corporation as it exists appeals to Justice [Louis D.] Brandeis of the United States Supreme Court as a state within a state.[2] A similar phrase has been used by Lord Rosebery in speaking of the completeness and coherence of the cooperative movement in England.[3] [Charles P.] Steinmetz [the noted engineer and Socialist], in his analysis of our present national problems, has separate chapters on the Political Government and the Industrial Government, though using the latter term in a narrower sense than it is used here.[4] These are all more than mere facile descriptive terms. They all point to a most substantial characteristic of facts.

Observe now the rough outlines of the industrial system: For railroads, 100 per cent is in corporate form; for public utilities, 100 per cent; for mining and manufacturing, 90 per cent; for commerce, we may suspect 60 per cent. The corporation formally organizes certain persons in their wealth relationships: bond-holders, preferred- and common-stock holders; and in managing relationships it organizes certain of these same persons and certain others through profit-sharing, commission, or bonus arrangements. Practically, rather than formally, it organizes great numbers of other persons in clerical, wage-labor and superintending capacities. Thence, through the various forms of gentlemen's agreements, combinations, and trusts, the corporation has passed to the super-corporation [e.g., the United States Steel Corporation] known as such not to law, but to business life; combining and organizing many plants and industries and populations far remote from one another into a common system. Above this appear interlocking directorates, holding companies, and the investment-banker system of promotion and control.

Behind them stand unproclaimed and mysterious background partnerships, quasi-corporations, and corporoid forms of agreement [e.g., cartels]. Just as the partnership developed into the corpora-tion through combination of interests, differentiation of functions, and the need of permanence for "the business," so corporations are passing through [an] analogous evolution out of themselves into a larger form. Through advertising, package-goods, and fixed-price control, they are organizing the marketing system and regulating the consumers' possibility of purchase; and thus in an external sense organizing the consumers themselves. They are controlling produc-tion, limiting output, and fixing prices by direct act of volition.* All of this organization results in an indirect, though no less power-ful, control beyond its immediate limits. In that part of commerce not already within the direct system, if a certain conformity is not yielded, a threat of destruction always impends. In agriculture, the indirect effects are so prominent today that while agriculture may

* Although anti-competitive business practices such as price-fixing and market-rigging have been more vigorously prosecuted under the antitrust laws in recent decades, Bentley's indictments remain pertinent. It is primarily the highly formal (and flagrant) agreements that have been attacked, and the subtler forms of col-lusion may continue to flourish.

not be said to be directly in the [industrial] system, neither can it be said to lie outside of it.

This then is the rough outline of the system: a system under which 8,300 stockholders own 52 per cent of the railroad stock of the country; under which 1.5 per cent of the stockholders of the largest of the proclaimed corporations, [U.S.] Steel, own 57 per cent of the stock;[5] under which, in ten years, out of all stock issues above $10 million in the country (a total of $3 billion) all but one were floated by the Morgan-Baker-Stillman [banking] interests;[6] [and] under which the meat supply of the country, and a growing control of other food supplies, is in the hands of a closely united Big Five with 750 dependent and affiliated companies and their agencies.

Let us now take our political government and characterize the relationships with which the relationships of the industrial government are to be brought into comparison. [The] political government [of the United States] is an organization of power, internal and external, covering all of a defined territory and all of the persons within that territory. Its citizens are assumed to be self-justified as citizens by the very fact of their existence, this being the meat of the Declaration of Independence phrase that all men are "created equal." They are bound together in a long list of relations under the civil and criminal laws, in various sections and branches of the government which they control or strive to control by vote and through representatives, direct and indirect, elective and appointive, of many kinds. Most of them now participate to some extent in the conduct of the government if by nothing more than by the use of the ballot, although in former times property and educational qualifications limited the franchise, and until recently women have been excluded, while minors, aliens, and certain defectives and delinquents are still excluded. The field of political government has included keeping the peace; keeping open the simplest highways, such as roads and streets; prohibiting such "industries" as theft, forgery, and the worst frauds; and maintaining certain general services like the Post Office and water supply, in addition, of course, to the tasks of external offense and defense. In recent years political government has extended its industrial regulations to include such matters as food adulterations, railroad rate discriminations, and sometimes local price discriminations; and it has placed certain positive requirements on citizens in matters like sanitation, where not to place them would be equivalent, under existing living conditions, to countenancing [an] indirect form of murder or theft. But it has not engaged itself constructively with the individual citizen's complexes of activity nor helped to build them up, except through devices like the protective tariff or of recent agencies for assembling information and giving advice.

In the industrial field, where exists what we have characterized as the industrial government, we can match all these facts. The whole people within the whole territory is involved, and the organization of power is immensely complex, stretching into other lands and underlying war and peace.[7] Aliens are as much in the organization as political citizens, and women and child wage-earners are directly on the same footing as adult men. Every resident, every citizen of the industrial government, if we may so put it, is self-justified as a getter of a living, a maintainer of life and enjoyment. All are bound together in a long list of relations involving property rights, wage systems, capitalizations, prices, and values.

The main difference between the two governments lies, of course, in the range of activities which are positively organized. For the industrial government, this range includes the whole field of industry, commerce, and finance in all of their forms; touching the political field in a thousand places, but developing itself positively and organizing itself separately, nevertheless, in its own way.

A secondary difference has to do with the manner in which power is exercised, or in other words with the "form" of government. Our political government is democratic: our industrial government is autocratic. Of course, neither democracy nor autocracy is consistent and thorough-going: the industrial government is no more autocratic at every point than the political government is democratic at every point, but the contrast of types of power is nevertheless well enough marked. Consider this in terms of the electoral franchise.

The shareholders of a corporation or some class or classes of them have the right of ballot. They meet at stated times and elect directors, who act as their representatives and elect officers. Bond-holders, and often preferred-stock holders, have surrendered this voting power in return for special security given them. Sometimes in small corporations, especially in case of emergency, this voting power is effective. Usually, however, it has much less possibility of [achieving a] result than the political franchise.* In the great mutual insurance companies where every voter counts one, it has always been impossible to vitalize it, and in large corporations it is rarely serviceable, except as between two compact rival interests. With subsidiary corporations, action follows upon commands that come from above; and with the investment banking system and the interlocking directorates, an even tighter control is exercised over corporations in the most essential matters of price and output.

If democracy shows itself in a very limited and imperfect way in the corporation so far as certain classes of investors are concerned, it shows itself not at all so far as wage-earners and consumers are concerned. Wage-earners are men who have no pretense of [corporate] control. Theoretically, they are free as individuals to take [orders] or leave [their employment], but practically, all together in the whole system, they are compelled to take [orders] and cannot leave. Not organized within the system, they have been driven to organization without [outside] it. To skillfully organized force they have offered [or] opposed raw force. Their [trade-union] organization is commonly regarded by rulers of the [American] industrial system as rebellious, and often it is treated in that way by the political system, until finally it has come to pass that some portions of the wage-earners' organizations [e.g., the Industrial Workers of the World] have boldly accepted the charge as truly characterizing their attitude.

With consumers the case is even more striking. They have not yet won to organizing their own interests in any definite way in the industrial government; except so far as experiments in co-operation have given them beginnings. They have vaguely relied on the political government, and through it have secured recognition for their

* The implications of the divorce between ownership and management of corporations are fully explored by A. A. Berle, Jr., and Gardiner C. Means, *The Modern Corporation and Private Property* (New York: Macmillan, 1933). Cf., J. A. Livingston, *The American Stockholder* (Philadelphia and New York: Lippincott, 1958); and Edward S. Mason, ed., *The Corporation in Modern Society* (Cambridge: Harvard University Press, 1960).

interests in the field of industrial government. They have some little indirect influence . . . [through] outcries or boycotts or potential competition, but very little compared to the extent of their interests in this field.[8]

Just as the democratic nature of the political government is given a theoretical expression in "equality before the law" and in equality of franchise, so the autocratic nature of the industrial government is evident in the fact that the industrial franchise, so far as it exists at all, is quantitative in terms of wealth. Men enter the industrial government not as "unit men," each man counting one, but as "propertied men," each one having a quantitative franchise in terms of dollars. On this footing of inequality, the great centralized power of the industrial government is built up.

This difference between autocracy and democracy does not invalidate our treatment of the two governments as separately coexisting in the same territory and period, but rather serves to emphasize it; and we may well believe that when the two types of power become the same, the two governments will coalesce: the possibilities before us being autocracy in both politics and industry, or democracy in both.

It may be objected that we have no right to regard the industrial system as a separate government alongside of the political government, because the corporation, its unit structure—its township, so to speak—is a creation of [legislative] statute and gets no power except from the political government. The answer is the answer of fact. The great system is there before our eyes. It is perfectly true that the corporation secures its permit to exist, its formal, as opposed to its substantial, creation from the political government. But the great forces that caused its existence and have led to its huge expansion have not worked through the political government. On the contrary, they have been excluded from it. The life of the corporation, as opposed to its formal title to existence, has been carried on in what we may call an "extra-legal" field: its legality has been barely enough to keep it from being positively illegal. Nor is this all. Even the idea of legal incorporation, and the name itself, came from old governmental types, such as the city corporation and the ecclesiastical corporation, all of them with governmental characteristics and functions. The political government took a business organization, the partnership, with the positive work of which it did not pretend to concern itself, [and] gave it a governmental form; and then, instead of keeping that new governing unit within its own system, or even under its steady control, launched it freely into the busy world of men and let it develop. The industrial government, rival of the political government, is the result as we actually have it in our land today.

Other objections may be raised, but they are equally aside from the issue, which is the best possible envisagement of the facts. The industrial government has no written constitution, while our American political governments all found themselves on the written word; but it must be remembered that written constitutions are not typical of government, but rather late manifestations and exceptional. Great Britain has no written constitution, to be found in one place and one text, even to this day; but she is no less a nation and a government for that. Our meat-packing industry may deny any formal combination, and by its cleverness of argument may drive us to talk of "harmonious competition" or "close competition," with a very special emphasis on the word "close," but it does not thereby alter any of the facts of limitation of output, division of field [markets], and control of prices.

Written or unwritten, that organization is just as perfect. To offset the lack of written constitution, the industrial government may indeed hold up to us its dogma, its elaborated creed of "property" and "rights;" terms distorted far from their true meanings, and worked up into idolatries and superstitions. To its dogma, all protest becomes anarchy, syndicalism, or bolshevism, or whatever [other] current epithet carries with it the greatest implications of horror. By it, all industrial dissenters [from oligopoly or monopoly capitalism], so far as may be, are proclaimed political traitors. By it, petty selfishness and petty fear are clothed with virtue: made, indeed, the peculiar virtues of its subjects. So pervasive is this dogma . . . that it has become the very atmosphere of all [public] discussion [in America], and its poisonous emanations blacken and stifle much that is honestly and clearly said or written about it.

Nor will any considerations of a theoretical nature concerning sovereignty militate against the view [that there is an industrial government]. Sovereignty, in a treatise on political science, is not something to rely upon, but something to wonder about. We must locate it in the population as a residuum of power, for even after a hundred and fifty years we do not all agree as to its exact residence as between federal and state agencies of government. From all that we know of the relations of international trade to war, and even from what we know of the rush of dollar-a-year men to Washington when war [World War I] began, we may locate as much sovereignty in the people industrially organized as in the people politically organized; and unless we are hopelessly attached to some meta-physical unity of sovereignty, there is nothing to worry us in re-garding it as hovering, a double-headed bird, between the two fields.*

Again it may be said that the political government stands before us fully evolved and formalized, while the industrial system answers no such tests. But despite our written constitution, with its many governing bodies and its full system of checks and balances, con-sider what we have observed in our own lifetime [from 1870 to 1920] of the submergence of state authority under federal au-thority: of the tremendous development of strength in the federal executive; and [of] the encroachments of the [national] judiciary upon the legislature, upon administration, and even, in the matter of punishments for contempt without trial by jury, upon the guarantees of our Bill of Rights. The modern state did not appear full-fledged in Europe, but arose out of long, sharp struggles. When some future historian describes the industrial development of the nineteenth and twentieth centuries, he will have a tale to tell similar in all essentials to that which our present historians now tell of the political development of Europe in the thirteenth to the sixteenth centuries. A comparison with France [as an emerging nation-state] is specially suggestive. The great barons built up their power, and were successively engulfed in the growing state or entered into it, much as rival corporations [in the United States] have been engulfed or consolidated, until finally the greatest of them all became the final center of power, of sovereignty; "L'État, c'est moi."

Such is the case, as a matter of description alone, for regarding the [American] industrial system as an industrial government, and

* Cf., A. F. Bentley, *The Process of Government*, p. 264; and Morris R. Cohen, *Law and the Social Order* (New York: Harcourt, Brace, 1933), pp. 41–68.

for recognizing its full working power in the field of man as earner of income and holder of property, the field which political organizations did not enter in any positive way. Of the reasons for the emergence of this system, we have said nothing except to refer them to the pressure of the population [within the United States] under the existing conditions of technology. Into this subject we need not enter, for we have not here a question as to the desirability or undesirability, the avoidability or unavoidability of the [American industrial] system. The system itself is the great achievement of the last half-century. In it, we all stand perforce as members, our eyes to the future, in the hope that that future will show itself constructive, and that the destructive tendencies arising out of the [oligopoly] system itself will be overcome, at least as fully as some of the destructive tendencies of the old industrial [laissez-faire] competition were overcome by the new industrial government.

The practical case, as opposed to the descriptive case for this point of view, is something that cannot be stated here, but must be judged by its fruits in later chapters. To refuse to include workers and consumers in a study of the industrial government is as much as to assume the point of view of a special interest or set of interests at the start, and to abandon all pretense of completeness. To discuss the [industrial] system solely as an organization of property rights resting in the political government, gives but a shadow of the facts, a phantom of words, not a living activity of people; not even the living activity of the owners of those rights.

If there is one valid objection to the [author's thesis or] point of view, it is the inclusion of those persons in occupations not yet directly centralized—agriculture, and a limited part of the trade— by virtue of the indirect effects of the system upon them, the indirect centralization. This again must rest [wait] for further judgment. The case lies in the mastery of the highways of manufacturing and commerce by the powers of centralization, a subject for later consideration.

One more aspect of the situation must be considered here, and that but briefly; the interrelations of the political and industrial governments. We all know enough of the phenomena of the [political] boss and the [political] lobby, of corruption, of the use of the saloon in city politics, of the ravishment [by unscrupulous business firms] of the public domain, and of [water] power and mineral rights. Treated ethically as outrageous things, fought against as possible of suppression, they proved nevertheless to be but the disorderly beginnings of the great struggle between the two governments. In the time of [President] McKinley the industrial government placed its blazoned representative, Mark Hanna, in control at the center of political power [in the Republican Party and in the United States Senate], and Hanna was followed, less spectacularly but more efficiently, by [Nelson W.] Aldrich in the same function [from 1904 to 1911]. Since Aldrich, the development of the [American] industrial autocracy alongside of the political democracy has been so overpowering, that no such conspicuous [counterpart to] Charles Martel has been needed by it beside the throne of the political holders of office, and its results have been reached smoothly and quietly in comparison with previous struggles.

Perhaps the greatest of the struggles, already well along towards becoming a recollection of the past, was the anti-monopoly fight in its various forms [from the Civil War to World War I]. The old arguments [in favor] of [laissez-faire] competition, of [the] service and efficiency [of competitive enterprises] and their rewards, as working out [to] the general public welfare, have been dropped; first by one part of the population and then by another, till now [1920] they are rarely heard. The ethical assaults on monopoly as destroying competition have failed.[9] In time of war [World War I] the political organization [the national government under President Wilson], so far from striving to pick the industrial system to pieces, fused with it. The industrial government [as represented by Big Business] moved into the political headquarters [of the war agencies] almost bodily, and while subjecting itself to some limitation on certain of its more extreme powers, handled the war almost as if it were its own.

In the relations between capital and labor—primarily a struggle within the industrial government—the political government has been involved, with unequal power, by seizures or appeals from both sides. In such a matter as child-labor, after almost a century of struggle, there is even yet but an imperfect control through the political government. The majority of the reforms introduced have come haltingly and in crippled form.* Within the industrial government many achievements of force are exhibited on both sides, while phases of what has been called a "benevolent despotism" have appeared.

The case of the consumers would be a much shorter story.† They have wrested, through the political government, some control of adulterations and short-weights; but even their attempts at cooperative buying are still, in this country, under very considerable handicap of the laws.

So stand at this time [1920] the two governments; the political democracy and the industrial autocracy.[10] We do not need to raise the question as to which is dominant over the other, for clearly neither is dominant. They are involved in a great complexity of struggle. But we do need to recognize (1) that the two governments [co]exist; (2) that just as the political government is an organization of all of the population, so the industrial government is a direct organization of the greater part of the population and an indirect organization of all of it; (3) that the methods of power of the two governments are fundamentally opposed; (4) that all of the problems of law and order, revolution, and reform in our times will be involved in their conflicts; and (5) that unless we are willing to envisage them clearly and completely for what they are, we can participate in their struggles but blindly, and with an individual helplessness ill-befitting our needs.

We do not need to wonder if the loyalties of citizens under the two governments tend dangerously to divergence and clash. If the man with little or no property, or any other man living the subject['s] life under the industrial government, comes to think of the political government with hatred, it need not fill us with surprise or moral indignation no matter how much we deplore it; but rather it should seem to us but the natural outcome, the counterpart, of the fact that [the] men living the ruler[s'] life under the industrial government have come to think of the political government with a proprietary sense—as though its prime function was the protec-

---

* Cf., Harold U. Faulkner, *The Decline of Laissez-Faire 1897–1917* (New York & Toronto: Rinehart, 1951), pp. 258 ff.
† *Ibid.*, pp. 352–355.

tion of their property powers. The attitude of revolt is hardly any further away than the attitude of proprietorship from that loyalty of citizenship, which we are all supposed to possess, [from] that love of government as the reasonable regulation of our powers, [and] as the protection of our lives and families and enjoyment of property from the unreasonable aggression of other men. To give adoration to political government as the protector of powers of exploitation, and to hate government as the protector of the powers of exploitation are [the] obverse and reverse of the same coin: if the latter attitude is seditious and subversive of liberty, the former must equally be so classed.

Notes

1. This applies, of course, to our own government, and is not always historically true. Patriarchal tribes and communal villages have worked up all industry, or almost all, very positively into their political systems.

2. ". . . you have created within the State a state so powerful that the ordinary forces existing are insufficient to meet it." Commission on Industrial Relations, *Final Report and Testimony* (12 vols., Washington, D.C.: Government Printing Office, 1916), Vol. I, p. 63.

3. Quoted by Emerson P. Harris, *Cooperation, The Hope of the Consumer* (New York: Macmillan, 1918), p. 92.

4. Charles P. Steinmetz, *America and the New Epoch* (New York: Harper, 1916), Chaps. XII and XIII. Steinmetz, who is consulting engineer of the General Electric Co., uses the term "cooperation," as a descriptive companion word to "corporation," thus bringing out the personal side of the working relation. He frankly describes [in this book] the purposes of a super-corporation as being the control of prices and the limitation of output (pp. 34–35), and discusses its functions under the headings: Financial, Administrative, Technical, and Social (p. 37). At the financial pole he sees the maximum of abuse and wastefulness when this function is too prominent in the minds of the corporation managers, and at the social pole he sees a benevolent recognition of the workers. . . . [He has an] interesting discussion of the weakness of our political government as an occasion for the independent development of the industrial government. . . . [He also has a] valuable analysis of the sectional interests of the United States prior to the Civil War and afterwards as making impossible a consistent national policy. . . . [Both critiques] are illuminating.

5. Commission on Industrial Relations, *Final Report*, 1916, p. 80.

6. See *Report of the* [Pujo] *Committee . . . to Investigate the Concentration of Control of Money and Credit*, House Report No. 1,593, 62 Cong., 3 Sess., p. 160.

7. For a careful discussion of the way in which excess profits lead to foreign investment and thence to the danger of war, see Walter E. Weyl, *American World Policies* (New York: Macmillan, 1917), pp. 186ff., also pp. 59ff. and pp. 203ff.

8. It is interesting to observe how even consumers' organizations are coming

to be regarded as of a rebellious nature by the rulers of the industrial system. A most striking illustration applying, however, not to consumers but to livestock growers, is to be found in the long statement filed by the [meat] packers with the Senate Committee on Agriculture and Forestry during the hearings on the Kendrick Bill (S. 5305) 1919: *Hearings on Government Control of the Meat Packing Industry*, 65th Cong., 3rd Sess., pp. 1995–2045, esp. p. 2023, in which, with much evidence of outraged innocence, the history of the livestock growers organizations is discussed as if they were a dangerous conspiracy against the peace and well-being of the land.

9. See C. P. Steinmetz, *op. cit.*, and Arthur J. Eddy, *The New Competition* (New York: Appleton, 1912).

10. Compare two such different points of view as those of Lindley M. Keasbey in "The Economic State," *Political Science Quarterly*, Vol. VIII, No. 4 (December, 1893), pp. 601–625, who holds that to the old economic "factors of production": land, labor, and capital, a fourth, "the economic state" should be added; and William D. Haywood and Frank Bohn in *Industrial Socialism* (Chicago: C. H. Kerr & Company, 1911), who characterize present industry as an "industrial empire."

IV

Property and Power

The industrial government has its footing in property. The citizen of the industrial government is man in his property-owning activities. Property ownership is closely associated with industrial power. Until we have examined the relations of property and power, our analysis of the political and industrial governments remains incomplete.

If by property one means primarily accumulations of capital goods and all the claims and privileges that grow out of them, [and] if by ownership one means a finished system of legal rights—stiff-frozen and sacred—his conception of the industrial government, and of the political government as well, will be determined for him in advance. He will see before him, whether clearly or vaguely, a caste system of the propertied and the property-less.

But if under property one comprehends the full ownership and enjoyment and use of [real and personal] property, including the property each man handles as a consumer and the income that he earns and uses, [and] if one sees the system of legal rights not as finished, but historically as an evolving system, then he will have a much better chance at an understanding of the many forces that are arrayed in society and of the many issues they involve. Instead of using terms and methods of thought that shut out in advance all possibility of agreement and compromise between the interests arrayed, he will have a chance to bring them to [before] his understanding, upon a common meeting ground.

The word "right" is specially misleading, for almost by definition it begs the question in advance: indeed, it begs all questions which

48

it touches. Not merely ownership in a limited sense, not merely the rights of property, must be examined, but that full complex of property rights-uses-powers as actually existing. "Powers" is by far the more comprehensive term; for while "rights" asserts the individual's position as it for the moment is, and while "uses" lays its stress on property goods as such, "powers" brings more clearly to mind the actor in his full relations both with the [capital and consumer] goods and with other men. We shall use the word "powers;" and we shall use it, to begin with, as objectively and as free from favorable or unfavorable implication as we use it when we speak of a power of attorney, or when in political science we discuss the powers of government.

We know very well that there is such a thing as power in society, and that indeed our whole life is shot through with it. Apart from courts, constabulary, and administrative offices, there are facets of power in all of our daily relations with each other. Wealth is power, work is power, and industrial knowledge is power. If I sign a note, I give someone else a certain power over me. If I contract to buy a house, I do the same thing. If I have a grocery store, I have one range of power over you as my customer, which I can heighten by some form of combination or understanding with the other grocers; while you, as my customer, have a certain power over me, which you can greatly heighten if you combine with other customers.

If you need work, I have power over you if I can employ and pay you; and if I work for you, I have various powers of diligence or malingering very important to you. If I am starving, who can say what power I will yield myself up to in order to secure bread, or what reserve fund of violence I will myself draw upon to get that bread?

The direct physical violences of muscle and of personal weapons have been largely, in [the] ordinary course [of affairs], eliminated from society. They form a technique of power which would, [if] in general use, involve the destruction of society, and are necessarily under control if society is to continue. Many of the trickeries and treacheries of brain-use have been similarly eliminated.

A tool is almost by definition an extension of a man's power. With it he can get more quantities and kinds of things than he could without it. He must possess it to use it, though that possession may range all the way from the most temporary handling up to the furthest extreme of private title.

The goods a man consumes are in the same way extensions of his power. His food nourishes him to work again. His store of food enables him to choose his times and ways of working. His consumption of pleasures may heighten his vitality. Many of his expenditures are for symbols of his power, displays of his person, and marks of his mastery of his environment.

These powers—under an elaborated protective system of private [property] titles, and under the many-sided system of exchange of commodities involved in society's production and consumption— evolve themselves into a far-reaching system of powers over other men, expressed through the whole terminology of values, prices, and capitalizations. To the power a man has to handle himself as a man among men, and to the power to produce for himself and for other men, is added power over the production and the results of the production of other men and over their consumption.

We have here no mere question of logical analysis of definitions, but a problem of assembling and grouping facts of the commonest everyday observation. More than this: so far as we pause to discuss the powers of property in terms of individual men, it must be understood that we are doing it entirely with reference to the great mass-facts of power which underlie the industrial and political problems of the times [the 1920's]. The minutiae of an individual's way with his property will be of significance to us only as they cast light on those operations of masses of people which have tangible effects on a large scale on our well-being, and which enter into the nature of our industrial institutions.

The distinction which is most apparent on the surface is that between the rights-uses-powers of property for consumption and the rights-uses-powers [of property] for production. This gave to political economy long ago the distinction between consumer goods and capital [goods], a distinction which could quite adequately be made concrete by picturing all the wealth of the country in two heaps, one destined for consumption by individuals or the public, the other destined for transformation into [producers'] goods that [produce goods that] ultimately will be consumed [either] directly or after still further transformations.

The next distinction in property rights-uses-powers is that between powers of production and powers of appropriation. This is one that cannot be so easily pictured in terms of heaps of goods, but it is nevertheless just as concrete as the preceding distinction, and it is represented just as fully in perfected differentiations within our industrial system today.

The selection of terms which will best convey meaning is, as always in this field, somewhat difficult, because all terms we can find shade into each other in complicated ways, or carry marked implications of approbation or disapprobation. If we wish to be schematic, we may perhaps comprise both the productive and the appropriative powers under the term "acquisitive." We will then first distinguish between consumption-powers and acquisition-powers, and within the latter, we will separate between powers of production and powers of appropriation. However, this [schema] matters little.

The fact that concerns us is that we use goods to sustain and promote life (consumption); we use them to produce other goods (production); and we use them to mediate the transfer of title of goods, either now existing, or in course of production, from others to ourselves (appropriation). These uses are well-differentiated, not only in individuals, but—what is the true test for us—in the largest functioning features of the industrial government: and the distinction between them is vital to all discussion of the industrial problems of the times. This distinction, it is of course manifest, is not a distinction between production in the sense of manufacturing, and appropriation in the sense of trade. The economist has long ago pointed out that commerce produces place and time utilities which are just as truly productive as the form utilities contributed by manufacture. Not only does the productive power of property exhibit itself in trade as well as [in] manufacture, but the appropriative power has found some of its most fertile fields in manipulating manufacturing industries. We have but to refer to many of the incidents of trust formation and "high finance"; to the financial function of the corporation as Steinmetz describes it; and to the phenomena of the investment bankers, in illustration [e.g., J. P. Morgan's formation of the United States Steel Corporation or John D. Rockefeller's creation of the Standard Oil Trust].

If one farmer cuts a lot of fence posts, hauls them to town, and failing to find a purchaser at the current price, gets a place to stack them, and then whenever he gets a chance, spends a little time hunting a farmer who needs them and will pay a fair price for them, we can certainly see in his whole activity a productive quality. If a town dealer purchases the posts and attends to the selling, we can also see a productive use of the property, though we may reserve a possible point or two for further information as to the way he uses the powers he acquires over them. But if a village idler gets permission to sell the posts, that is, gets permission to use certain property powers involved in them, and then spends two or three days sitting on the village square, awaiting the appearance of a man who, he hears, needs them and who is, he thinks, an "easy mark" for a high price, we have something very different. We have distinctly an appropriative use of the property rights, not a productive use. We have it in a differentiated form as a man's activity. The whole productive service could have been accomplished by a word to the fence post-maker or a postcard to the possible user, but that would not have secured the hoped-for appropriative profit.

If a manufacturer makes goods and puts them on the market and sells them, he is working productively; but if he builds up an elaborated protective system of tied agents and fixed prices with penalties for violation, he is adding a very special appropriative activity to his productive activity. And if he enters in this way a field already well-supplied and by new cleverness in his methods gains a stronghold in it, he is perhaps predominantly appropriative in what he does.[1]

Again when a trade-mark brand of an ordinary food is built up into a hugely profitable business by some specialty of advertising reiteration, we may have the appropriative corporation functioning without a single productive accompaniment; or at any rate with very slight productive accompaniments. Adulterations, short weights, misrepresentations, so far as they occur, are very definite appropriative uses of property.

When an oil company is organized to secure a lease, and starts [digging] a hole which it never expects to finish; when it sends out a flock of stock salesmen whose receipts from the sale of stock go one-third in commissions, one-third to the "salting" of the plant and to overhead expense, and the other third in profits to the promoters —and such adventures are notoriously common—we have purely appropriative uses of all the property involved. The whole adventure rests on the appropriative power involved in the property owner- ship, and in the appropriative methods and organization built thereon.

Let the distinction stand for what it is, a clue rather than a test, and let us look further, and from another point of view, into the property phase of industrial organization.[2]

A corporation has property to start with, that is, a going corpo- ration has property. There have been corporations started on fond hopes, the stock all water, the property all to be acquired. There have even been banks in which the notes of the incorporators were the only capital provided. But setting such cases aside, we may as- sume that a corporation starts with gold on hand [and] with build- ings or machinery or land or materials to be worked up or traded in. The value of its property rests in the use of it, in the power to use it and get returns from it. Now while the mere corporate form as such does not give any added value, nevertheless the corporate form is normally adopted in order to gain certain special advantages in management, control, and transfer of title; and so we may say at once that for using and income-producing purposes a certain ele- ment of value, at least a potential value, is added by incorporation.* We have therefore in our corporation at the start, or at least in its early working stages, a value which is not merely the sum of the values, assuming them to be ascertainable, of the items of property owned, but a premium, an addition due to the position acquired for industrial purposes.

It is, of course, not right to distinguish between a corporation technically in this respect and a partnership or syndicate [or] any other business organization. The corporation is merely the standard- ized organization, prepared, in its various more highly developed forms, to reap to the full and [to] consolidate and maintain the advantages of organization. In the case of any successful enterprise,

---

* Incorporation may also offer significant income tax advantages (vis-à-vis partnership or proprietorship). Bentley seems to equate the corporation with the large, powerful firm. This may have made more sense in 1920 than it does today, when we have numerous small business units incorporated.

the value of the sum of the assets taken separately is usually less than its value as a going concern. Even an unsuccessful enterprise is apt to show somewhat more value than its assets would have [shown] if appraised when scrapped.

From this we may pass through a long series of [business] phenomena: of surplus accumulations capitalized; of market valuation representing much more than par of capitalization and surpluses; of stock issued against high earning capacity of the present, regardless of valuation of assets; of stock issued against anticipated high future [growth]; of stock issues representing franchise grants in public utilities; of stock issues representing good will; of stock issues representing the good will or trade names of rivals purchased and absorbed; of stock issues representing merely the cost of acquiring rivals and putting them out of business without any further use of them; of stock issues against promotion costs; and of all the various kinds of "water" and "blue-sky" [additions to securities not represented by corresponding increases in assets] that may enter into capitalization.*

All of this valuation is worked out and adjusted, not on the basis of the material assets involved at separate appraisement, but on the basis of the income-earning capacity or the estimation of that capacity given to the organization, management, and industrial position of the company, with reference not only to other companies, but to available working forces and to available consumers for [the company's] products.

Now the point that stands out most clearly here is that the corporation must be regarded not primarily as an affair of property, but primarily as an element in the industrial government. It [the company] is appraised and valued; it has power for or against, favorable or unfavorable, in accordance, not with computations of [the money value of its] property goods, but in accordance with its position and functioning in the whole industrial system, which, as

---

* Corporations seeking to raise funds on major capital markets (i.e., those whose securities are "listed") are subject to relatively tight control by the Securities and Exchange Commission, as regards valuation of assets and any representation of company position. A pervasive system of regulation was enacted by Congress in the years following the Great Depression of 1929, when numerous fraudulent and deceptive practices came to light. Bentley's objection to valuation procedures appears, however, to go beyond those practices prohibited by the SEC.

an organization of all the workers and property owners and consumers, is the industrial government. Property as commodities rests at the basis of [this] system, much as the gold in the bank vault or in the national treasury rests at the basis of the elaborated credit system; but it is the organization that counts, not as a negative system of rights under the political government, but as a positive system of functional power under the industrial government.

Out of the mountainous heaps of interesting illustrations to which everybody could contribute from experience, let us take just three and put them briefly.

The Sulzberger and Sons Company, successor to Schwarzschild and Sulzberger, one of the Big Five packers, for reasons still largely concealed in the *histoire intime* of industrial royalty, was in trouble. After a raid on its stock by Swift [& Company] which just failed of securing control, and after some preliminary experiences with [New York] investment bankers, which culminated in its being significantly listed as Teutonic in sympathy by Great Britain and put on that country's barred [black] list of dealers [during World War I], its owners surrendered [in 1916]. The bankers, besides arranging a very comfortable 10 per cent profit on flotation and refunding of bond issues [for Sulzberger and Sons Company], took over some $10,000,000 of [its] stock—a little over half of the total issue—at between $5 and $6 a share. They then arranged to pay Thomas E. Wilson, [previously] president of Morris and Company, $125,000 a year [in] salary, to give him outright $1,500,000 par value of stock, and to sell him $3,500,000 more at $10 a share. No sooner was this stock of the new "Wilson and Company" on the market, after the reorganization and the establishing of satisfactory relations with the other four members of the Big Five, than it began to sell at prices ranging from $45 to $87.50 a share. Mr. Wilson testified before the Senate investigating committee that the assets could not have been valued at over $70 a share in 1916 when the transaction was made, but that the stock at the time of his testimony (January 1919) had a book value above $150 a share, though selling at $70 on the market.

We have here, clearly enough, something very different from a mere fact of property goods. Again, when the elder J. Pierpont Morgan bought control of the Equitable [Life] Assurance Society in 1910, he paid about $3 million for $51,000 of stock, limited by law to a 7 per cent dividend and never capable of being paid off to him on dissolution of the company at more than par value. He made an investment that would pay him less than one-eights of one per cent [in] direct income, but an enormous indirect income. What he bought was not property, but power; not the power of property as commodities, not productive power, but the power of appropriation, based on a kernel of property rights, and organized corporatively for action, and, so to speak guaranteed [its income-generating power] under the industrial government, and there only.[3]

And once again, in a different field. It has been estimated that if the business of the British cooperative societies was incorporated and placed on the market on a joint-stock [company] basis, it would capitalize for ten times the value of the assets now [in 1920] carried on its balance sheets. This would be a measure of its earning capacity, not in the sense of productive power, but in the sense of the appropriative power of its property organization.[4]

Some measure of the [stock market] value of going enterprises as entirely distinct from their property basis is shown in the fluctuations of stocks on Wall Street under varying conditions. There may be a wide range of price within a year, with substantially no change in the actual assets [of any one company or of many companies].

Another measure [of the same phenomenon] is seen in the great excess of the industrial valuations of the country over the property valuations calculated by the [U.S.] Census [Bureau] on the basis of [tax] assessment figures, as indicated in Chapter II. Along with the steady increment of land values goes prominently a similar increment of [stock-market] values arising out of the organized power of industries as such.

Again, the startling showing of income centralization as compared with [or as based on] property centralization is an evidence of what is taking place, especially when we take the maintenance of life among the workers at a decent standard as [something that should be considered a] part of the costs of production.

In what has just been said, we have touched on two contrasts—one, between the productive uses or powers of [private] property and the appropriative uses or powers—the other, between the property basis of a corporation, super-corporation, or [some] other

part of the industrial structure; and its special powers, not attribut-
able to property direct, but rather directly to its organized functioning strength. We have accepted here [market] value and price as
measures of all of these combined uses and powers because we see
them so used as a fact in society, and without any need of going
into the details of any [special] theory of value or price. In all of
these matters it is income-producing capacity that furnishes the test
in the background; ranging all the way from that income which is
a commodity produced by a man for his own use, to that income
which is an entry on a balance sheet marking the acquisition;
not of commodities for his use or for other peoples' uses, but
rather the acquisition of appropriative claims to heightened appropriative powers which can appear in capitalization and balance-
sheet figures, and which can in turn give rise to more such claims
and powers and capitalizations, ad infinitum.

The word "property" today covers a wide range of facts, all the
way from a flint knife or a haunch of venison in primitive hands to
a vested [economic] interest, such as the power that [J. P.]
Morgan acquired over the assets of the Equitable, or . . . the well-
advertised, well-clinched, well-capitalized capacity [of a company]
to sell a limitless number of 30-cent safety razors at $5 a piece,
world without end, or the capitalized earning power of some patent
medicine [or] brand of breakfast foods, for which "there's a reason"
in the profits.

When our Constitution was adopted, property was almost entirely goods, commodities, tools, land, buildings. It is in the sense
of property of this kind that Professor [Charles A.] Beard must be
understood when he says that "The Constitution was essentially an
economic document based upon the concept that the fundamental
private rights of property are anterior to the government and
morally beyond the reach of popular majorities."[5] In the course of
time, corporative undertakings began their evolution; property came
to be regarded as much in its quality of a claim to rights, such as a
stock certificate gave, as in its quality of a material good; the
franchise grant, first given to permit some large scheme of development to have [financial] security over a long enough period to
assure it success, came to [have] a very high direct value of its own
apart from [the] property commodities owned in connection with

it; and the Dartmouth College case [4 Wheaton 518 (1819)] established the inviolability of such franchises as property against the
corrective action of the state. With further development of vested
interests and corporation organization, the Fifth Amendment to
the Constitution: "Nor [shall any person] be deprived of life, liberty,
or property without due process of law" came to be the political
stronghold of property interests, rather than of [personal] liberty;
and when there was a question of state powers over property, the
Fourteenth Amendment [Section 1] was increasingly appealed to
before the Federal Courts: "Nor shall any State deprive any person
of life, liberty or property without due process of law." Both of
these amendments were primarily intended for the protection of
personal rights, but President Hadley of Yale University has pointed
out how the latter [amendment] especially has "[come] to be the
reliance of [champions of] property rights in their most extended
appropriative forms.[6]

Justice Brandeis has drawn a distinction interesting in this connection between active and passive capital, using the Morgan activities as the type [an example] of the former, and the Astor wealth
as the type of the latter. This distinction, valid at a glance as one of
our big-scale facts, is made as between the creative moment in
appropriative power and the vested rights that follow. The Astor
wealth is largely in high-valued land and is a special case of vested
rights, resting on a different form of organization from what we are
now discussing [and] one which we will defer for later consideration; but similar estates of passive wealth may consist of the soundly
protected and safely held increments of industrial organizing capacity and active appropriative power of the past.

The range of meanings for the word "property" runs therefore,
as we have said, from the simplest material goods to vested rights
and to active appropriative rights not yet vested. It runs from concrete items of wealth to the most immaterial, yet most powerful
claims to income, backed by the structure of industrial government
through their expanded interpretations of the meaning of the term
"property." Let this rest as fact, without implications as to goodness, badness, or indifference. The qualities of goodness, badness,
or indifference must be attributed not by us, but by the interests of
the various groups of the population affected by them, and ultimately by the dominant [group] interest that determinates their fate.

The ultimate decision is not for any writer or any theory to make, but for history [the interactions of different pressure groups in a society] to evolve.

One aspect of the situation involving a more immediate judgment as to goodness or badness needs, however, to be indicated, because it is the actual judgment of a large part of the citizenship today and knits very closely with similar judgments of the citizenship in the past; judgments firmly asserted under the greatest of privations and with the greatest sacrifice of blood. It has already been mentioned that the unit man of the political government, "created equal," gives way to the propertied man with quantitatively measured power in the industrial government. We now find that this quantitative power does not attach to property in the sense of the rhapsodist or humble moralist, but to property in a very complex appropriative system built up elaborately in [market] prices, values, and capitalizations. And this judgment (the judgment of millions of citizens) [appears] that, just to the extent that the political government (through the interpretations of law and constitution by its courts) has taken up into itself this quantitative differentiation between the citizens, just to that extent it has split away from the constitutional provision that each citizen stands as a unit in the tests of life and liberty.

To illustrate the magnitude of the quantities of power involved, and by the same token the magnitude of the resistance that is being developed, the following bits of dialogue from public records will serve. The first deals with power in industrial life:

J. OGDEN ARMOUR: Of course, Mr. Heney, a big man, I suppose, if he has got enough money, can kill off a small man: if he has money enough to do it—if that is what you mean.

FRANCIS J. HENEY: Certainly I do.

MR. ARMOUR: That is a power that a man would have not only in the packing business, but in everyday life.[7]

The second lies in the field of political government:

MR. HENEY: I have abandoned prosecutions as being useless where there are $100,000,000 involved. Senator Kenyon happens to know my viewpoint on that and was very much amazed to hear me state this away back in 1910. I do not believe you can convict $100,000,000.

SENATOR KENYON: I have found out you could not, too.
(Laughter)

MR. HENEY: You cannot convict $10,000,000 if the owner of
the $10,000,000 has two qualities—boldness and persistence. . . .
and consequently I was not concerned with any question of prosecuting the packers at all: and I do not take any interest in it now,
and I do not divide men into good and bad, and I do not think our
economic troubles come from that.[8]

To clinch the proof for this treatment of the appropriative
powers of property in the industrial system, it is fortunate that a
great case of appropriative power exists which is just as much a
functioning part of the industrial government as any other, and
which nevertheless has not a shred of defensive property logic or
property moralization behind it. This is the case of the power of
organized labor to secure increments of wages and to maintain
possession of those increments when secured. It has arisen not
upon a property footing, not as a struggle against property, but as
a struggle against the organized appropriative powers of property.
To organization on a property footing it has opposed organization
without property, and it has met its opponent in the common and
deeper-lying field of income.

The workers, through their method of organization and their
weapons such as the strike, have made good their claims with
greater or less success in various parts of the system, both as regards wages and as regards hours of labor and other working conditions. They have done this in the face of unfriendly judicial interpretations of the law, which have often upheld property rights and
rights footed in property as superior to other rights. Take the
special case of the railroad employees. Through favorable conditions of employment in a service, definite in its extent at any time,
and definite in its programs of expansion from year to year—a service requiring certain marked qualities of skill, reliability, and
sobriety in its workers—the organized railroad employees have
come to acquire a favored position among all the workers of the
land to such an extent that they are often referred to as forming an
aristocracy of labor, and indeed, in the last year or two, as a minor
aristocracy in the whole industrial system. Their strength in enforcing their demands under early war [World War I] conditions is
very well known indeed. Their power and right in the premises is

structurally and functionally of identical kind with the power and right of receivers of income from great appropriators' capitalizations, even though the latter refer back in title to property goods and the former do not. It is easy indeed to compare more exactly still the claims of the organized railroad wage-earners with those of the holders of capital securities of the Northern Pacific [Railroad], whose holdings do not represent a single dollar of expenditure on the construction of the road, inasmuch as it has been estimated that the public-land grants to the road more than paid its entire cost of construction, leaving a credit balance in the treasury of $25,000,000. Both claims [are] based on power of organization, offensive and defensive in industry.[9]

The recent history of the American Federation of Labor clearly sets forth this situation. The [Samuel] Gompers policy, well maintained and fortified, is a policy (1) of differentiation inside of the industrial government; (2) of harmonization with it in all respects except the division of the relative shares of the total industrial income; (3) of using its own organization power against the similar organization power of the [property-]title holders and managers; (4) of identifying itself as an appropriative power alongside of another appropriative power, although not as a property owner alongside of a property owner in the narrower sense. In the person of its leader, the Federation has shared on this basis not only in national, but in international policies during the war [World War I] and during the [Paris] peace negotiations; and after the war [it] has kept its footing solidly against all revolutionary tendencies as a structural part of the [American] industrial government. It is now, we may say, a component branch of that government, a true "estate" under it in the old [feudal] political sense [of a great class vested with distinct political powers]. Skipping the phase of footing in property goods, it has its footing solidly in income appropriation.

Notes

1. An illustration is a company that recently undertook the manufacture of lighting and starting batteries for automobiles. It produced a battery substantially identical with that of the largest manufacturing distributor in this field, put it on the market at a slightly shaded price, and devoted its main efforts to placing agents at all promising points. It tied these agents to a fixed price and the exclusive sale

of the one battery, gave them 55 per cent of the selling price for their commission, and set aside the greater part of the balance for overhead and distribution expenses. The result is that the consumer pays for his battery five times its manufacturing cost; the company's capitalization includes the heavy expenses of breaking into the field upon which dividends must permanently hereafter be earned; the country has saddled upon it two such capitalized organizations instead of one (to disregard the smaller competitors), and the camel's back of national industry is just that much nearer the breaking point. Incidentally, the local agent has a scale of repair charges upon which he gets about as much for the most trifling repair as an entire new battery would cost to manufacture. It is all very profitable to the backers of the enterprise, though five or ten dollars or perhaps more of national income is wasted for every one dollar of appropriative profit the company earns.

2. No objection based on ability on the part of managers or proprietors will apply in reference to this distinction, for huge ability finds as ready fields in appropriation as in production; though it is true that the greater abilities, providing they have no obstacles of temperaments or individual moral standards, seem today to tend to turn into the former field.

3. See [Pujo] *Report of the Committee to Investigate the Concentration of Control of Money*, House Report No. 1.593, 65th Cong., 3rd Sess., 1919, pp. 60, 83–84.

4. Estimate cited by Emerson P. Harris, *Co-operation, The Hope of the Consumer*, p. 224 n.

5. Charles A. Beard, *An Economic Interpretation of the Constitution of the United States* (New York: Macmillan, 1913), p. 324. The Constitution was ratified by a vote of one-sixth of the adult males, and was "the work of a consolidated group whose interests knew no state boundaries and were truly national in their scope."

6. Arthur T. Hadley, *Undercurrents of American Politics* (New Haven: Yale University Press, 1915), Lecture II. See also Hadley, "The Constitutional Position of Property in the United States," *Independent*, Vol. XLIV, No. 3098 (April 16, 1908), pp. 834-838, and [the] discussion in Walter Weyl, *The New Democracy* (New York: Macmillan, 1912), pp. 114ff. Cf., Charles W. Collins, *The Fourteenth Amendment and the States* (Boston: Little, Brown and Company, 1912), p. 137: "The Fourteenth Amendment, although a humanitarian measure in origin and purpose, has been within recent years practically appropriated by the corporations." Cited in Commission on Industrial Relations, *Final Report*, 1916, pp. 48–49. Cf., Levy Mayer in Senate Committee on Agriculture and Forestry, *Hearings on Government Control of the Meat Packing Industry*, 65th Cong., 3rd Sess., 1919, p. 1794.

7. U.S. Senate *Hearings on Government Control of the Meat Packing Industry*, p. 679.

8. *Ibid.*, pp. 25–26.

9. See Department of the Interior *Report* to Congress Feb. 3, 1881, printed in Thomas Donaldson, *The Public Domain* (Washington: Government Printing Office, 1884), pp. 912–933. At that date [1881] the value of the Northern Pacific land-grant lands remaining unsold was estimated at $99,750,000, and the total cost of the road when completed was estimated at $75,000,000. For a recent analysis of this problem, see Paul W. Gates, "The Railroad Land Grant Legend," *Journal of Economic History*, Vol. XIV, No. 2 (Spring, 1954), pp. 143–146.

V

Profits and Profiteering

Profiteering is a word that gained currency during the war [World War I] along with patrioteering, and undoubtedly with reminiscence of privateering. A willingness to seize exceptional profits whenever opportunity offers, whether in war or peace, is no new thing. However, such a willingness is not a sufficient characterization of the profiteering of the war, of the days since the war, and, for that matter, of the years immediately preceding the war. The profiteering that the country knows today is the splendid fruit of the industrial government, whether the particular plant in question has suddenly shot up in war soil, or whether it is deep-rooted and strong-stalked from long history [of growth].

One peculiarity of our present profiteering is that comparatively few people have participated in it, because, we can freely admit, comparatively few people have had the sufficient opportunity. We have seen it in a few great central points with radiating waves, ever-lessening, reaching out from these points.

To get at the nature of profiteering, to get at the qualities which have given to it its opprobrious name, we must go back of the war and look deeply into the whole industrial organization. We must seek to distinguish clearly between profit and profiteering, not merely as a matter of magnitudes, but in terms of the causes of these differences in magnitudes. We shall find, I think, that one great characteristic of profiteering is that it tends to perpetuate itself, while profits, on the other hand, as we currently know them and as the economists describe them to us, have a tendency to disappear; or at least ever to disappear and reappear, by the tests of efficiency and service in the productive process.[1] Profiteering, in short, is a great resultant of the working of the industrial organization, not a function of property ownership, not a function of the productive processes, but a function of the great consolidated appropriative powers based on property, reared through corporate and super-corporate organization and maintained in effectiveness by the ruling of the industrial government. It is the special financial reward to those who possess strong positions in the industrial organization, which they are prepared to defend and maintain against all comers.

Our purposes have not made it necessary for us to discuss sovereignty or the economic theory of value. Nor will they require us to discuss, in a theoretical way, profits or any of the companion forms of economic reward: rent, interest, and wages. But a few words toward avoiding obscurities do seem requisite. When the theories of political economy were first definitely formulated [by Ricardo and J. S. Mill], interest seemed fluid, equalizing itself for all capital, while ground-rent seemed to specialize or individualize itself for each piece of property. Interest seemed to tend toward a level under the given conditions of business, but rent, varying per acre between one piece of farm land and another and between one piece of city property and another, seemed dependent upon the position of each piece of land with respect to such factors as fertility, location, roads, markets, and the mechanics of farming.

However, interest, as is well known, shows distinctive rent features as between different countries and different sections of a country in different stages of development, and the abuses of the power of position held by owners of loanable wealth in early periods have been given witness by the usury laws. On the other hand, rent, through the capitalization of rental values, tends to take on the appearance of an interest return, and the tendency for rentals to seek an approximate level under such conditions as those of the opening of the Great West has shown itself clearly. At the present time, by the test of the balance sheets of great corporations, rents and interests are not practically considered worth distinguishing from the business point of view.

Now, these opposing tendencies as to equalizing or individualizing, originally held up to view as between interest and rent but later distinguished as existing inside each of them are also distinguished with equal clearness in profit and wages. On the one side, given equality of opportunity or any approximation to it, we have a tendency for returns to seek a level. On the other side, given any specially strong position, there is a tendency for a favored return, a typical rent, to appear. The whole problem is one not of property abstractly or apart from its special ownership, but of organizing men and their powers secured through the holding and the maintainance of organization. Wages, so far as we can use the term, were mere subsistence for slaves. Wages under certain conditions of increasing population, with the laborer passively awaiting use or disuse like any other commodity, have tended towards mere subsistence. But wages, when the laborers actively exert themselves and become themselves an organized part of the industrial system, take on a rent quality as between different groups of wage earners, and secure position values for the respective appropriative powers of the employees towards the employers.

With profits and profiteering it is the same. Assume profits, in the old way, as that part of the product which a man gets for his special ability, skill, or luck in managing his enterprise, and we have something of a rent while it lasts; modified by a tendency to wipe it out with the free spread of knowledge and training, except indeed as the profit-maker continually keeps ahead of the procession. But with progressing industrial organization we have elements, not merely of efficiency in service, but of prestige, of good will, of control of a market or of a series of markets; and finally, of control of output and prices, subject to such modifications as self-limitation of wants and needs by consumers may give. If we follow this series of conditions through, we may place profits at the one end, tending to equalize or efface themselves, while at the other end, as the positions held by the organized industries are consolidated and maintained, we approximate ever more closely a positive control with its rewards in profiteering.

The whole study, then, of interest and usury, rent and rack-rent, subsistence-wage and war-workers wage, profit and profiteering, is one of power in industry—the power of position: position derived from property ownership, and position derived from industrial organization. Given positional power which is lost or held by merit in the free struggle of men with men, and we have theoretically one kind of industrial society. Given positional power so consolidated and maintained that it is absolved from these daily, weekly, and yearly tests of merit and service, and we have something very different.

That in these poles of income-return—interest and usury, profit and profiteering, rent and rack-rent, subsistence-wage and strike-enforced wage—we have phenomena connected with the distinction between the productive powers of property and the appropriative powers, is clear. We have something connected also with the distinction between property as goods of use or production and property as a vested claim to part of the national income. But we do not have, any more in this distinction than in the others, any standard of equity or social desirability, any norm for industrial or political policy. Every judgment passed upon these income types, either in their extreme or in their less conspicuously marked forms, must inevitably be an expression of the underlying group interests of the persons who maintain the judgment actively, and who, by the various processes of suggestion involved in education and argument, may perhaps succeed in imposing it on wider circles than their own.

In applying in terms of group interest the distinction between the productive and appropriative powers of property to the various forms of income, we find that any group of men without capitalized property, and so situated as to make the attainment of such property on any noticeable scale improbable in the ordinary course of events, will naturally come to regard all return to the owners of capital goods as an appropriative use of property. This is due to the fact that groups of the owners of capital goods seem to occupy a fixed and commanding position as against the ownerless groups. Similarly, the more completely land titles tend to be concentrated, and, especially, the more the titles to the best-located city lands and the best-located and most fertile farming lands tend to be concentrated, the more it will be said that income to landowners has the appearance of an appropriative rather than a productive use of property powers. And similarly with profits. So long as men generally can enter, or consider entering, any field of enterprise and can expect a reasonable success with reasonable ability and good fortune, profits have a different appearance from what they have when the fields narrow down and close up. And as regards wages, we can easily forecast a future in which many strong labor organizations [e.g., the American Federation of Labor] might hold the field with wage policies of "More, always more," and among them a few especially strong organizations which were actually getting their "more" all the time, at the expense of the "more" of weaker organizations. In such a future, quite manifestly the power of position would find very strong condemnation from whatever groups of the people [e.g., unskilled and semi-skilled workers] were most unfavorably affected by it.

Position is the thing that counts. Strong position with respect to other working groups or organizations, whether that position rests on high organization of a group of workmen; a superiority in training and habits of one group of workmen over another; a variation in the quality or location of privately owned pieces of land; the ownership of patent rights; the occupation of the only water power in a community; the title to the exclusive franchise to provide a community with some service such as light or street transportation; a special business form of organization; a clientele secured under an advertised trade-name and maintained by a continuing expenditure for psychologic suggestion; the control of private car-lines and stockyards which all competitors must use; or an enormous system of centralized business interests.

The huge profiteering of the war years was simply a vivid illustration showing how well-prepared the appropriative organizations were to take advantage of an exceptional opportunity. A study by Basil Manly, Joint-Chairman of the National War Labor Board [1918–19], of the profits of eighty-two corporations in the years 1911 to 1918 (his list including every corporation in the country for which he could get figures for the eight years) shows that the average net [corporate] income in the prewar years was $325 million, but that the [corresponding] 1916 income was more than $1 billion, the 1917 income $975 million and the 1918 income $736 million, after the deduction of all federal and state taxes and "of every conceivable charge which these companies could devise for reducing and concealing their apparent profits." So great were the reserves for depreciation, amortization, and other contingencies in 1917 and 1918 that Mr. Manly belives the true profits of those years would equal or exceed those of 1916.[2] An illustration of profiteering within a corporation, which both reduced the return to investors and concealed the true profits from the public is given by the Federal Trade Commission in the case of the American Metal Company for 1917. Fifteen officers and managers of this company received salaries and commission of $1,798,680, ranging from $38,000 to $364,000, with an average of $119,912.[3]

It will be readily apparent that we have raised here the facts around which discussions of competition and monopoly have revolved, and that we have attempted to bring them together into a workable background of industry and politics as complete as possible. It is equally apparent that we have also been concerned with the standard of democracy, that of equal opportunity, and that we have used it not for any judgment of our own, but as the basis on which group judgments of the population most surely evolve.

The profit system has long enjoyed its panegyrics because of the stimulus it has given to the extension of industrial enterprise in new fields. The newly discovered forces of nature have required practical utilization, and practical utilization has been a great adventure, and great adventures require great rewards [for the entrepreneurs and investors of capital] to compensate them for the chances of great failure they involve. Great rewards have been gladly paid. But when every great adventure makes everybody pay, and when many great adventures mass together and perpetuate their requirements of reward, then the payment which society must make becomes enormous in its total. There was a time when the great adventurers were, in the end—always presumably, and to a large extent actually—mastered by the industrial process in which they were a part.

But now there has come a time when they have banded themselves together to master that process itself. They have uplifted themselves and coordinated themselves in a hierarchy of mastery, which has become the industrial government. They are ruling that government on a method not akin to the old system of profit, but frankly on the new system of profiteering. Their ruling offices are not the offices of productive control, but the offices of finance. Their use of property powers, their definition of property rights, rests not on the productive powers of property ownership, but on the appropriative powers. The profitmaker, in the old sense, has been as much an object for the aggression of the profiteer as has any other citizen.

In all this development, one may say society has been so set on getting its work done that it has cared comparatively little up to date as to who has got hurt in the process. It has protected an invention against infringement, but it has cared comparatively little about the fate of the inventor. The public has had to pay a double price: the price for the productive use of the invention, and the price for the appropriative organization which has been built upon it.

Not that we have not had bitter fights against profiteering. One may almost say that it is against profiteering that all labor and industrial and business legislation is directed. The worst abuses—those that the country has felt to be most of a personal character, most crude, those that we have been able to assimilate in type to old-fashioned crimes against property—have been made criminal by law. Other abuses, not so readily to be identified with the common ideas of crime, have been attacked with various restrictive measures. Legislation against child labor is in this class, and also legislation against hurtful labor of women. Here are the various attempts at the control of trusts and combination. Regulation of banks, usury laws, "blue-sky" laws, laws against rate discrimination and against local price discrimination are there. Factory safety and sanitary regulations are included. Not only legislation, but many political programs, many trade agreements, and many strikes and other contests over wages are aimed at the same end. Though efforts to promote profiteering are common, those against the profiteers are universal.

Revolutionary movements also take their roots here. A reform directed against profiteering which becomes hopeless of success through legislation or politics will readily identify the legislative and political processes with the profiteers, and will strike at the government along with the profiteers. An extreme and unintelligent form of revolution will attempt haphazard violence. A violent revolution against profiteering, when through perseverance it has become successful, will look extremely respectable and admirable to its beneficiaries and their descendants. We may say with confidence that no revolution, violent or peaceful, is conceivable as directed against property-uses and property-powers in the productive sense. The revolution must really run against the consolidated and established results of the appropriative use of property powers, even when it faultily uses the word "property" as a symbol of the evil it strikes at. To locate the appropriative powers, to undermine their fortifications, and to remove them by ordinary methods of political government in accordance with old standards and tests would assuredly seem the best practical method of avoiding the destructive by-products which even a constructive revolution will involve.

Our test of profiteering has been that of the occupation of a favored [strategic] position, which can be strongly held, which tends to maintain itself permanently, and which by its maintenance affects unfavorably [those] people who cannot win to favored position of their own.[4] We have touched upon a profiteering element in many sources of income in which there is still a partial opportunity for many, if not all of the citizens, to gain a somewhat similar footing. We have also considered profiteering positions in which there is no opportunity for anyone whatever but the existing holders to secure a footing.

Hereafter we shall be concerned in the main with that second part of the profiteering that arises upon profit, which is of most vital importance in our present industrial government, and which lies at the heart of our programs of industrial reform as well as of all revolutionary efforts which we may anticipate or fear. This is the profiteering incident to the occupation of the most favorable strategic positions in the industrial world; the mastery of the great highways of industry.

Before we turn to an examination of our highways of manufacture and trade, and the condition in which they are now held, it will be desirable first to examine what statistics we can secure in regard to the use of the national income . . . [Then we can] bring out the enormous wastes to which it has been subjected, in connection with the development of the profiteering system. Without these facts it will be impossible to realize how vitally the welfare of the entire citizenship is affected under our present industrial government.

Notes

1. "The outstanding feature on the score of profit revealed in the regular work of the [Federal Trade] commission under the statute creating it and the Clayton act, is the trade tendency to increase and to maintain prices against the forces of competition." Federal Trade Commission, *Report on Profiteering, Senate Document* No. 248, 65 Cong., 2 Sess. (Washington: Government Printing Office, 1918), p. 5.

2. Address before National Conference on Social Work, Atlantic City, June 2, 1919. Printed in "America's Industrial Unrest," *Nation*, Vol. CVIII, No. 2815 (June 14, 1919), pp. 933–35.

3. *Report on Profiteering*, p. 19.

4. The United States Council of National Defense in its *Analysis of the High Cost of Living Problem*, (Washington: Government Printing Office, August 1919), p. 9, defined profiteering thus: "It should be clear that increased purchasing power derived from reduced service is the very essence of profiteering, and is possible on no other basis than the deprivation of others." See discussion of this report in Chapter XIV.

VI

Waste and Welfare

Are we, as a people, getting our money's worth out of our industry as we have it organized today? If we are not, we may be expected to hunt for the leak, if there is one, and stop it.

Beyond question some of our businessmen are getting their money's worth and more. Equally beyond question, by the test of high prices, large parts of our people feel that they are not getting their money's worth.

However, the question in terms of "money's worth" is superficial. It will answer for the individual citizen, but when we seek knowledge of all the citizens, we must go behind money and prices and put the question: "Are we, as a people, getting the worth of our energy and time and of the wealth we apply towards getting our common livings?"

The answer to this latter question is not only that we are not getting our effort's worth, but that we are not getting anywhere near our effort's worth. Something can be done towards estimating the discrepancy of efforts over accomplishments in ratios of two, five, ten, or twenty [to one] and the results are so astounding that one hesitates to write them down. Merely to assemble the wastes here and the wastes there that can be estimated definitely, and to add them together, gives such an astonishing total that the adding machine fears to be branded a liar. The conclusions seem utopian. We may hedge such estimates with every precaution, scale them down at every point, and yet show that we could easily get two or three times as much welfare for our industrial efforts as we now do get.

A sketch, a crude and partial and extremely conservative sketch, of our present-day wastes in industry and business is to be made in this chapter. It is to be made on the following basis:

No wastes will be considered which do not rise directly out of essential characteristics of the present ownership and control of industry and business.

No estimate of any special waste will be accepted which is not moderate, even as compared with the most moderate opinions of investigators in the special branch of business affairs under consideration.

No estimate will be made merely of something that "might be otherwise."

Instead, every estimate will be made on the basis of mechanism that is practical to substitute for that now used. The test of what is practical will not be, however, ability to survive in a hostile, profiteering environment. [The] practical [criteria] will require that the proposed alternative mechanism have already shown its workability or already indicated itself as on the point of introduction. But it will be judged by its possibilities under an assured national organization distinctly bent on subduing profiteering and substituting productive service.[1]

The justification for this test lies not merely in the immense losses [to consumers] through present profiteering, but in the deep injury to our industrial life it is causing; in the whirlwind course towards industrial crisis; in the involvement with threatening revolution; in the compulsion we are under, as a nation, to solve in some way the problem it produces or else be torn by destructive convulsions.

And finally. Not the winnings of profiteering, but the costs of profiteering, are what will mostly concern us.

If we should add all of the earnings and all of the profits of all our people together, no matter how gratifying a total they might make, they would give no indication whatever that the people were getting the worth of their efforts out of what they do. The figures, to start with, would merely tell how much better off some men were than others. They would be in terms of a common yardstick, the dollar; and their total would be only a yardstick total. They would tell about dollars, but not about welfare. The real question at issue is one of comforts, conveniences, and luxuries, including both goods and services. It is the question of the total of these secured, as compared with the greater total that similar efforts and wealth and skill might achieve if better organized. It is the question of [economic and social] welfare versus waste. It is the question of the costs to us of what we get. To answer it, we must study the friction inside our industrial organization and determine how much it lowers output. We must decide how much of its waste is inevitable, and how much is artificially excited within the system and hence capable of being removed, if we deliberately want to remove it.

What is cost to the individual man, and, from the point of view of his profits, reasonable and necessary cost, may be waste from the point of view of total social product and social service. If the goods had to travel the way they did, then perhaps the cost was socially necessary. But the goods did not have to travel the way they did. They could have traveled a much cheaper way. Therefore the cost was not a true [necessary] cost, but a waste. Therefore the nation, in permitting these costs to be incurred, has wasted much of what it might otherwise have had for its enjoyment and welfare.

Advertising, the malicious imp attendant upon modern [1920] business, is a type of such waste. It represents at least 10 per cent of the costs of all goods after they leave the producers' hands until they reach the consumers. If it did not result in profits to the advertiser, it would not be used. But that is very different from saying that it results in more goods to the consumer. As a matter of fact, nine-tenths of it results in higher prices, which is another way of saying less goods to the consumer. Consider the million a year or more apiece said to be paid by certain Minneapolis milling firms for advertising—not to tell people what flour is, or what better flour is, or how better to enjoy flour, but to maintain brands. To the miller it is a cost. He recoups it in his prices. He protects his inflated capitalizations by it. Another and another big miller follows after in imitation. They do not produce as cheaply as their smaller rivals. They cannot sell as cheaply. But they play their game in a business system that permits the piling up of these costs, and the reaping of profits upon them, and the strengthening of their corporations, and all the appearances of stability and prosperity—until when? Just until the burden of waste breaks the consumers' back.

Then the collapse. Not the collapse of one advertising branch of trade or another; not the collapse of advertising trades alone; but [collapse] of the specialized, high-cost selling trades—of the over-capitalized, profiteering trades—in short, of the industrial-profit protective system in which all are bound. Such a collapse may be a crisis. It may ultimately be a revolution. Of this, later.

Or take the $1,700,000 which, by sworn statement, Swift [and Company] spent for advertising in 1918; not to introduce meat to strangers to it, not to explain meat, nor to further [the] meat trade, but to influence Congress against legislation to interfere with future profits in meat. All this cost was charged onto the price of meat and operated to increase prices and reduce supplies. It was big enough in itself, and yet it was only one drop in the bucket of those costs that are wastes of welfare.

Undoubtedly there is a resistance, an isolation, a friction between man and man to be overcome in trade as in all other social intercourse. Undoubtedly, the growth of a nation-wide complex of industry, with products from everywhere going everywhere, has offered greater problems of this kind of friction to be solved than the world [has] ever had before. But also undoubtedly, the system that solved them has appropriated and capitalized and exploited them. Instead of surmounting and wiping out frictions of this kind, assuming the costs . . . [when] necessary, but getting rid of them as fast as possible, it has built itself upon them, and laid its foundations in waste—no more secure than if they were in sand.

Does not knowledge of slang, familiarity with popular songs, acquaintance with books, popularity of dramas, cross the continent by simple channels of intercourse without the hammering of suggestive, compulsive, hypnotic advertising? Cannot we know of our breads, our meats, our clothes, without this gnawing expense? And if this expense is 10 per cent of the costs beyond producers' hands, is not that one waste alone equal to 5 per cent or 6 per cent or 7 per cent of all the goods and welfares that we now secure? Save it, and could we not have that much more of welfare goods? That much, if we reckon only with our normal conditions. Much more, if we reckon with the atrocious abuses of advertising by the excess-profits [tax-] dodgers in 1918, 1919, and 1920? For remember, advertising is not something academic, ethereal, a mere matter of dollar charges. It is trees, and men cutting down trees. It is pulp mills, and men working in them. It is paper, and railway transportation. It is printing presses, and printers, and circulators. And all of this wealth and these services might be producing real goods to use and enjoy.[2]

I do not propose to reckon advertising costs separately. Part of its wastes may be subsumed under trade wastes, part under wastes of consumers, falsely stimulated and wrongly stimulated to buy. If one should start with the detail of advertising and add detail after detail, the total would be too enormous. Consider advertising as mere illustration of a typical waste for profiteering's sake, and let it go at that.

Observe some types of waste directly connected with our way of handling business. First waste motions, waste activity, such as [occurred] once in the paralleling of [America's] railroads, and [in] the duplication of factories and of public-service plants, and now more commonly in duplications of stores, milk routes, and commercial traveler-service. Next, frictions in rivalries for the profits of business by underminings and lurings, with the high rewards to the successful operators on these lines. Next the harassing and tricking of the consumer by specialized salesmanship into purchases unfit for him, and fit only for the profit-taker's purposes. Next the wastes of trade failures, misrepresentations, adulterations, short-weighting, and shoddy—the last-mentioned, alone, almost a national calamity—and of the destructions of food in city markets and fields for price-maintenance's sake. Then the wastes of strikes, lockouts, and sabotage, and of the high turnover of labor and of unemployment at the behest of price manipulators. The wastes of inefficiency due to malnutrition, those of display extravagance due to excessive incomes—and beyond them, of imitations of display stimulated by traders among consumers of smaller incomes. The wastes of resources unutilized because of profiteering control. The wastes of legal services [suits for fraud, damage, etc.] entirely under profiteering motivation, and of those caused by the spider-web traders whose whole function is lying in wait for victims. The wastes of absurd multiplication of types by insignificant detail variations for trading purposes, illustrated in automobile batteries in which half to two-thirds of the cost of purchase, upkeep, and repair could be saved by intelligent standardization. These are all but [merely] hints at the items on the list.

In this welter of wastes let us choose five classes for rough examination, with a view to reasonable guesses at possible waste elimination, and [at] consequent welfare augmentation in accord with the tests above laid down for guidance. These will be: (1) trade between producers' hands and consumers; (2) manufacturing; (3) distorted consuming capacity; (4) misapplied and unutilized resources; and (5) shoddy. But before entering upon them, three opinions from observers of very different types may profitably be considered:

[First] Charles P. Steinmetz, Consulting Engineer of the General Electric Company:

"One hundred years ago the average work-day was ten to eleven hours. Now [19?] it is eight to nine hours. It has decreased about 20 per cent. The productivity of work in the [past] hundred years by the steam engine and the infinite number of inventions and improvements following it has increased at least tenfold—probably more nearly twenty to thirty fold—but for illustration let us assume only a tenfold increase. Thus with only an average of one hour's work during the day we could produce as much as we did in ten hours work a hundred years ago, and we should live in the same manner and with the same standard of living which satisfied us 100 years ago by working only one hour a day."

And again:

"We can see a world with a standard fully as satisfactory as ours but working only four hours a day, only 200 days during the year. This is far away but it is no idle dream."[3]

[Second] Thorstein Veblen:

"Today [1918] under compulsion of patriotic devotion, fear, shame and bitter need [this was written during the war] and under the unprecedentedly shrewd surveillance of public officers, bent on maximum production, the great essential industries controlled by the vested interests may one with another be considered to approach—perhaps even conceivably to exceed—a fifty per cent efficiency as counted on the basis of what should ordinarily be accomplished by use of an equally costly equipment, having the disposal of an equally large and efficient labor force and equally good natural resources, in case the organization were managed with an eye single to turning out a serviceable product, instead of as usual being managed with an eye single to private gains in terms of prices. To experts in industrial engineering who are in the habit of inquiring in terms of material cost and mechanical output this rating will seem extravagantly high. Publicly and concessively the latter speak of a 25 per cent efficiency; in private and confidentially they appear disposed to say that the rating should be nearer ten per cent than 25 per cent. The apparatus and procedure for capturing and dividing this share of the community's annual dividend is costly—one is tempted to say unduly costly. It foots up to perhaps something like one-half of the work done."[4]

[Third] A great English manufacturer, quoted by Frank A. Vanderlip:

"Today the brains of the country are being wasted. In a factory employing say 7,000 men, the work is being directed by perhaps not over one hundred. If such a adjustment could be made that the brains of the whole 7,000 were engaged with the problems of industry, if all the workers had an intelligent grasp of at least some parts of these problems, and all cheerfully applied their energy and brains to the welfare of the industry because they were satisfied with their working conditions, and felt that they occupied a just relationship to the results obtained by the enterprise, then the profits for both capital and labor would be far beyond anything that the present system can produce."

The speaker goes on further to predict that the country that first puts its industrial brains to work will "forge so far ahead of other nations that men will wonder that society could ever have endured the present system."[5]

For 1916, while the total of trading transactions, all buying and selling, has been reckoned at $507 billions, and while national income, including that from various investments, has been placed at about $50 billions, the total of goods going to consumers at retail is placed somewhere around $25 billions. Advertising costs were around $1.5 billions, and transportation charges were between $2 and $2.5 billions.*

Before estimating waste we need some idea as to how much of

* Numerous sources are cited in support of Bentley's estimates in an unpublished manuscript, Appendix K, including: Irving Fisher, *The Purchasing Power of Money* (New York: Macmillan, 1911), on trade turnover; Theodore H. Price, "The Mail Order Business," *The Outlook*, Vol. 112 (January 26, 1916), pp. 227–32; Harris, *Co-operation*, and B. M. Anderson in *The Annalist*, Vol. 9, No. 208 (January 8, 1917), pp. 32, 53–54, on retail trade; and Harris, *op. cit.*, on advertising.

the retail price goes to manufacturer, wholesaler, and retailer. As guide here we may use percentages established by [the economist, W. H. Ingersoll], taking 40 typical factories in 1916 and tracing their products step by step into consumers' hands. These factories included foods, hardware supplies, drugs, fuel, house furnishings, clothing, jewelry, shoes, dry goods, notions, and auto supplies. . . .

TABLE I

How Retail Prices Are Divided Among
Manufacturers and Merchants[6]

Branch of Industry	Per cent of Retail Price Accounted for by:		
Manufacturing			
Cost to produce	37		
Cost to sell	12		
Profit	4	53	
Wholesaling			
Expense of Doing Business	10		
Profit	3	13	
Retailing			
Expense of Doing Business	28		
Profit	6	34	100

Regrouping these figures, taking 8 per cent of the retail price as the total transportation costs at all stages, and assuming that a little more than half of this transportation cost is incurred after the goods leave the factories, we get the following:

TABLE II

Guide-Post To Waste

Cost of Manufacturing Goods	37	
Cost of Transporting Finished Goods	5	42
All Selling Costs		45
All Profits		13
Total		100

Selling costs here appear as greater than manufacturing and transporting costs combined, and three and one-half times as great as all profits at all stages combined.

How is it, we are compelled to ask, that men in one organized society, engaged in making goods for each other and using each others' goods, have come to such a pass that it costs them more to induce each other to buy the goods once made than it costs to make and deliver the goods themselves? Is it inevitable that they should show such stiff resistance to each other in the one matter that most deeply concerns them all, namely, getting from each other their daily and weekly and yearly supplies of necessities and pleasures? Or is there something in the way? Are the wheels rusted? Is there a strong arm of interference? Can they find the trouble and get rid of it? Most of these questions are for other chapters to discuss. What concerns us here is the proportion of the friction, and the amount it may reasonably be reduced according to the tests already listed.

So far as trading wastes are concerned, the best road to the answer comes from considering what has already been accomplished towards reducing costs by cooperatives, chain stores, and . . . mail-order houses.

The record of the British local cooperatives tells one part of the story. From 1862 to 1915, 53 years, with sales of $15 billion, they have returned average profits to customers in the form of patronage dividends on the Rochdale plan of 9.73 per cent. The average dividend in 1918 was 9.82 per cent. This in the face of a continuous offensive war waged on them by private industry; struggles when producers and jobbers refused to sell to them, struggles when laws were enacted to hamper them, struggles when bank credit was snatched away from them. This, also, above and beyond their large expenditures for propaganda and education, to spread their spirit and ideals among men.

Or contrast with our wholesale costs, the distributive expenses of the Cooperative Wholesale Societies Limited of England. In 1916 on sales of $250,000,000 this Society showed distributive expenses of less than $4,000,000, which is little more than 1.5 per cent.

This table does not include the expense of branches and depots, but allowing for these on the basis of employees engaged in pro-

TABLE III

Distributive Expense of the C. W. S. of England[7]

Kind of Expense	Per cent of Selling Price of Goods
Wages, Salaries, Committee Fees, Traveling Expenses and Dining Room	0.89
Price Lists, Advertising, Show Cards, the *Wheat Sheaf*, Stationary, Postage, Telegraph, and Sundries	0.15
Rent and Taxes	0.07
Legal Expenses	0.00025
Repairs, Insurance, Depreciation, and Interest on Capital Investment	0.45
Total	1.56

portion to the figures given, the expense comparable to the 13 per cent in the Ingersoll Table would still be below 3 per cent.

Next, our American chain-store systems and mail-order houses, handling as high as a fifth of the business in some cities and in some rural districts, and certainly doing a tenth of the total retail business of the nation today. The figures for four concerns whose financial reports permit analysis, shows the cost to them of the goods they buy at [range] from 65 per cent to 70 per cent of the prices they charge, instead of the 53 per cent of the Ingersoll tables. . . .

This more favorable showing has been made by eliminating some wastes, but by retaining and profiting from many others. Consider some of the capitalizations as contrasted with actual capital (in the old sense of stored-up wealth) which such corporations use. When Woolworth incorporated in its present form, it put in $15 million of actual or possible assets, and added $50 million of good will, issuing a total of $65 million of capital stock. It still carries the $50 million of good will in its balance sheet. This is equivalent to an assertion of its power to make, not one normal profit on investment, but four and one-third profits continuously. Its 1917 report shows a net profit creditable to common stock of 16.72 per cent. Sears, Roebuck and Company in its 1917 balance sheet carries "property, plant, machinery, good will, patents, etc.," at $41,328,731, and of this $30,000,000 is represented by "good will, patents, etc." The United Cigar Stores Company carries [on its books] trade-marks and good will at $21,400,000.

To read the possibilities for trade out of these facts, note first that mail-order houses with their comprehensively developed catalogs, and chain stores with their routine buying and selling tests—which have largely replaced the merchandising instinct first relied on by them—have been transforming themselves into what we may regard as bureaucratic institutions, and have come to compare very closely in administrative respects with the British cooperatives. Next note that the actual wealth-employment in their business is much less than their capitalizations of appropriative power. Next, remember that under the great, superficial variety of advertised and pushed products in this country is a real standardization of needs and supplies, which is given this costly appearance of variety only because that way lies profit to the clever manipulator of appearances and inducements. Our real, though camouflaged, standardization of products may be estimated as covering 90 per cent of all articles in trade. To allow 10 per cent for novelties and improvements needing true introductory service on merit would be extremely liberal.

Now supposing society, under compulsion of such necessity of production in peace as it has already felt in war, should determine to squeeze the foolishness out of trade; regarding welfare of consumers as more important to it than profits of manipulators, it could readily adopt and expand the system of mail-order and chain stores. With this it could cover 90 per cent of our trade. For this we need not confine the assumption to government operation of business by salaried officials, or to cooperative enterprise by salaried employers of the cooperatives; but we can include private enterprise by independent business managers with commission or bonus profits for their productive efficiency. In all three cases, or in possibly still other forms of enterprise, [we can do so] only [by] assuming that the government supplies information, guidance, and insistence on a spirit of productive service, and represses . . . [opponents] who use hurtful methods, and gives favoring legislation.

We may assume further that, by bond issues or by currency based on the commercial principles that . . . give needed elasticity to our present Federal Reserve currency (only extending them and diverting them from the uses of individual appropriators to those of productive service), the government could supply or supplement the real capital needed for these trading operations in this 90 per cent of business.

Let us not try to estimate the actual saving under such assumptions or value them for any purpose, but merely hold that these assumptions, taken together with the existing tendencies in our present trade, would justify us in believing that we can, if we will, get goods from producers to consumers at the actual cost-percentages of our present chain [stores] and mail-order houses. What would this mean to us?

The average gross expense of such establishments was about 37 per cent of the cost of their merchandise to them. If we now take an effort and investment figure of 42 units (Table II) to represent cost of merchandise plus transportation—or, say, 46 [units] to include manufacturers' profit—and if goods can be marketed to consumers for 38 per cent of that cost, or . . . 17.5 units, we would get a price to consumers representing 63.5 units in place of the 100 of the table. And this is the same as to say that for every two measures of commodity and service the consumer now gets, he would then be getting three. He would be half-again as well off with the same investment, effort, and skill the country now has, given only the substitution of a purpose to serve in place of a purpose to profiteer.

Let me modify this, first to allow for the 10 per cent of novelty trade; then for the fact that chain-store, mail-order, and cooperative service to consumers now exists; and for the supply of some standard articles, as for instance sugar in the grocery . . . at a close margin. Let us cut our [one-]third saving to a quarter, and estimate our investment of welfare at only a third of the present [amount] instead of a half. It [this figure] is extremely reasonable.[9]

The second section of the hunt for wastes concerns manufacturing. If the factory cost of most articles we buy is only 37 per cent of the retail price, to use the Ingersoll percentages, can we not congratulate ourselves on great economy and efficiency in this field? We cannot. We must even fear [that] the wastes here are the worst wastes of all.

Sabotage is the trouble with manufacturing, and sabotage not merely as the war-weapon of the more reckless workers' organizations, but as the settled "financial function" of profiteering industrial control. Sabotage may be described as the destruction or hampering or decreasing of product undertaken by any party to the manufacturing process for purposes of private gain. [Thorstein] Veblen has broadened the term from the misdeeds of labor to those of capital,[10] and the Supreme Court of the United States has written down some of the facts authoritatively for the benefit of future generations in the Standard Oil and Tobacco Trust decisions.

Deliberate sabotage by labor has sometimes been destructive, and sometimes it has been the disingenuous observance of the letter of rules which, when so observed, decrease output. It is waste of national resources. The strike is waste. It is the acute form of what becomes chronic when each worker strikes as much as he can against output, while still putting in his hours and drawing his pay. Malingering of workers in many forms, conscious or unconscious, is the predecessor among individuals of what has since become all too widely organized. Union contracts often aim to limit output, and the length of the working day—which from the standpoint of efficiency has been most wisely reduced from the older customs—may be forced down by present tendencies [to a level] too low for the good of either worker or society.[11]

On the other side, that of the employer, sabotage used to take the violent forms of arsons and the incitement of strikes against rivals. It appeared also in the scrapping of factories, not because of the actual over-production as tested by consumers' needs, but by the test of inflated profit requirements.[12] It settled down into the systematic control and limitation of output with respect to price and profit, exercised through chairmen of the boards of directors, as distinct from presidents and managers, and gradually centered for all the greatest industries in one close financial harmony of management. Permanently, deliberately, tribute is levied by it on the comforts, conveniences, and necessities of the entire population; tribute that benefits the recipients only in small fraction of the injury it inflicts on the tribute-payer.

All of these wastes of possible output, whether on the side of employer or of worker, may be, indeed must be, interpreted in terms of stimulus. Either the right stimulus is lacking, or the wrong is overemphasized. The employer is intent on profit obtainable only under conditions that have made high costs profitable to him, though wasteful to the nation. The high costs limit the use of his products, and his profits come to depend on his not making too much product, rather than on his ability to make a great product cheaply. The worker, on the other hand, whose services are bought for a price, is after that price, and that only. Through his union he fights for less work and more pay. And finally, when rising prices make the "more pay" a verbal rather than an actual benefit, he takes his revenge in less work and still less. He has no proper stimulus to do more work.

To measure the wastes of present manufacturing methods, we must proceed in part by estimating stimulus and what could be accomplished by better stimulus, so far as we can practically assume its introduction. But stimulus, on both sides to the waste, is not to be understood as a matter of individual psychology. Stimulus is the same thing as the industrial organization, the environment which determines the possible inducements and forms of industrial conduct. How far we can change [the] stimulus depends on how far we can reasonably assume changes in this industrial organization by compulsion of the people through their government.

But first we have two definitely measurable wastes directly chargeable to the existing type of industrial organization. One is unemployment, and the other is the labor turnover. Unemployment, due to factories having more men permanently attached than they can offer full-time work, absorbs at the very least, and in its remediable forms, 10 per cent of our working capacity. [W. J.] Lauck and [E.] Sydenstricker's estimate for the average male worker in basic industries, of more regular employment, has already been quoted as from one-sixth to one-third of their time each year. The coal strike of 1919 spread wide knowledge of unemployment conditions in the bituminous mines and what it meant in wages and cost of coal.[13]

As for the labor turnover, Slichter's investigations of 105 factories with 250,000 employees showed an average turnover of 100 per cent a year. H. L. Gantt, the efficiency engineer, states that "many of our industrial plants have estimated that the cost of breaking in a new employee in very high—running from about $35 up."[14] Considering the actual working days per man per year, this may be equivalent to the value of 5 per cent of a man's time. Cut it in two, as we did with unemployment conditions, and say only half is due to the present industrial organization, and still unemployment and labor turnover prove to be wasting 12.5 per cent of our productive power; or enough, if put to use, to raise present output nearly 15 per cent. And if there is any hesitation, we can throw in the strike waste for good measure.

With this waste in furnishing men [with] work and keeping them at work, what is the shortage of actual accomplishment of the men at their machines compared with what they might accomplish? The scientific management systems beginning with that of [Frederick W.] Taylor, which strove to push labor, to gather and appropriate its bench-knowledge, and to keep the compensation down in the old way, have only shown the loss, but not helped it. They have failed to give stimulus and instead have provoked the most bitter resistance and hatred. On the other hand, for methods like those of [H. L.] Gantt—who establishes a standard day's task and gives a bonus to the worker each day he meets it, and bonuses also to foremen and superintendents who keep skill and spirit alive —there have been excellent results. Gantt tells us that the average worker at the end of a full day's achievement under good methods and proper stimulus is less wearied than the man who has slouched through a day of slovenly work and low output. He tells us also that factories using this bonus system have uniformly reaped prosperity from it. An examination of his typical charts in red and black, showing the progress of workers under the system, indicates what can be gained.[15] Here is easily another 15 per cent of possible increment in output, and that by introducing only a limited inducement to workers under a system still unfavorable to their interested participation in most of its aspects.

What else must be reckoned? Brains. Recall the predictions of Vanderlip's English manufacturer [that we have] already quoted.

Recall the words of Professor [Alfred] Marshall, the distinguished British economist, that our greatest waste product is "the higher ability of the working classes, the latent and undeveloped, the choked-up and wasted faculties for higher work that for lack of opportunity have come to nothing."[16] An efficiency engineer quoted by Helen Marot[17] estimates the loss of wealth due to the inability of the businessman to grasp the creative possibilities in industry at 50 per cent. Suppose we take the lost brains among workmen and put with them the losses directly due to the fact that the factory superintendency is thwarted and hampered by financial control, counting only the actual administration and organization of machines and labor under such superintendency. Let us estimate all of these as costing us a present loss, and a consequent decrease in possible output, of only some 15 or 20 per cent.

We have, in these three groups of factors, indications of a possible increment of 50 per cent in our present product. Many other items might be estimated, but omit them all. Omit even any attempt to an estimate of the loss occasioned directly by that "financial function," sabotage of the corporation, which limits the output [in order] to control the price. Assume that such latter losses are included either under losses of trade or under the losses in the factory operation direct. This 50 per cent possibility of increment remains low enough. Certainly when we remember the habitual estimate of efficiency engineers that our industrial efficiency is not above 10 or 25 or, at the outside, 50 per cent of the possible.

Is it low enough so that we are justified in saying that we as a nation ought today, beyond any chances arising from the peril of the adventure, be able to secure that saving of waste, that addition to welfare, if we set ourselves to it? The indications of practicability lie in the many tendencies towards democratization of industry, in the shop-steward experiments of England and similar shop-committee efforts in this country, in projects such as the Plumb Plan for railroad control (envisaging the Plumb Plan not as a profiteering weapon of railroad workmen against railroad investors and operators, but as a project for developing the interest of the workers in the management of an industry), [and] in the success of the government's arsenal administration during the war [World War I].

As in preceding cases, compulsion to practical action is given by the growing forcefulness of labor [union] opposition to capital, and by the destructive possibilities of the future. The method that might be followed is given us by war experience. Assume an industry financed by the government so that profiteering possibilities could be avoided. Let the necessary height of its output, and its adjustment to the output of other industries, be studied and determined by government experts for the public good. Assume its control given to production engineers, instead of to professional moneymakers (as was the unhappy fact for our war [World War I] efforts in this direction).[18] Let it work with joy in working and pride of achievement, and with reward to its workers and managers, on any one of many possible bases for their true achievement. Could it not then certainly assure us, in view of all the considerations set forth, an increase in productiveness of 50 per cent? Such an estimate will be regarded [as] moderate by all persons who have investigated this field.

If this estimate covers manufactures, mines, and transportation, what discount shall be made for agriculture and the hand-trades? The hand-trades we may disregard. They fill their place, and will keep up with the productivity of organized industry according to the possibilities of individual workers' temperaments and capacity, or merge into it. Agricultural productivity suffers today from bad marketing facilities, from price robbery and consequent uncertainty of result in marketing,[19] [and] from labor shortage caused by the seducing away of its laborers by industries that enjoy greater profiteering possibilities.[20] If—instead of being a victim of [the] Beef Trust's sabotage against it, and of the high cost of securing standard supplies which ought to flow to it easily and cheaply on a warehousing basis—agriculture could be stimulated by the cooperation of industry organized on a true productive basis, it would probably, not as a matter of interior technique and capacity of workers, but as a result of favoring trading environment, keep equal pace in increased productiveness. At any rate, if it did not fully do so, so moderate is our estimate for manufacturing that the deficiency should easily be covered under the figures assumed.

Under trading we assumed a [one-]third increment of welfare goods by better trading methods. If now we apply this trading increment to a 50 per cent increment in production, we would get a possibility of double our present production from the two types of waste-elimination combined.[21]

The third field of waste to examine is that which grows out of distorted consumers' capacity [arising from] incomes too small and incomes too large, but examined [here] only so far as they are directly involved in the excesses of our present industrial and trading organization. The question is not: Do some people suffer because of deficient incomes, or [are] others able to enjoy things some one else disapproves of because of their large incomes? But rather: Assuming such sufferings and enjoyments as fact, what effects do they have on our productivity, on the total quantity of consumers' welfare that we create each year? Are they waste, not by the test of anyone's moral judgment, but as factors in production by the test of a needlessly lowered output?

Begin with the deficient incomes. A quarter of our families [in 1919–20] admittedly have incomes that do not permit a decent standard of health and comfort. Six million children, according to the Federal Child Bureau, go to school each day insufficiently fed. Such children, their teachers will commonly estimate, fall 50 per cent below the progress they ought to make in their studies. How about malnutrition among workers . . . [and] its effects on their product? How about sickness, the result of improper care and lack of medical attention?[22] Sluggish hands, lack of interest and ambition, [and] inattention to essentials are incidental effects, and the result is lessened output. The amount may well be considerable; and this is so evident that the mere mention of it suffices.

For the effects of excessive incomes, the nature of the waste needs analysis, though . . . under the characterization of "national extravagance" many people will point to it out-of-hand as the source of all our high-price ills.[23] The trouble, however, with the arguments about extravagance is that, as a usual thing, they stress it for people who can't afford it; for the laborer with high wages, for the stenographer with her $21-pair of shoddy-stylish shoes, for the poor man's wife aping the rich; treating it as moral delinquency on the part of individuals to be cured by preaching, and not tracing it back to plain business causes. These causes lie in profiteering, in excessive incomes, and more particularly in "get-rich-quick" incomes, from which radiating waves of imitative waste pass over all society; not merely because it is easy and natural for them [the low- and middle-income groups] so to do, but because such extravagance is continually stimulated by the existing business system with its advertising, its clever salesmanship, and its high-cost bulwarks . . . [Business] finds in [these activities] some of its best chances of inflated profits. Easy come, easy go. Business knows it and profits by it. More "easy come." And worse "easy go." And so ad infinitum.

The type of expenditure which we have a right to isolate here for treatment is display expenditure. The case is not against display as a satisfaction of the individual: in this respect that satisfaction is as much justified as any other so far as this inquiry is concerned. But it is display which is a mere dollar display, not only in origin and in common denominator of all of its forms, but in its exploitation by business enterprise. A pale pink automobile, with most of its lure in paint, upholstery, and high selling expense; a spasm of furs in summer; an elaboration of country estates, a pest of servants; or for that matter, a cream-colored washing machine with a bird of paradise handpainted on its east façade—all of these, and a thousand things like them, have their reason for existence in display, and their common denominator in their expensiveness. . . . [In part] our present business system [is based] on the poverty of individual ingenuity in personal display [and is] combined with the gluttonous hunt for display by "easy money." . . . [to the extent that business] standardizes its possibilities in costliness, stimulates them by luring advertisements, protects its high-cost systems through this method, and manufactures more easy money and more display stimulation, we have a definitely located waste for which we may blame the system.

Along with this should be reckoned all that useless expenditure forced on the customer through the system of fixed retail prices and manufacturers' advertising; the urging of unnecessary goods and unnecessary forms of goods, the praising of expensiveness as quality, the inflation of costs, and the protection of many profits. To the extent that the customer's power of buying actual satisfactions is diverted into the costs and profits of such business, we see a calculable waste directly arising out of the business organization.

Without setting any percentage of waste, even of the most schematic kind, for the above items of deficient and excessive incomes,[24] we may turn next to the wastes of misapplied and unutilized resources [while] still staying strictly within the limits of the business system. The waste of our rivers and canals under our railroad-profiteering system has been enormous, as Director-General [Walker D.] Hines of the Federal Railroad Administration has repeatedly shown. The wastes of resources in the old railroad routings, which the government took in hand during the war, is analogous. Wastes of agricultural and city building land could be traced also in enormous amounts and here, as in other cases, certain investigators would think they could find the greatest wastes of all. We may list also the human resources which we now permit to waste themselves in certain highly specialized trading operations, including the professional trader: known to every town, great and small, a spider who weaves his web and sits in it watching for fat victims. The wastes of effort and capital in "blue-sky" enterprises are notorious. Legal services are supposed to be nine-tenths waste, reckoning only such as are employed in appropriative processes. The "fashionable doctor" system of the cities, which involves a high cost in office and personal display to maintain prestige, is somewhat similar. Food destructions in field and market to maintain high prices might be mentioned. It is impossible to classify wastes logically, so complex is the wirr-warr of wastes in our organization, and some of these could properly perhaps be subsumed under preceding headings.

Pass again for the moment any estimate of the loss from resources misapplied or unutilized directly because of the way we run our national industry and business, and consider shoddy. We might reasonably say: "The more shoddy, the worse our industrial life." Shoddy is, at first sight, the symbol of poverty. But we are not a pauper nation. Shoddy for us is the symbol of waste. It is not directly a matter of trading costs, nor of manufacturing inefficiency, nor of consumers' incapacity, nor of unutilized resources. But it is directly the thing we are getting in ever-increasing proportion from the work we do . . . [and] the way we do it. It is a chief fruit of our industrial and business system.

Profit comes as readily from rotten products as from sound products. Advertising, our main strength in selling, is just as effective with shoddy as with substance. Are our costs high? Take it out of quality. Push the poor goods, put them in place of the good goods. Nineteen-nineteen was a great era of shoddy. High prices were bad enough, but shoddy was worse. A western farmers' organization, which buys wool from its wool-growing members and contracts for the yarn, the cloth and the garment-making, sells back to its members a 39-inch mackinaw coat, made of nothing but the best of the live wool, for $15. But that is not part of our business organization of today. Such a coat cannot be bought on the market. If it could, it would cost, it is estimated, $50 or $60 at retail. A shoddy coat of its type actually costs $20 to $30. What would we be getting today if our industry were set to encourage the making of quality goods, as compared with what we are getting? One may well believe that the 200 per cent of the present product that we might get with better manufacturing and trading methods might be doubled again, if all the released effort and wealth were applied to the one matter of quality. The 200 per cent might become 400 per cent by quality alone. It is a possibility, but pass it over here.

How far are we justified, under the tests we have set up, in attempting [to estimate] the increments of welfare that would come from all three of these last wastes combined; from better utilization of resources, and from the overthrow of the reign of shoddy? The present wastes clearly enough grow out of the industrial organization which we have built up and which we still choose to maintain. But do we see practical signs of their elimination, practical tendencies towards better things? We may avoid the direct answer and the direct estimate. So far as we suppress the profiteering control and substitute the purposeful productive control, we shall indirectly reap improvement here and improvement there. Let us be moderate, and say that the extreme limit of all of them together may be as much more saving as we have held possible from the trading and producing reforms, with a range from nothing-at-all to that amount [200–400 per cent].

We can sum up then with the belief that, counting both the direct and the incidental effects of a set purpose to eliminate profiteering and its ideals and system, we may easily secure ourselves from two to three times our present welfare goods with the same effort and wealth and skill we now employ.

This is a most moderate conclusion, and it is one that depends on no fixed idea as to how we would do it. It does not postulate socialism, or syndicalism, or cooperation, or government-ownership. So far from proposing the overthrow of individual enterprise or initiative, it stresses such capacities and seeks to give them play; but in the field of production and the rewards of production, rather than in that of appropriation and the rewards of appropriation. It assumes, in short, only such an attitude towards our welfare in peace as we perforce were driven to take towards our welfare in war; but it assumes it, with the elimination of that one thing which most hampered our securing productivity and resultant welfare in war—the presence of the hordes of emotionally touched business men at the head of affairs, striving no doubt for honest productiveness in their efforts, but constitutionally and hopelessly incompetent to achieve it.

Notes

1. By profiteering we shall not mean excessively high profits, however. We shall mean instead such rewards as are based on power to take, rather than on power to produce advantageously. The huge winnings of the Ford [Motor] Company, tinged though they are with profiteering, are a type of true profit in this sense, as compared with those of the meat industries, which are today profiteering in every essential respect.

2. "For many years the Royal Baking Powder Co. spent $750,000 a year in advertising and William Ziegler, principal owner, left a fortune of $30,000,000. A government report says the Tobacco Trust spent for advertising in 1910 $11,000,000 and that the companies succeeding the trust spent for advertising in 1913 $23,000,000. The Procter and Gamble Co. recently testified that they spent $3,000,000 in five years to put "Crisco" on the market. The American Sugar Refinery Company have just appropriated $1,000,000 for 'trade-mark' advertising." Emerson P. Harris, *Co-operation, The Hope of the Consumer*, p. 52, n.

"C. W. Post of Grape Nuts started poor and left an estate of $18,000,000. Quaker Oats are said to pay annual dividends of $1,900,000, while each letter of the word Uneeda is said to be valued at $1,000,000. *Ibid.*, p. 198. Some interesting specimens of results of special sales pushed by advertising are given by W. Sammons, *Keeping Up With Rising Costs* (New York: A. W. Shaw, 1915),

p. 13. A department store spent $1,519 for advertising to sell $8,891 of women's and misses' coats, or 19 per cent of the resulting sales. In a special sale of men's shirts, $1,169 was spent to sell $8,640, and in a sale of dresses $1,356 was spent to sell $14,001. A general sale that was an annual event, and merely used widespread price announcements in catalog form, sold $92,671 at an advertising cost of $2,172.

3. Charles P. Steinmetz, *America and the New Epoch* (New York: Harper's, 1916), p. 57.

4. From one of Mr. Veblen's brilliant series of essays "The Modern Point of View and the New Order," in *Dial,* beginning October 1918. Quotation from *Dial,* Vol. 65, No. 778 (November 30, 1918), pp. 482–89.

5. *What Happened to Europe* (New York: Macmillan, 1919), p. 141.

6. . . . These percentages were gathered by W. H. Ingersoll, and the results were published by him in "Dissecting the Consumer's $," in *National Civic Federation Review,* Vol. 4 (June 30, 1919), p. 7. They are used here in preference to the figures previously assembled by the writer—from which they are not greatly different—because they are the outcome of a direct recent investigation, because they carry with them an assurance that good business judgment was used in selecting the industries to be included, and because their agency of publication precludes any possibility of unfriendliness to the existing industrial system of the country. Although they are figures for manufactured products only, we may apply them generally for the following reasons: gross manufactures (including duplications) were 65 per cent, gross agricultural products (crops plus livestock) were 27 per cent, and gross mineral products 8 per cent; of the combined gross total of these branches in 1914. See figures in *U.S. Statistical Abstract, 1918* (Washington: Government Printing Office, 1919) pp. 183, 199, 240, 242. Of the mineral products, all but part of the coal went into manufacture. Of the agricultural products, a large part went into manufacture. For the part of the agricultural products that went direct through trade to consumers, a 50 per cent attribution to the producer is about right. By starting with manufacturers' selling price as the producers' price for food products, we more than offset any possible correction of the table for directly sold food products.

7. The C.W.S. handles large plantations and factories of its own. In October, 1917, it had 29,638 employees of whom 3,365 were in its distributive department, 5,519 in branches and depots, 16,897 in producing enterprises, and 3,847 in tea and cocoa plantations owned jointly with the Scottish wholesale.

8. [Data derived from *The Moody's Industrials* (New York: Moody's Investors Service, 1917, 1918).]

9. [Various estimates of costs and waste in trade are presented. These writings include: Sidney A. Reeve, *The Cost of Competition* (New York: McClure, Phillips and Co., 1906); Willford I. King, in Richard T. Ely, *Property and Contract in Their Relations to the Distribution of Wealth,* Vol. II (New York: Macmillan, 1914) pp. 523–52; and Harris, *op. cit.* Mark-up and profit estimates of numerous sources are cited, including: *Printers Ink,* 1914; *Bulletins,* Harvard Graduate School of Business Administration; and Wheeler Sammons, *Keeping Up With Rising Costs* (Chicago: A. W. Shaw, 1915). The inference of the data cited is that Bentley's estimates of waste and possible savings are quite conservative.]

Some of our fields of savings, concretely put, would be duplicated stores and the losses by failure resultant from them; duplicated delivery routes not actually more . . . necessary or desirable to us than duplicated mail service would be; standardization of types and supplies and packages, where no purpose except one of profiteering is now served by variety (as in automobile tires and batteries); inflated rentals, where due to present types of competition; specious advertising; . . . the cost of trick salesmanship; [and] duplications of commercial traveler expense. The wastes of inefficiency in retail-store management alone are estimated as high as 5 per cent by Harris, *op. cit.*, p. 57.

10. See his discussion "On The Nature and Uses of Sabotage," *The Dial,* Vol. 66, No. 787 (April 5, 1919) pp. 341–46.

11. The following very forceful interpretation of the British workers' point of view is from Walter Weyl's article "In the King's Robing Room," *New Republic* Vol. 19, No. 246 (July 23, 1919), pp. 389–92: "The general strike, such as we have never yet seen it, is neither more nor less than an economic blockade of the whole nation. Back of this giant strike, moreover, lies an even more subtle, deadly, and uncontrollable weapon—the refusal of men greatly to exert themselves. This growing reluctance of wage-earners to give more than they get is the Achilles-foot of our modern industrial system. It is the weapon which in the end injures those who use it as well as those against whom it is used, and it is the more dangerous because it destroys habits of industry and injures the morale which a century of capitalism has strengthened among workers. But how can you overcome the wage-earner's refusal to work hard and his acquired habit of taking things easy if he believes that the chief thing he is working for is the profit of the mine-owners, already over-rich? You can conscript labor, but you can't conscript enthusiasm, and without enthusiasm labor today is a dead limb. The mine leaders have predicted, and in a sense promised, that the men will work with all their might if the management is theirs and the profits are public profits, but not otherwise. It is, of course, a threat more than a prophecy, for without enthusiastic labor private ownership of the mines will be unprofitable. It is compulsion. But the miners believe, rightly or wrongly, that they have never gained anything except by compulsion."

12. The following from the majority opinion of the U.S. Supreme Court declaring the United [States] Steel Corporation not an illegal corporation under the Sherman Act, delivered March 1, 1920, lists some of the offensive destructive acts of other corporations. (*U.S.* v. *United States Steel Corp.,* 251 U.S. 417) "It (the Steel Corporation) resorted to none of the brutalities or tyrannies that the cases illustrate of other combinations. It did not secure freight rebates; it did not increase its profits by reducing the wages of its employees—whatever it did was not at the expense of labor; it did not increase its profits by lowering the quality of its products, nor create an artificial scarcity of them; it did not oppress or coerce its competitors—its competition, though vigorous, was fair; it did not undersell its competitors in some localities by reducing its prices there below those maintained elsewhere, or require its customers to enter into contracts limiting their purchases or restricting them in resale prices; it did not obtain customers by secret rebates or departures from its published prices; there was no evidence that it attempted to crush its competitors or drive them out of the market; nor did it take customers from its competitors by unfair means, and in its competition it seemed to make no difference between large and small competitors." It should be remembered that, at that, only four out of seven justices participating felt that the Steel Corporation, even with all the record of abstinence from evil, was entitled to further existence under the law; and the two justices who did not participate were both against that corporation's legality.

13. Cf., *U.S. Geological Survey,* "Coal in 1917"; Averages by Walter N. Polakov, *The Dial* Vol. 67, No. 802, (November 1, 1919), pp. 395–404, esp. p. 397.

14. Henry L. Gantt, *Organizing for Work* (New York: Harcourt, Brace, and Howe), p. 88.

15. See charts in his *Work, Wages and Profits* (New York: Engineering Magazine, 1910) and in his *Industrial Leadership* (New York: Yale University Press, 1916).

16. Quoted by Emerson P. Harris, *Co-operation, The Hope of the Consumer,* p. 155.

17. Helen Marot, *The Creative Impulse in Industry* (New York: E. P. Dutton, 1918), pp. 15–16.

18. See on both these points Gantt, *Organizing for Work.*

19. Herbert Hoover asserts that "the American farmer receives a less proportion of the consumers purchase price than the farmer of most civilized countries." Chicago address, February 27, 1920. [Cf., *New York Times,* February 29, 1920.]

20. An extreme case is a group of counties due to produce much below normal in 1920 because men and teams have been pulled from them by a road contractor, who secured a large contract on a semi-political, profiteering basis, which enables him to offer unheard-of wages.

21. It is not easy to offer statistical proof as to whether our industries are becoming more or less productive, but King has a computation of the total product of factories for sixty years, per person engaged in industry, translated from the prices of the particular year, by means of the wholesale price index into terms of the price scale of 1890–99. His index figures of product per person rose steadily, except for the Civil War time, from 329 in 1850 to 891 in 1900, but dropped in 1910 to 849. [Willford I.] King, *The Wealth and Income of the People of the United States* (New York: The Macmillan Co., 1915), p. 144.

22. Dr. William Farr's estimate for England is often quoted. For every annual death, he holds two persons are continously suffering from severe illness, and three [are] ill enough to need medical care. [Cf., his *Vital Statistics* (London: The Sanitary Institute, 1885).]

23. The Federal Reserve Board continually insists on extravagance as a cause of high prices. See especially the letter of its governor to Senator McLean, August 11, 1919. The district banks of the system almost invariably insist on it in their current discussions of financial conditions. The U.S. Council of National Defense in *An Analysis of the High Cost of Living Problem,* emphasized it as one factor.

24. Some measure of the possible influence of excessive income may be found in the fact that in normal years half, and in some years more than half, of our national income is in the form of return on investments and in profits; as contrasted with the wage and salary receipts, which roughly make the other half.

VII

The Masters of the Highways

Profiteering, we have seen, rests upon the occupation of strong, strategic positions in the industrial world. National wastes are the costs of its success. Taking its origin in the appropriative powers of property, profiteering comes to maturity in the organized system of the industrial government. The little profits of man with man disappear; the little freedoms of man in trade with man disappear. The great profiteering, the autocratic control of centralized industry, takes their place. Against itself, by the very fact of its dominion, the centralized, profiteering industrial government raises the threat of revolution, industrial and political, with all its dangers of violence and destruction.

We have now to study more in detail these strategic positions; to determine where they are located, how fortified and maintained, and what exactly are their public and private aspects. We shall find them on the great highways of industry, the trade routes that all products must follow from maker to user, the routes of communication in that system of technology, without which we could not all work together as functioning parts of one common society.

In the Middle Ages, under a very simple system of manufacture and trade which nevertheless spread itself over wide territories, a baron could build a castle on a commanding hill overlooking a trade route. From there he could make forays for plunder, or, less crudely, he could levy tolls upon passing caravans in return for the protection he gave them—a protection which was often rather against himself than against any other peril.

In modern times the highways are no longer so simple, nor so easily held. They include . . . roads and railroads; Post Office,

97

telegraph, and telephone; complex institutions of commerce like grain and produce exchanges, warehouses, and terminals; [and] all the institutions of credit without the services of which no industrial activities can go far. Their control rests not merely in enough steep hill or moated land for a castle, but in the ownership of the great equipments of the highways; in the administration of the natural resources of the nation: its coal and oil, gas and ores, timber and water power; in the possession of the organization which functions through them; and in the appropriation of technology and trade information in all of its most useful and most profitable features.

Now merely to sketch in this way the scope of the highways shows how very easily we may range the whole universe while on this subject and perhaps never come to earth at any definite point. We shall therefore hold to two tests to guide us in examining [the] highways of industry, and in studying questions of the where and why of the strategic control that has been established over them. One is the test of the great vital problems of today; the problems of wealth and waste, and [of] power and revolution. The other is the test of the individual man, the self-justified gainer of a livelihood, the man who, on a level with every other man, and in accordance with his own powers and capacities—providing they are powers and capacities not hurtful to others—stands justified in his desire and willingness to play a full man's share in the adventure of life.

It is with considerable misgiving that an attempt is here made to classify these highways, and the following list is set forth without any pretense of completeness and without any emphasis on its details of arrangement. This subject might well justify a volume in itself. Here all that concerns us is the background of the main problems of the day. We might arrange the highways with reference to the services performed upon them, and with reference to the equipment they use. We might also arrange them with reference to the kinds of tolls or charges levied upon them. We might finally arrange them with reference to their footing; upon the resources of the land, or the resources of the scientific and technological nature which have been seized and organized for holding control of them. We shall, however, merely roughly classify the main highways and indicate without classification certain types of footing they make us of.

Types of Highways

1. Highways for Physical Transfer of Persons and Goods: Roads and Streets, Railroads, Streetcar Lines, Rivers and Harbors.
2. Highways for Communication: Post office, Telegraph, Telephone.
3. Highways for Special Services: Light, Power, Heat.
4. Highways for Trade: Grain Exchanges and Boards of Trade, Stock Yards and Terminals, Private Car-Lines, Warehouses and Elevators, Provision Exchanges, Egg and Butter Boards, Public Markets.
5. Highways for Industrial Information: Private Information Systems of Technology and Trade, Technical Schools, Government Bureaus of Markets and Information.
6. Highways for Credit: The Commercial Banking System, The Investment Banking and Promotion System, Domestic and Foreign.

The Footing of Highway Control

1. All Land As a Possibility
2. Right-of-Ways in Particular
3. Seizable Contents of the Earth: Coal, Ore, Gas, Oil, Timber, Water Power.
4. Centralized Organization
5. Technology and Market Information
6. Reiteration and Suggestion: Commercial Advertising, Educational Advertising.

No apology is needed for the way the criteria of classification cut across each other in the above lists. Intensely complex is the organization of industrial government, and intensely complex also is [the] fortification of industrial strategic positions upon its highways. Roads and streets, rivers and harbors are open to all by public determination, even though farm- or office- or dock-owner may still secure profit by reason of advantageous location with reference to them. Post Office [service] has also been made free to the nation, so far as [such] service goes, with single-zone tariff for letters and a limited number of zones for parcels. Streetcars and railroads hold [control of their land] by virtue of right-of-ways granted them, both now coming under a troubled and uncertain public control; the former with its flat tariffs, the latter with its complex rates worked out first on appropriative basis and later modified by public requirements of service. Telegraph and telephone are in the same wavering field of control. Those other services—light, power, and heat—are recognized as in this field by the very descriptive term "public utilities," so commonly applied to them, along with streetcars and [the] telegraph and telephone.

The "master man" who holds the ownership position between the "producing man" and the "consuming man" has been compelled to accept the label of public utility, however much he resists the limitations placed upon his mastery. In commerce, the great food markets for grain and meat were perforce recognized practically as in the nature of public utilities by the government during the war [World War I], and brought under the administration of war boards. In the matter of information, both that of technology and that of trade conditions, elaborate private systems have been built up as aids to mastery, and much of what is theoretically a public possession has been seized so far as its utilization is concerned by private owners. Against these private systems, technical schools assert the public's right, and new government bureaus are tentatively endeavoring to equalize opportunities in some of the main marketing lines.[1]

Behind all [business and industry] are the highways of credit which have become the very central fortification of the industrial government. The commercial banking system was early regulated to correct its more startling and irresponsible abuses towards its patrons, and then thoroughly systematized under [Senator Nelson W.] Aldrich to wipe out still more of these abuses, and [to] give it coherent strength as a department of industrial government. But the investment banking system, which rules it, has thus far had practically no limitation placed upon it save in such legislation as that against interlocking directorates, which has simply removed a symptom, not produced any deeper change. And in this field, so

34254

marked is the nature of the appropriative power at issue, that no way of effectively banning even the worst of the "blue-sky" [fraudulent] enterprises . . . has yet [1920] been found; . . . [nor any] satisfactory and workable line of demarcation to use in legislation.

If the street in front of my house were owned by someone else, and the alley behind it, and the lots on both sides of it; if these were not owned simply for possession and use, but with the full appropriative power of property as against me and other people, my position would indeed be intolerable. The owner of the street could take such toll of me as he desired; he could in the extreme case confine me and bear [drive] me down to ill-health, weakness, and even death. But society has long ago taken care of this need of social existence by making the streets and roads free, and even stripping off, almost everywhere, the last vestiges of the old toll privileges on privately built roads. (Indeed, the freedom of the roads and streets may be regarded rather as a survival of the general freedom of the land from which private holdings have been carved out, than as a special freedom established in the midst of private holdings.) For the movement, not merely of persons but of commodities, these highways, as opportunities free to all, are vital to our industrial life.

Now, this simple primitive case has seemingly within it the whole principle upon which the solution of our industrial problems can be worked out. We are, all of us, makers and users. Living together, we have, all of us, power for good or evil over the rest of us. Wherever a position [in the economy] is found upon which this power can be exercised for personal advantage, it is bound to be exercised. And if a position can be found from which others can be shut out (not only with respect to the particular advantageous position in question), and if this position is of such a nature that other citizens must use its facilities and consequently must pay a tribute to the possessor of it, we have a typical case [analogy] of the [medieval baron and the] highway for the industrial relations of man with man. When such situations arise, and they are always arising, always being forced upon us as new masters appear in new positions, it is for society to deal with them. It may be [dealing] confusedly, hesitatingly, and partially; it may be clearly and deliberately; it may be a bit here and a bit there until the end is attained; or it may be, if the power of mastery has become too

Lincoln Christian College

strong and too resistant, with harsh determination or even with violence. It must always be, in the end, with recognition that the full, ultimate authority of society over all of its [economic] highways of whatsoever kind and description, is the essential condition of social existence and prosperity.

Take the railroad as a highway. Without going into the history of the relations of the railroads with the public, the slightest reflection recalls the long list of abuses [by the railroads] before the nation took a hand in defense of the welfare of citizen-workers and citizen-users of products. This town was ruined by rate discriminations to the benefit of that other. This city developed a trade in some line with which no other could compete because of railroad action. The farmlands of the East [according to some critics] were forced into a decline, for the benefit of the long-haul interests of the roads in handling western produce in bulk.[2] With the aid of the roads—through rate discriminations, or special rebates, or special service for private car-lines—this or that corporation [e.g., the Standard Oil Trust] dominated the whole field, or almost the whole field, of its industry in the nation.

Consider the public utilities of our cities. They filled a place which had, inherent in it, needs of unification and consolidation. They developed into huge power and huge wastes, and the result was the most urgent need of public control. They could not exist without using the original highways, the streets; and on that use they built huge private positions of dominance. Today under belated control, many of them stand suppliants at the door of the public, carrying on their backs the piled-up capitalized wastes [watered stock] of the past; urging that they should be allowed to fatten forever on their capitalized misdeeds of the past; asking the cities to relax their recently exerted regulative powers so that this fattening can continue.

The essence of their position is that they perform a mediating service between one citizen and another, and the citizens must have these services; . . . unregulated, they are the masters of the citizens, and . . . if the citizens are to function freely and efficiently in their dealings with one another, this mastery must be destroyed. The answer of George W. Perkins [a partner of J. P. Morgan] to the question put to him by Victor Murdock [chairman] of the Federal

Trade Commission [1919–20], "How to bust a trust?" illustrates the character of the power. The answer was: "cut the telephone wires of the country."[3]

Turning to trade, consider the North Dakota farmer who has wheat to sell. First he hauls it over the country road and the city street. Then he places it in the local elevator by sale or deposit, for transfer to the railroad cars. Railroad and country roads are both part of his highway to market, but, by the same token, so is the country elevator. The farmer is interested directly in the the price the local dealer pays, but he, with all his fellow farmers, is interested much more deeply in the price that becomes possible as a result of the passage of his produce over all the highways into the hands of the consumers. If he finds the local elevator interfering with his business enterprise, while being absolutely necessary to it, he will inevitably treat it as a highway. As a matter of fact, most of the North Dakota country elevators are now owned and managed co-operatively by the farmers; and wherever a private elevator or one of the old-line elevators still exists, if the farmer decides to enter the field himself, the old elevator simply shuts up and quits. The cooperative venture upon the highways of trade, so far as local elevators are concerned, has been very successful, not only in North Dakota, but in many of the western states where heavy production of a limited range of crops is the usual status.[4] But the wheat has still a long road to follow before it reaches the consumer.

From the railroad it goes through the hands of a commission man in Minneapolis. This man must be a member of the Minneapolis Chamber of Commerce. Nominally, this is a body open to the public; actually, no increase of its members has occurred for years, and no commission dealer offering more favorable terms to the farmer than the rules require will be permitted to retain his seat. This Chamber of Commerce is a body maintaining its own courts with what are substantially extra-territorial rights for its own citizens; and if a final issue arises, the state courts merely enforce its decrees—not only as against its own members, but incidentally and indirectly as against all non-citizens of the Chamber.[5]

On the Chamber of Commerce, the wheat is graded in a way that classifies it as to its probable price, and it is docked in weight for any foreign grain or seeds it contains, even though the presence of those foreign seeds had already affected its grading. All of this is under a regulation by [the] state and lately by [the] nation, which the farmer holds is, in the main, not for [the] producers' or consumers' benefit but for [the] traders' benefit. The farmer's wheat must pass this way, and hence he regards the Chamber of Commerce in Minneapolis—and along with it the boards of trade of Chicago, Milwaukee and Duluth and other cities—as part of the highways he must follow. For the control of this part of the highways, he has made a cooperative experiment in the form of his own selling agency, the Equity Cooperative Exchange. But the exchange has never been able to get its members admitted to the Chamber of Commerce, and the terminal elevator it has erected at St. Paul has never had a fair chance to function as part of the wheat-marketing system of the country; because of the discriminations against it, direct and indirect, originating from the masters of the highways, who had to fight to keep from losing their mastery.

Through terminal elevator or mill elevator the wheat passes either to export or to manufacture into flour. There is a little work of a manufacturing nature in the elevators, cleaning and combining [it] into new grades; there is more in the mills where various types of wheat, usually from various localities, are mixed and milled. Thence follows passage through warehouses and on railroads into wholesale stores and retail stores and via delivery wagons to private houses, or else through bakeries to the same destination. The wheat and its products are ever on the highways.

When [in 1915] the North Dakota farmer found his plans for cooperative handling of his products at the central market point were nullified by the controllers of the market, he turned to politics. The Non-Partisan League,* strictly a farmers' organization—which fully dominates the politics of North Dakota [in 1919], and which has shown great strength in Minnesota, Montana, South Dakota and other states—has a platform which consists almost exclusively of planks that have to do with the mastery of the highways of trade between producer and consumer. If the farmer is not permitted

* Cf., Robert Morlan, *Prairie Fire: The Non-Partisan League, 1915–1922* (Minneapolis: University of Minnesota Press, 1955); Theodore Saloutos and John D. Hicks, *Agricultural Discontent in the Middle West 1900–1939* (Lincoln; University of Nebraska Press, 1951).

under the industrial government to establish a cooperative terminal elevator, he proposes under the political government to establish it and to back it with the full power of the state.

Knowing that no one element in the industrial complex can be successful except under sound working relations with the other elements, he has arrogated to himself the political power to build state flour mills and establish state selling agencies, and above all to create a state credit system which will enable him to guarantee his other enterprises against raids at any weak points that may appear along the line. He has added regulative legislation upon railroad rates to prevent discriminations against him, and he has revised and made more effective the state laws against local price discriminations in products that may be sent into the state to compete with him.

Not one of these projects has been undertaken because he likes the idea of state business enterprise. On the contrary, he has proceeded reluctantly, but under what he conceives to be the ultimate compulsion upon him from without. He welcomes competition: he is willing to face any kind of competition that is fair. He insists only that he be safeguarded from the kind of competition that ruins him and then proceeds to profit many fold from the ruin. That is his program in its main outlines; strictly and solely a program of control of the highways.

Such a program as this, which within its limits and considering its purposes would seem a reasonable use of the powers of the political government, has made the farmer an Anarchist, a Socialist, a Bolshevist, and pro-German traitor—all at one and the same time—in the eyes of the rulers of the industrial government whose seats [of power] are in the mills and terminal elevators, in the Chamber of Commerce and in the bank directorates of Minneapolis. The most elaborate organizations have been formed to defeat him. One of them, reputed to have raised a million dollars for the fight, sent a pretended "farmers weekly" of many pages to hundreds of thousands of northwestern farmers, and only abandoned it when its scheme had been widely exposed and all hope of getting paying subscribers was over.

The Minneapolis Board of Safety and the governor of the state joined, during the war [World War I], in the most relentless prosecutions of active League members. On a pretense that the League was seditious, its workers were mobbed, their property was destroyed, and dozens of them were arrested on charges of espionage. Practically none of the cases held finally in the courts. Every possible agency of publicity and of the suppression of publicity was used against them. In a third of the counties of Minnesota, during the fall campaign of 1918, the League was not permitted to hold a political meeting. Mexico [at this time] could hardly show anything more high-handed. Later on, a "Kept Chautauqua" [subsidized lecture program] was established with many subscriptions back of it, and all of its speakers were carefully trained to undermine the League insidiously wherever they went.

So the case stands now [*circa* 1920] in the Northwest, with two governments clearly opposed. To the farmers the industrial government is an autocratic usurper of the [economic] highways. To the Minneapolis bankers, millers, and grain men and all their connections, the farmers who have mastered the political government are socialists, syndicalists, criminal revolutionists, and traitors.

Let us now consider with more attention for a moment the special functions of highway control, as compared with the productive functions that appear at all points in the handling of goods on the highways.

The railroad, now fully comprehended by the public as a highway rather than a purely private enterprise, is manifestly productive. Its use makes possible the production of greater quantities of goods and their wider distribution. It is almost impossible to estimate the total increase in the productiveness of the workers of the country, the total increase in consumer goods for the users of the country, due to our railroad development. Before the railroad became subjected to the public's interest in its highways of trade, railroad rates were built up out of a mixture of open or, more often, hidden purposes of an appropriative nature, many of them arising entirely outside of the transportation field. "What the traffic will bear" was a test. A town site some man was interested in, a subsidy from industries in some city, the purposes of a construction company, the power some great industry had developed to swing its traffic between rival lines, were all important factors.

All of this was appropriative highway control. It belonged under the so-called "financial function" of the corporation. It had no contacts except incidentally with the productive services. Observe how the study of rate-making stood with reference to theoretical economics. One would think that if any economic theory of value [e.g., Alfred Marshall's] was valid, it would cover railroad rates. Yet, as a matter of fact, economic theories of value hardly ventured into this field: they were bewildered when they approached it; and [until John R. Commons' *Legal Foundations of Capitalism* (1924) and A. C. Pigou's *Economics of Welfare* (1st ed., 1920) appeared] they left the books on railroad rates to specialists who dealt directly with very raw, very brutal facts, and tried to classify them.

Now that state and national commissions have worked with rates to bring some measure of equity into them, we are approximating commodity classifications with strict distance tariffs inside of each classification, or we are approximating zone tariffs such as the parcel post uses. Labor costs are a factor, and material and maintenance costs. The relation of total tonnage carried to investment value also figures in, but investment value is so confused with capitalization on the basis of past earning powers that it needs much prying into. The whole question of railroad rates—the problem of economic value in railroad rates—is clearly one of two poles; at the one extreme the appropriative power, not of property as such, but of property in a strategic [exploitative] position on the highways, and at the other extreme, equality of opportunity to all makers and users.

In the flour mills we have a not dissimilar situation. The productive work is done, but it is under the price control of [business] interests whose main stress is upon the appropriative possibilities of their situation. The great mills of Minneapolis are what they are to a similar extent because of water power and electricity derived from it; to a larger extent because of the great mass of hard wheat available from the territory west of the city; and to a comparable, and possibly even greater, extent because of the possibilities, (dependent on transportation facilities) of mixing the hard wheats with softer wheats from Nebraska and Kansas on the most economical basis. The possibilities of these positions are capitalized in the form of watered stock, and maintained against local competition in various parts of the country by excessively wasteful expenditures for advertising whose purpose is appropriative, not productive.

Turn next to the Minneapolis Chamber of Commerce. The commission firms which operate upon [within] it perform a necessary service. Both its necessity for the public and the cancerous effects of the way it is performed upon the public were sufficiently demonstrated during the war when the federal government took its central function into direct public operation, and placed its various attendant motions under regulation through the creation [in August, 1917] of the [United States] Food Administration, and later of the [United States] Grain Corporation. Grain must be graded, cleaned, mixed and directed into the channels that lead to its use. Prices must be established in accordance with national and world needs dependent upon the year's crop, and [upon] the holdover from the preceding year. A clue must be given to producers to guide them in the amount they sow for the following year. Information is what the Chamber of Commerce specializes in. It is the source of the incomes of its members. But this information is not the public's own information of its own activities, past, present, and future, used with equal value to all for the common good. It is partial information secured by many specialists, supplemented by much guessing; guessing . . . of the hour, of the day, of the month and of the year. It is used directly and expressly for the guesser's advantage. Upon it each guesser bases his appropriative power. The best-informed man, the best guesser, the boldest guesser, soon gets a precedence in reward which (by continuation of those qualities) he may make ever greater; utilizing the proceeds of past appropriations and the credit established thereupon for further appropriations. Without a close organization of interests between the millers, the terminal elevator operators and the bankers, not only in Minneapolis, but in the other great centers of the trade, this appropriative use of the powers of the highway could not be successfully made.

In the field where once "corners" [of the market] were known, there now exists what is in a sense a perpetual corner; moderated only in action by whatever happens to be the judgment of appropriators as to their welfare, or by sporadic interferences from the government.[6] As the various elements stand knit together into a firm but elastic organization, they frankly admit the evils that result, but call them incidental. They argue in terms of the service the country needs, and which they are now the agency for giving, but they assume credit for that service as their own. They assert that their system of government is "the" government, and they accuse of treason all who would try to change it or substitute something else for it.

The North Dakota farmer says: "I cannot get storage: You control it. I cannot get credit to hold my grain till spring: you control it, and my notes are all made due in the fall. I cannot control the grading of my wheat: You control it. I cannot get pay for rye in my wheat or wheat in my rye, for flax in either, or for the cockle which the chickens eat: You take these out, keep them and sell them, but do not pay for them."

In the two years from September 1, 1910 to August 31, 1912, the receipts of the high-graded and high-priced wheat—No. 1 Northern and No. 1 Hard, at Minneapolis—combined, were 16 million bushels, and the farmer was paid for this amount. But the shipments of these high grades were 20 million bushels; and for the 25 per cent excess the dealers, not the farmers, got the higher prices. For the low grades, No. 3 and No. 4 Northern, the receipts in those years were 12.5 million bushels, and the shipments only 8.25 million, while on "rejected" and "no grade" wheat the receipts were 6 millions, and the shipments only a little over 1.5 millions. The masters of the highways bought [wheat] as cheap grades and sold [it] as high grades. The producer was the loser. The user [also] was the loser. The masters made the profit.[7]

In the eleven marketing seasons between 1906–1907 and 1916–17, the average spread between September and May low prices of wheat on the Chicago market was 20 points, and the average spread of high prices for those months was 27 points. Or, leaving out the exceptional war year, 1918, the average was: for low prices 10 points, and for high prices 11 points. This is about three times the carrying charges. There were only three of the eleven years in which traders would have taken a loss, even if they had made their trades like automatons; and there was never less than an 11-point spread between the low of September and the high of May, to help out the skillful.

"Feed D" wheat, a special grade created in 1916, a year of light-

weight grain, will long be remembered by the North Dakota producers. The farmer received perhaps 80 cents a bushel when No. 1
was bringing $1.70, with a 7-cent freight rate in between; but when
the millers sold the flour, they advertised it is exceptionally fine because of the high gluten content which had been characteristic of
Feed D and the other poorer grades. The North Dakota Agricultural
Experiment Station made a series of careful tests and proved that
Feed D Wheat milled 60 per cent of flour as against 69 per cent
for No. 1, and that millers' profits on Feed D would be 112 per
cent as against 21 per cent on No. 1[8]

President Ladd, of North Dakota Agricultural College, estimates
that the farmers have lost as high as $50 million in a single year by
market manipulations. Herbert Hoover, addressing the Senate Committee on Agriculture June 19, 1917, estimated that $250 million
would be extracted from the consumer in excess of normal trade
and distribution profits in the last six months of that year if the
government did not take action to control wheat and flour prices.
Frederic C. Howe has estimated an unjust taking of $37,800,000 on
wheat in September 1915 alone, and a loss in the last six months of
1915 of $302,832,000.[9]

We shall [look] carefully into the technique and results of this
highway control in the two succeeding chapters, dealing with the
nation's meat supply. Here we shall be content with a few other
illustrations. All over the country, for all lines of foods, produce
and commission exchanges have developed. [Professor L. D. H.]
Weld, in his volume on the marketing of farm products, has several
chapters devoted to their description. Most of them [the ex-
changes] have originated for the correction of intolerable conditions in the commission men's own business. Some few have continued to a career of generally useful work. Others have been but
stepping stones to an appropriative control of the markets, and have
either disappeared or continued to exist as mere formalities; deceptive appearances of markets, used to delude now sellers, now buyers,
as to what true [competitive] prices are. The Elgin Butter Board,
existing where there is no real butter market, is typical. "The principal reason for having the quotation at all," says Weld, "is that
such a large part of the country has become accustomed to the use
of the quotation that there has been a demand for its continuance."[10]

Deliberate destructions of great quantities of perishable foods in the city [food] markets are frequent attendants upon this form of appropriators' control. Even in time of war needs there was no restraining hand from within the trade. The producer may lose his carload and his year's profit, the rich consumer may pay high prices, the poor consumer may go without [needed food], but the appropriator preserves his basis for profit. Only through [his] domination of a highway which both producer and consumer must use, does such an abuse become possible. The many war [World War I] boards of the government for the stabilizing of prices developed in this field; all aimed to check the appropriative powers, which under war conditions were a visible menace to the nation's success in the conduct of the war; and all of which, by the same token, remain as a continuing menace to the national welfare in the business of peace.

In all such establishments as warehouse terminals and [commodity] markets, the test as to how far a business is private and how far it has become touched with public character lies in the necessity the public is under of making use of its facilities. If the consumer can get along without [them], and if he cannot substitute other agencies, he will inevitably regard it as public; and the fact that he so regards it will, in the ultimate analysis, be the proof that it is public: that fact is all the proof needed. It is all the proof that any public institution ever has had for itself. Let an abuse appear through dominance founded on ownership, let the abuse become known, and the struggle begins. Our mail-order houses and our chain stores for cigars, drugs, and, to a lesser extent, groceries are, at the present time, private institutions rendering services in their respective ways. But if any of the predictions that are made as to the suppression of wholesale and retail grocery trade in this country come true, and if the same thing occurs in the other lines, chain stores and mail-order houses may later appear as candidates for inclusion on the list of institutions on the highways of trade. They might even today [1920] be listed as possibilities of the near future. Their transfer into cooperative organizations, or their . . . [being supplanted] by cooperative organizations under government protection would then be an easy matter of prediction. Indeed, in England, this very development which the United States is having through chain stores and mail-order houses has taken place through the Wholesale Cooperative and its affiliated societies.

We seem to be, in truth, at the point of a great extension of the idea of what constitutes of public utility into the field of these high-ways of commerce. In the congressional hearings over bills for the regulation of the packing industry in January 1919, the phrase "public utility" was heard every day. Walter L. Fisher referred to a Supreme Court decision which laid it down "as a fundamental prop-osition that a railroad, so far as it is a common carrier, is exer-cising a function of government." [He] insisted that the Food Ad-ministration Law must not lapse without something to take its place; and compared present-day arguments for private initiative with those used in earlier days when private "tax-farmers" held that it was not a proper "governmental activity" for a government to collect its own taxes.[11]

Levy Mayer, representing Armour and Co., devoted much time in opposition [to this position, by] arguing that the meat business was not "clothed with a public use"; his points being derived, of course, from the existing legal status. Branch houses, stockyards, and terminals were all described by witnesses at one time or another as public utilities, along with refrigerator cars.[12] Much time was also given by the [meat] packers to explaining why the govern-ment's success with its war boards could not possibly be duplicated in time of peace.[13]

The points that stood out in these discussions were those of efficiency—the admitted appropriative efficiency of the highway masters, with frequent recognition of their productive inefficiency; the effect of their methods on output; . . . their control of prices by arbitrary methods; their excessive wastes of productive power in order to heighten their appropriative power; and the limitation of national savings through these wastes. Of all of these matters, illustration will be [made] evident from time to time.

Notes

1. "In my judgment, turning the spotlight of publicity on to the markets, even if no authority went with it at all, and if it were merely a gathering and publishing every day of market prices, supplies, movements and all that goes on in the markets, would cure about fifty per cent of the troubles that exist. I do not think that is enough to cure them all, but I think it is the most important point at which to begin with the correction of market evils, because you cannot correct an evil

unless you know just what it is." [Statement by] Louis D. Hall, specialist in marketing, Bureau of Markets, Department of Agriculture, House Committee on Interstate and Foreign Commerce, *Hearings on Government Control of the Meat Packing Industry*, (on Sims Bill, H.R. 13324), 1919, p. 1957.

2. See Frederic C. Howe, *The High Cost of Living* (New York: C. Scribners Sons, 1917), Chapter IX. [On the other side, see Fred A. Shannon, *The Farmer's Last Frontier* (New York & Toronto: Farrar & Rinehart, 1945), Chapters VIII & XI.]

3. House Hearings on Sims Bill, p. 2378.

4. In 1912 there were 2,020 of these farmers' cooperative elevators in western states affiliated with various farmers' associations. U.S. Department of Agriculture, *Year Book 1913* (Washington, Government Printing Office, 1914), p. 249.

5. The same [control over members] is true of the New York Produce Exchange.

6. In May 1919, Julius Barnes, National Grain Administrator, told the Chicago Board of Trade that unless the rapid fluctuations in prices were stopped—and he had a case of a 10- or 12-cent break in corn prices on the day he spoke as an illustration—he would use his power under the Food Control Act to prohibit dealings in futures entirely. Moreover, he said that if flour and wheat prices did not come into better accord, other administrative measures would be used. He treated the situation throughout as one which the Board of Trade, as a body of dealers working together, could control by their act of volition. "Editorial Notes," *New Republic*, Vol. 19, No. 239 (May 31, 1919), p. 133.

7. Louis D. H. Weld, *The Marketing of Farm Products* (New York: Macmillan, 1916), p. 379.

8. E. F. Ladd, "North Dakota Wheat for 1916," North Dakota Agricultural Experiment Station, *Bulletin No. 119*, November, 1916.

9. Frederic C. Howe, *The High Cost of Living*, pp. 32–38.

10. L. D. H. Weld, *op. cit.*, p. 306. Weld, it will be recalled, is a strenuous defender of the existing order, so his testimony in this part is especially significant. Compare also Howe, *The High Cost of Living*, p. 56.

11. *Hearings on Government Control of the Meat Packing Industry*, pp. 294–295.

12. *Ibid.*, pp. 891, 1251, 2355, 2409.

13. *Ibid.*, pp. 889–896.

VIII

The Nation's Meat

[Bentley devoted a large chapter, about fifty manuscript pages, to an exhaustive analysis of profiteering in the meatpacking industry, based on a scholarly study of extensive government investigations. He concluded that the deficiency in the meat ration of large parts of the city populations was due to the inefficient and excessively costly meat-handling system of this country prevailing in the first two decades of the twentieth century. Since important changes in the whole national food supply have occurred since 1920, the editor has deemed it advisable to omit the major part of this chapter, except for the last few pages, comparing the elder Henry Ford's activities with those of the big meatpackers.

[In place of Bentley's extended critique, we have reproduced the highlights of the Federal Trade Commission's condensed statement in its *Report . . . on the Meat-Packing Industry**** as follows]:

"It appears that five great packing concerns of the country— Swift, Armour, Morris, Cudahy, and Wilson—have attained such a dominant position that they control at will the market in which they buy their supplies, the market in which they sell their products, and hold the fortunes of their competitors in their hands.

"Not only is the business of gathering, preparing, and selling meat products in their control, but an almost countless number of by-product industries are similarly dominated; and not content with reaching out for mastery as to commodities which substitute for meat and its by-products, they have invaded allied industries and even unrelated ones.

* "Letter to the President," *Summary and Part I* (Washington: Government Printing Office, 1919), pp. 24–27.

"The combination has not stopped at the most minute integration but has gone on into a stage of conglomeration, so that unrelated heterogenous enterprises are brought under control.

"As we have followed these five great corporations through their amazing and devious ramifications—followed them through important branches of industry, of commerce, and of finance—we have been able to trace back to its source the great power which has made possible their growth. We have found that it is not so much the means of production and preparation, nor the sheer momentum of great wealth, but the advantage which is obtained through a monopolistic control of the market places and means of transportation and distribution.

"If these five great concerns owned no packing plants and killed no cattle and still retained control of the instruments of transportation, of marketing, and of storage, their position would not be less strong than it is.

"The producer of live stock is at the mercy of these five companies because they control the market and the marketing facilities and, to some extent, the rolling stock which transports the product to the market.

"The competitors of these five concerns are at their mercy because of the control of the market places, storage facilities, and the refrigerator cars for distribution.

"The consumer of meat products is at the mercy of these five because both producer and competitor are helpless to bring relief.

"The stock car is a part of the equipment of the common carrier whose services are necessary to the producer of meat animals so that he may reach the market. The railroads furnish suitable cars for the transportation of other kinds of freight, and as to the use of such cars the miner of coal or the manufacturer of furniture are on an equality, but in the matter of transportation of livestock to a small degree there comes in a private ownership and a control and a manipulation of the means of transportation—the stock car—so it is that we recommend:

1. That the Government acquire, through the Railroad Administration, all rolling stock used for the transportation of meat animals and that such ownership be declared a Government monopoly.

"In the transportation of all other kinds of freight the transportation companies provide proper and suitable freight depots. The proper and suitable freight depot for live stock is a stockyard with its equipment of exchange buildings, terminal railways, and means of distributing full, unbiased, helpful market information, etc. We therefore recommend:

2. That the Government acquire, through the Railroad Administration, the principal and necessary stockyards of the country, to be treated as freight depots and to be operated under such conditions as will insure open, competitive markets, with uniform scale of charges of all services performed, and the acquisition or establishment of such additional yards from time to time as the future development of livestock production in the United States may require. This to include customary adjuncts of stockyards.

"A requisite for the proper transportation of fresh meats and dairy products is that type of rolling stock known as refrigerator cars. The railroads supply proper, special types of cars for other classes of freight, but the beef refrigerator cars and icing facilities, which are absolutely necessary for the transportation and distribution of fresh meats, are in private ownership. This ownership furnishes these five great packing companies one of their most powerful means for controls, manipulations, and restraints. Lacking access on equal terms to these facilities competitors of the five great packers are at their mercy, and, competition being stifled, the consumer similarly is helpless. We therefore recommend:

3. That the Government acquire, through the Railroad Administration, all privately owned refrigerator cars and all necessary equipment for their proper operation and that such ownership be declared a Government monopoly.

"Proper freight houses are provided by common carriers for the various sorts of freight except meat and perishable products. The indicated freight depot for such commodities is a cold-storage house. Such a depot used as a distributing station, if free of access to all, would constitute an agency for fair and free competition. Such a depot in private hands, as now, constitutes an invincible weapon for monopoly and control and manipulation. We therefore recommend:

4. That the Federal Government acquire such of the branch houses, cold-storage plants, and warehouses as are necessary to provide facilities for the competitive marketing and storage of food products in the principal centers of distribution and consumption. The same to be operated by the Government as public markets and storage placed under such conditions as will afford an outlet for all manufacturers and handlers of food products on equal terms. Supplementing the marketing and storage facilities thus acquired, the Federal Government establish, through the Railroad Administration, at the terminals of all principal points of distribution and consumption, central wholesale markets, and storage plants, with facilities open to all upon payment of just and fair charges.

"The Commission believes that these four suggestions strike so deeply at the root of the tree of monopoly that they constitute an adequate and simple solution of a problem the gravity of which will be unfolded to you [President Wilson] in the pages which follow.

"Out of the mass of information in our hands, one fact stands out with all possible emphasis. The small dominant group of American meat packers are now international in their activities, while remaining American in identity. Blame which now attaches to them for their practices abroad as well as at home inevitably will attach to our country if the practices continue. The purely domestic problems in their increasing magnitude, their monopolization of markets and their manipulations and controls, grave as those problems are, are not more serious than those presented by the added aspect of international activity. This urgently argues for a solution which will increase and not diminish the high regard in which this people is held in international comity.

"Some show of competition is staged by the five great packing companies. It is superficial. There is the natural rivalry of officials and departments, and this is made much of as indicating the existence of real competition. It is not real. How sham it is will be fully set out in the accompanying summary and the complete reports.

"Some independent packers exist by sufferance of the five, and a few hardy ones have survived in real competition. Around such few of these as remain the lines are drawing in."

[Bentley's Concluding Reflections]

The packers themselves have taken pleasure in comparing their business with that of Henry Ford by way of showing their moderation and the value of their national service. We may well conclude this attempt to estimate what they [the packers] really stand for in our national life by taking their own comparison in the figures just as they give them, without regard to turnover, and adding a word of interpretation. They say that with $2 million capital[ization] and $111 million surplus, Ford made $55 million in 1916. They say that on the same scale, Armour ought to have made $137,500,000 instead of $15 million or $20 million.[1]

Ford offers his goods on a market in which his customers can buy or not buy as they choose. The packers offer theirs in a market in which the customers, taking the country as a whole, have no choice.

Ford is primarily a manufacturer, and his profits are, to a large extent at least, producers' profits; subject, so far as modern conditions ever permit, to the [competitive] checks that control such profits. The packers are, in their present [state of] development, only incidentally manufacturers. Their main reliance for their profit is [on] strategic position and the weapons of highway appropriators.

Ford unquestionably renders service. The packers are just as unquestionably inefficient in giving service. Their presence [existence] now lies in their ability to keep other people from rendering service.

Ford is tending to one business. The packers are extending their methods over the earth. Ford enlarges the market for materials. The packers have their hands at the throat of producers, and act upon them according to their will, aiming to keep them alive just to the point that provides the highest appropriators' profit for themselves. Ford, so far as we know, reports all of his profits. The packers report what fraction they please.

Ford, so far as evidence goes, is investing his profits in producers' wealth [plant and equipment]. The packers, we know, are investing huge sums which they call expenses and deduct from their admitted profits, in a super-Teutonic propaganda (educational advertising being one of its forms) aimed at increased industrial autocracy.

Ford, while striving to get the greatest possible products from his wage-earners, has stimulated them with high wages and good working conditions, and has been helpful to them as far, perhaps, as he knew how to be, under the defective system he was working in. The packers have been among the hardest employers in the country with whom labor has had to deal.[2]

The consumers of Ford's product get more from him than they can get elsewhere for their money. The consumers of the packers' products get less than they would get if the highways were not blocked.

Ford regards his wealth as an industrial investment. He sees it dimly, perhaps, but nevertheless practically, as equipment which the nation is using while he is holding it.[3] The packers regard their wealth first, last, and all the time as a tool of power: theirs by divine right; and interference with their autocratic use of it, a treason.

Ford's business, the system by which he controls it, the power and profits he gets out of it, may be far from the best type the nation can set up. The packers' business, even if we compare it with Ford's in its worst aspects, is as darkness compared with light.*

And finally, if there are any lessons in Bolshevist Russia, the continued existence and power of the packers' organization and privilege is the worst possible enemy to the future prosperity of Ford and of all the lesser producers of his type.

Notes

1. Senate Committee on Agriculture and Forestry, *Hearings on Government Control of the Meat Packing Industry*, 65th Cong., 3d Sess., 1919 (Washington: Government Printing Office, 1919), p. 1792.
2. See John C. Kennedy *et al.*, *Wages and Family Budgets in the Chicago*

* For contrasting evaluations of the big meat-packing companies, see Rudolf A. Clemen, *The American Livestock and Meat Industry* (New York: Ronald Press, 1923); Lewis Corey, *Meat and Man: A Study of Monopoly, Unionism, and Food Policy* (New York: Viking, 1950); William F. Williams and Thomas T. Stout, *Economics of the Livestock-Meat Industry* (New York: Macmillan, 1964).

Stockyards District (Chicago: University of Chicago Press, 1914); Commission on Industrial Relations, *Final Report and Testimony*, Vol. IV, pp. 3465–85; and Hearings before Judge Samuel Alschuler on wages at the Stock Yards, 1918–19. Cf., *New York Times*, February 18, 1919. Wilson had appointed Judge Aschuler Administrator for the Meat Industry.

3. See his interview in *Reconstruction*, Vol. 1 (May, 1919), p. 130.

IX

A Batch of Field Notes

[This chapter consists of excerpts from the 1919 *Hearings* before the Senate Committee on Agriculture and Forestry, and the House Committee on Interstate and Foreign Commerce, 65th Cong., 3d Sess., and the 1919–20 Federal Trade Commission Report on the meat packing industry. The first part of the chapter, "Of Combination and Competition," presents testimony from officials of the leading packers denying that any combination or collusion existed in the industry. Sharp questioning, however, seemed to indicate that at least a tacit and informal arrangement to avoid competition may have been in effect.

[A section on advertising presents testimony showing that promotional expenditures in meat-packing companies were both extensive and expensive to consumers of meat. Other parts of the chapter present statements on the packers' dealings with the public and government, and on their general social philosophy. The evidence presented by Bentley in this chapter, in its unpublished form, confirms the points already made in Chapter VIII. The additional details given are not essential to his main argument in this book.]

X

The Highways of Credit

Back of all industry, in any but its most simple form of a man's work for direct satisfaction of his own needs, lies [business and bank] credit. Credit, thus broadly viewed, is the social adaptation of one man to another for the joint industrial task. Time is required for the production of supplies, and the condition of successful production is that each man shall rely on what others will accomplish to offset [complement] his own efforts. Each man must have faith in his industrial environment [complementary enterprises and industries] and give credit to it as completing and realizing his purposes. Credit is the very atmosphere of industry, without which we would be industrially stifled. It, like our technical knowledge of the world and our established types of workmanship, is a condition presupposed to all discussion of industrial organization.

To say this is equivalent to saying that credit has typical highway characteristics, since men perforce pass through it in their industrial relations with one another, and since any strongly established position upon the credit highways will give mastery to its holder over other men—except and insofar [as] he has been brought under an adequate public control.

It is also equivalent to saying that credit is not peculiarly a possibility of the particular [American] industrial system under which we are living. It is not peculiarly bound up with our present currency, banking and capitalization system [of the 1920's]. On the contrary, it may adapt itself to any form of industrial life. It may range in its applications from the grossest of abuses to the most beneficent of public services. It may be found, whether in hurtful or in beneficent forms (and probably always in both), as well in

Bolshevist Russia as in democratic [capitalistic] America. This is true both of personal credit resting on general expectations of income, and on institutionalized credit, specially supported . . . [by] property or . . . [by] claims to property or to income. We are not concerned with the possibilities of credit under any socialist or communist government, but we are very much concerned with the possible development of credit, both personal and institutional, for productive purposes; as opposed to its appropriation and manipulation for private appropriative purposes. We have seen credit institutions in this country transform themselves very greatly in the last fifty years, as they have adapted themselves to the centralized industrial system, and we may just as easily see them transform themselves still further as that centralized system is put under adequate public control.

So far as personal credit is concerned, it is of course not the quality of the man as apart from all property or all income that counts. It is the working man, the income-securing man, who is trusted; but the trust goes to him without designation of any specific part of his property or expected income to guarantee it. He is relied on to gain his income and to apply it as agreed. Equality of credit is hardly more to be thought of than any other kind of dogmatic equality, but if today the man who can shrewdly get and keep secures the most confidence, it would equally be possible in the future for the man who assuredly can produce with efficiency to be entitled to the most confidence. And what this change of emphasis would mean for the public weal goes without saying.

The history of institutionalized credit in this country is one of developing public control, but of a control which, however sound and successful within its field, has nevertheless been limited both in the extent of that field and in its purposes. The great needs for currency in the swift development of the West led to the free issue of notes by bankers. But the appropriative possibilities of such note issues were so great, and the abuse of these possibilities so great that confusion was brought upon all businessmen. The highways of credit transfer under these conditions became hard to travel. Hence government control, not to the hurt of business, but for the salvation of business. Next developed our great bank deposit and checking system, and this was perforce carried on under increasing

rigidity of regulation, involving continuous national and state inspections and publicity of reports; to safeguard the depositor, not
so much in his capacity of investor as in his capacity of businessman.
This culminated in many western states in the system of guarantee
of bank deposits, which, at first the despair of the old-line banker,
proved itself most surprisingly successful in nearly every case. State
guarantee was indeed not the revolutionary thing it seemed; not
a destruction of private enterprise, but only one little touch the more
to that system of control which gave safety and fluidity to the use
of the credit system. The banker was necessary to the other businessmen: they had to use his institution; they left him free to show
his ability and win his success; but they eliminated the worst of the
methods by which he could throw them into confusion or maltreat
them by excessive power.

With centralization of the industrial government, a further development in the organization and control of our credit system became
necessary, and this we secured [in 1913] in the Federal Reserve System to which the great majority of the banks now belong.
The system has worked excellently within the limits set for it by
the industrial government,[1] but it is primarily an agency for pooling
all of the credit of the great centralized industrial organizations as
the service of their masters. Helpful as it is to the individual producers, through the greater efficiency and serviceability it gives to
the local banks, that feature is an incidental element which is kept
subordinated to the other.

Moreover, back of the Federal Reserve system and controlling
it, rather than being controlled along with it, is the investment banking and promotion system of the country in its two branches; the
commercial promotion banking, and the international banking. The
Morgan, Baker, and Stillman institutions* are still most prominent;
the first, however, now [since World War I] more in the international
field than in the field of domestic industry. The way in which power
is exercised in this field in the interest of the appropriational control
of industry rather than that of productive control is typified by a
story told recently by Senator [Thomas P.] Gore, [a Democrat from

---

* J. P. Morgan and Company, the First National Bank, the National City Bank,
the National Bank of Commerce, the Chase National Bank, the Guaranty Trust
Company, and the Bankers Trust Company.

Oklahoma] concerning the experience of an inventor of an improvement in agricultural machinery. This man went unsuccessfully from one New York bank to another seeking capital to back him. At each bank the inquiry was not into the value of his invention and the free possibility of his commercial success with it, but whether he had taken it up with the International Harvester Company. Always, on his negative answer, he was turned away unsatisfied. The credit highways were not open to him. It is because of such power as this that Supreme Court Justice Brandeis says of the investment bankers: "We must break the Money Trust or the Money Trust will break us."[2]

Of credit institutions differently motivated and forecasting something of what the future may more generally develop, many illustrations might be given, apart from the old established land banks and rural credit associations of Germany and other European countries. The Building and Loan associations in the United States have done fine work, except in that period of a decade or so when the "nationals," with appropriators' motivation behind them, bade fair to wreck them all.[3] Cooperatives have, in several countries, been driven by unfair treatment from existing banks to start their own banking establishments. The British cooperators carry on banking business on a large scale, and very successfully. Our Federal Farm Loan system [established in 1916] gives a service of this kind, modified by the fact that it is almost as much at the speculator's use as at the use of the true [full-time] farmer. North Dakota's new state bank, designed to finance both a farm loaning system and the state industrial enterprises, is unfortunately created, not on a basis of solid safety but for purposes of aggressive defense against the hostile appropriative powers (the bankers, millers, commission men, and elevator men at Minneapolis), and it will be subject to grave perils which will require much self-denial on the part of the management to surmount if the bank is to develop into a permanently serviceable agency for the people.

In Chapter II . . . [we] presented a national balance sheet which shows the relation which capitalizations of property and capitalized claims upon the future income bear to the real value [the original cost] of the people's property. It [the national balance sheet] showed it, indeed, only in the very limited way in which the figures of government reports cover the facts. An effort will be made in a later chapter to bring out the meaning of these facts for the industrial life of the immediate future. At this place we may briefly connect them with the other phenomena of credit.

Our point of view persistently held is that tools and the man must be considered together—not the man alone, and not property alone. The fundamental thing, the synthesis of the two, is production; it is income. Credit, no matter what property security may be given, is an affair of future income. The property value itself rests solely in the fact that the goods can be consumed, or that goods produced from them can be consumed as parts of income. Even in the case of a mortgage on a farm, while the mortgage represents part of the farm land and so, in a sense, involves a division of ownership of existing goods, yet both values—the mortgage value with its fixed dollar statement, and the residual farm value, with its possibilities of increase or decrease—represent rights of participation in the future income of the country.

While the real-estate mortgage can therefore in one sense, and in one sense only, be directly attributed to existing property, there are many forms of credit—possibly in preponderating total—which cannot be so attributed, but must be considered solely and directly in terms of income. Bank credit—the deposit and bank loan system —is built up in total values far beyond existing property values. With a national income for 1912 estimated at some $33 billions, and a total wealth of some $187 billions, we had bank clearings . . . [of many more billions than either the national income or national wealth estimates] . . . and total trade transactions of some $600 billions. The bank deposits and loans cancel out the duplications as business transactions go forward, and their reference is always to coming production, and to coming appropriations out of production.

The capitalizations of our great industrial enterprises are credit instruments also referring forward to income. We have seen that by the test of property they were excessive in 1912 even at market valuations, and we have reason to think that this inflation has mounted steadily, although facts are now withheld from us. Further concealment of the facts is assured through the present tendency of new corporations to issue shares of "no-par value." Such shares are not at all different from common stock shares of $100 valuation each. Like the latter they have whatever valuation they can establish out of earnings. But they free themselves from the charge of falsely stating themselves as worth $100 in advance, and they likewise free themselves from the demand that they hold themselves hereafter down to a $100 value if by any chance they can make themselves valid at ten or twenty times that figure. By this method $50 million of good will can be added to $15 million of property without, as in the case of the Woolworth Company, openly admitting it.[4]

The shares of these corporations are liabilities to them, but they go to the investor as his assets. Their limit of value under the present control of business is what can be appropriated from the future income of the nation. When in the first part of [the] last century the country was flooded with the currency of banks of free issue, the [paper money] values could not be maintained; liquidation began at once with excess of issue. But now with these enormous capitalization credits, there is behind them a system for enforcing payment from the people in the future through profiteering. Our whole credit system is shot through with them. Sound as our credit system is within its own range, it is hateful to think of what it may be by the test of future income.

We come back, therefore, to the question of strategic highway position. Credit must be used by men in all their interrelated business transactions, as much when they produce for a future market without borrowing as when they borrow. But their highway of credit is now possessed and manipulated by appropriators of the future income of the nation, who maintain themselves strongly on it today by their centralized [corporate-directorate] organization. The costs mount. The burden increases. Today or hereafter, peacefully or violently, a reckoning is sure.

Notes

1. This should be qualified by the facts as to its encouragement of speculation in 1919–20, the issue of which is not yet ready for judgment.
2. Louis D. Brandeis, *Other People's Money* (New York: Frederick A. Stokes

Company, 1914), p. 201. Many abuses of credit in special fields still exist apart from the general overhead control of the investment bankers. The case of the North Dakota farmers has been mentioned. The approach to industrial slavery among tenant farmers in the Southwest may be studied in the *Report of the Comptroller of the Currency, 1915* (Washington: Government Printing Office, 1916), pp. 20–31, 149ff, and 218ff; [and] in the *Final Report and Testimony of the Commission on Industrial Relations*, 1916, Vol. X. See also F. C. Howe, *The High Cost of Living*, pp. 220, 242. Other illustrations are the control of Negro labor on southern plantations by commodity advances, and the use made by the coal mines in the past of compulsory company stores. With respect to these latter, it is interesting to note that just in those fields in which the company store system was the worst, consumers' cooperation is now having one of its most successful developments.

3. Building and Loan associations have now [1920] almost 4 million members and almost $2 billion . . . [in] assets.

4. See Chapter VI. An interesting recent case is the American Safety Razor Corporation, figures for which are given in Chapter XIII.

XI

Land and Opportunity

Another great subject, which in this volume may be discussed only enough to bring it into relation with the problems in which we are specially concerned, is that of land ownership—land as a highway, land as a stronghold for appropriative power, land in its relations to the industrial opportunities of the people.

The followers of Henry George [champion of the single-tax] have felt that if the nation would assume to itself the unearned increment of value in land, if it would make unused agricultural lands more readily available to producers and vacant city lands more readily available to home-builders and businessmen, it would secure [the production of a] greater product from nature and have more of the comforts of life for its people. Their program has been a form of taxation to absorb the [increased money] value that the population gives to the land by its presence, and to leave to the holder only the product that he can secure from its use. Their analysis is clear, their policy cogent and practical, and yet they have not won to a clear trial of what they advocate.[1]

The reasons for this failure to succeed seem to be of a double nature. First, opportunity for land investment is still open to a great part of the people, so that what a man loses to . . . [another], he may hope to make back . . . through [acquiring] land-holdings of his own; and second, other forms of highway control have been much more spectacular in [their] methods and in [their] swift development.

It is said that within the limits of Greater New York [as of 1919], eight million people could be housed, ten families to the acre— hardly more than village density; that within easy commutation distance, thirty millions more could live; and that land speculation

129

is largely responsible for the vacant areas on the one hand, and for the slums on the other. With the land speculation goes encouragement of building speculation and discouragement of true home-building. Everywhere are visible evidences of the social loss under the system. Going northward in Chicago, one hardly gets out of the business section before he comes across vacant properties that might have been used to relieve the congestion that is met when one goes westward. In any small town, instances of [similar social] evils may be found. In a hill village where good sites are few, perhaps an agricultural implement dealer with an established business sees his location rented away from him over his head. The first vacant property he inquires [about] is for sale at a speculative price, and he can only get month-to-month tenure, not sufficient to justify putting his sheds on it. The next site he finds is priced prohibitively. Finally, he is driven to an inconvenient location remote from the trade he needs to attract. Maker and user suffer, and only a few landholders profit. In agricultural lands many instances, great and small, could be given of lessened productivity incidental to the system.

Nevertheless, almost everywhere men can get their homes and their business sites on terms satisfactory to them as consumers or producers; and in agriculture, the tendency between the last two census years, whatever the coming [1920] census may show, was slightly away from centralization rather than towards it; and even on the speculative side, while that is largely in the hands of professionals, and while some of the very worst appropriative abuses we know of are attendant upon it, nevertheless, there is still opening everywhere for "man, the adventurer" to find his opportunity or at least his hope.

Even in the matter of city congestion, some of the worst abuses are much more readily traced to other forms of highway control than to the landowning system. The streetcar-fare has much to do with it. An extra penny added to the nickle will mean more slum-living, more vice, more sickness, lessened productive power, and greater dependence of the people in the crowded districts on their food purveyors.[2] When that extra penny is traceable to waste or robbery, or to the capitalized results of past waste or past robbery, there is a visible dragon's head to strike at which attracts much more attention than the various indirect effects of individual speculations and titles. There is an enemy in one place to attack, with the hope that victory once gained will be decisive, instead of scattered enemies—each one small, but enormous in their mass—over which victory is hard to win.

The greatest centralization that we have in the ownership of the surface of the land is in the timber-holdings. These, handled as they are now, will mean an enormous drain upon the income of the nation in the future. The government has gathered the facts, and the problem will in time become an acute one; more difficult to handle the longer it is delayed. The ore- and power-holdings have been closely gathered in by the great organizations of the centralized industrial government. They present themselves to us now, not so much as a separate highway problem, but rather as one of the footings of the general power that has been established on the highways of trade and finance.

As an isolated movement, a great effort was made a decade ago —at the time when [water and electric] power sites, especially, were being privately acquired on a huge scale—to preserve the public's interest. Much limitation was placed on these private acquisitions; but instead of the development of a national policy for highway control since then, the limitations have been relaxed and evasions permitted: which merely means that the whole problem will become more critical later on, with "equities" in possession and the charge of inequity struggling to make itself allowed against them under unfavorable odds.

As the case stands, and speaking not as a matter of logic but in terms of the present interests and viewpoints of the [people of the] United States, the land problem—however fundamental—is rather one aspect of the greater problem of industrial highway control than a separate highway problem in itself; and it interests us here mainly as a vivid illustration of the importance that freedom of opportunity, even though relative in extent and deceptive in true value, may have in determining the expressed interests and programs of the nation.

Notes

1. [*Progress and Poverty* (1879) was the most important book published by Henry George (1839–97), American economist and social reformer.] A National Single Tax Party held its first convention in New York, June 1919, with sixteen states represented. [Cf., A. N. Young, *History of the Single Tax Movement in the United States* (Princeton: Princeton University Press, 1916).]

2. See Ralph Adams Cram, quoted in *Literary Digest,* Vol. 61, No. 1511 (April 5, 1919), p. 36.

XII

The Highways of Information

If the reader will refer back to the rough classification in the table [Types of Highways] at the beginning of Chapter VII and to the preceding remarks, he will see that we have now covered in a scattered way all the phases of the subject there indicated except the highways of information and technology, these having received only incidental mention. Most stress has been placed on the highways of trade, because on them the most vital public problems of the time are found. Desirable as a systematic treatment of all of this material would have been, it is prohibited by . . . this focus of attention (1) on the present interests of the various groups of the population, and (2) on the viewpoints and programs they are developing.

We have spoken of our massed knowledge of the world and our technology as an atmosphere without which we would be industrially stifled. We deal with figures of speech when we talk either of atmosphere or highways in connection with our industrial information. But atmosphere is indeed a highway of life as much as is land, and the joint figures of speech are apt enough for the comparisons in question. We pass through our industrial knowledge in all the work we do; we may take it into account expressly, or we may accept it tacitly, much as we accept the roadway under our feet; but without it we would get nowhere. We have to consider briefly common education, technology, trade information, and advertising, both from the point of view of strategic positions of highway dominance and from the point of view of developing public functions to prevent such dominance.

Public school education has been made the common privilege of all of the [American] people by the political government, through the rejection of all class-claims to special privilege in its field. Beyond that, the political government attempts, though still unsuccessfully, to compel every child to acquire the rudiments of the arts and sciences on the theory that [if each child is] given the fair opportunity for success in life for himself, he will also contribute more to the success of others. True it is that the proffered education has not been at all what the citizens have needed under the developing industrial government. Planned to fit early conditions of comparatively free opportunity, this system of education has become dazed and increasingly aimless in the actual industrial world. Within the last decade or two, attention from the controlling elements of the industrial government has been directed to the subject [of education], with the purpose of adapting the German system of specialized trade education for the working classes to our American needs at it sees them. That these new tendencies would develop a class of workers fitted into the industrial organization, but atrophied in their pioneering possibilities, has been felt in many quarters, and vigorous resistance to this system is appearing.[1]

In higher education, many activities of the Rockefeller and Carnegie foundations have been used for the benefit of [those possessing] the existing control of industrial government, taking much the form and spirit of that type of propaganda which Germany developed as an aid to world control.[2] In the field of technology, schools have been founded for the purpose of fitting young men for varied industrial opportunity, and some of them still exist with this as their true purpose; while others have become . . . appendages to great industrial enterprises, preparing human material for its uses. Technological progress rests partly in these schools and partly in the laboratories of the large enterprises themselves, where, to a very great extent, it has developed for the benefit of the proprietors.

Inventions do not spring like Athena, full-valued deities, from the head of Jove. They require all the knowledge and technique that has gone before; they get value only as they meet social needs. Society, by its patent laws, aims to preserve to an inventor, for a term of years, a reward for his productive service; with the understanding that when the time is up, the use and value of the invention shall become common property. But it is well known how rare it is for the inventor to be the man to profit by his [own] achievement. And further than this, the patent issued by the political government has, under our industrial government, actually become of small importance. Many a patent to an article in wide and ever-increasing use has expired without any effect on the price of the article. Remove the patent and the technical knowledge remains still, as it was before, not a common possession but an appropriated thing, in the sense that the appropriators alone can profitable use it.

With the increasing centralization of industrial organization, a larger and larger proportion of all the knowledge mankind has acquired about nature, and a larger and larger proportion of all the control he has secured over nature, is passing into the possession of the masters of this organization so far as any profit or gain can be secured from it. This point has been very fully brought out by Thorstein Veblen in his brilliant . . . essays, "The Modern Point of View and the New Order," [and "The Captains of Finance and the Engineers"] in *The Dial* [from October 19, 1918, to January 25, 1919, and June 14, 1919]. "The technology—the state of the industrial arts—which takes effect in this mechanical industry is in an eminent sense a joint stock of knowledge and experience held in common by the civilized peoples," says Mr. Veblen. "It requires the use of trained and instructed workmen—born, bred, trained, and instructed at the cost of the people at large. So also it requires, with a continually more exacting insistence, a corps of highly trained and specially gifted experts, of divers and various kinds. These too are born, bred and trained at the cost of the community at large, and they draw their requisite special knowledge from the community's joint stock of accumulated experience."[3]

That is one side of the picture. But here is the other: "The usufruct of the community's technological knowledge has come to vest in the owners of such material wealth as is held in sufficiently large blocks for the purpose." The owners of this wealth "have in effect become 'seized and possessed of' [this knowledge]. . . . It is not as intelligent persons, but only as owners of material ways and means, as vested interests, that they come into the case."[4] "The owners, now represented in effect by the syndicated investment bankers, continue to control the industrial experts, and limit their discretion arbitrarily, for their own commercial gain, regardless of the needs of the community."[5]

The appropriation of this knowledge and skill is to some extent systematically planned and carried out. One of the functions of [Frederick W.] Taylor's scientific management system, for instance, is to gather up and systemize knowledge formerly scattered around in the possession of the workers.[6] The gathering . . . is of course good, but the appropriation is very far indeed from good, for any persons except the appropriators.

The situation with regard to market information differs from that in regard to technology because, while the latter is a definite accretion of methods and powers, the former is a changing thing of the day. The organization for securing it persists and is specialized as a mighty aid to mastery, but the content of the information secured is ever-differing. How such information is used, beginning with the days when the elder Armour developed it as one of the great aids to his success, has been touched on repeatedly in earlier pages, especially with reference to grain and provision boards and with reference to the packing industry. In this field the government can enter directly, and it is so entering through various activities of the Department of Agriculture, especially in the Bureau of Markets.

However, while the privately secured information goes directly and immediately to the appropriators who utilize it in the form in which they need it, the publicly secured information goes by devious channels to the scattered producers, who must often interpret it further before they can act upon it. It may well be that theoretically, a complete democracy of information—if we may so speak—would solve all the country's problems; but practically, the strongholds for effective use of information still exist, no matter what the government may do to gather it and make it current.*

* The role of information is of course crucial in the economic theory of market operations. "Perfect competition," for example, requires "perfect information," and its results may be distorted if such information is not present. Bentley seems to go beyond this, touching on a frequent and useful analogy between the free, or "competitive" market tin which consumers cast "dollar votes," and a political system of democracy. His notion that a "democracy of information" might mitigate certain economic distortions finds strong support in theory.

For recent pertinent discussions of democracy in the market place and in the political system, see Gary S. Becker, "Competition and Democracy," *Journal of*

Of advertising, a few words only may be said. The fact that a large part of it is misinformation by intention and by implication does not alter its position; it passes for information to those to whom it is given and who accept it. Commercial advertising, for spreading the knowledge of goods and for inducing people to buy them, rests in suggestion. Suggest a thing, repeat the suggestion often enough, get followers and imitators, and before long a habit is established. Then capitalize the consumer's habit on the balance sheet of the industrial beneficiary, and the process is complete, except so far as continual driblets of suggestion are needed to keep the habit from lapsing. Such driblets of $1 million or $2 million a year, spent by great Minneapolis flour mills to sell their wheat flour to the public—that is to say, to keep people from forgetting the names of Pillsbury and Washburn when they go to market— are typical of the system and its results.

We have discussed advertising as a waste; but it is more than a waste. It is an instrument of highway-control and of industrial domination, and, indirectly, through its influence on newspaper policy, a great tool for the permanent befuddlement of a nation. One may recognize liberally the residuum of real service [that exists] in commercial advertising, but that will not offset to any great extent the other characteristics which are today so prominent.

And finally, there is educational advertising, as the packers have developed it, an activity which can only be adequately described by again using the comparison with Teutonic propaganda. What it stands for in national life is manifest enough.

Nothing is clearer than that, just as our political government, when it became democratic, made free common school education one of the greatest articles of its faith, so our industrial government, if it is to be democratized, must insist in every way possible on the free possession and use of trade and technological information. To this end, institutions as mighty and perhaps as expensive as those of the public schools may have to be established. And no more in this case than in that of the public schools will such expenditure be looked upon with regret, save so far as the institutions maintained

Law and Economics, Vol. 1 (October, 1958), pp. 105–109; and Anthony Downs, "An Economic Theory of Political Action in a Democracy," Journal of Political Economy, Vol. 67, No. 2 (Apr., 1957), pp. 135–50.

fail to be properly adapted to the ends in view. Not only is knowledge power, but the power that comes from it must be socialized and equalized in opportunity to all of the people. And the more it is so equalized, the more its benefits will be diffused. To equalize it will require the determined action of the people in their collective organization.

Notes

1. Compare Helen Marot, *Creative Impulse in Industry* (New York: E. P. Dutton, 1918).

2. See Commission on Industrial Relations, *Final Report*, 64th Cong., 1st Sess., Senate Doc. 415 (Washington: Government Printing Office, 1916), I, 81–85, 235–261.

3. Thorstein Veblen, "The Captains of Finance and the Engineer," *Dial* LXVI, No. 792 (June 14, 1919), p. 603.

4. *Veblen*, "The Modern Point of View and the New Order III,'" *Dial*, LXV, No. 777 (November 16, 1918), p. 414.

5. Veblen, "The Captains of Finance and the Engineer," *op cit.*, p. 603.

6. See Robert F. Hoxie, *Scientific Management and Labor* (New York and London: D. Appleton and Co., 1915).

XIII

The Situation of Retail Trade

Attention has thus far been directed mainly to the strategic positions which are held for the advantage of the great profiteers. Under the shelter of these great profiteers, the retail tradesman derives certain incidental profiteering advantages of his own; but to offset this, his field of operations has already been cut down, and further and greater inroads impend upon him.

Certain well-known facts about retail trade may be brought to mind. The retail dealers, proper, number [in 1919] about a million and a quarter, and with them may be grouped about half a million other tradesmen running their own private business enterprises. Approximately 1 per cent become bankrupt every year, but sometimes as [many] as 20 per cent go out of business and disappear from the commercial agency lists in a year; and the average existence of an independent retail business enterprise is certainly not over ten years and probably nearer five years.[1]

Probably 10 per cent of all retail trade, and in many localities 20 per cent or more, is now in the hands of chain stores or mail-order houses, with the proportion of such trade rapidly growing. Certain of these chains, especially in the shoe trade, are manufacturers' agencies; but most of them deal directly with many manufacturers, cutting out the jobber altogether. There are, in addition, between two and three thousand cooperative stores which are now grouping themselves through the present six or eight cooperative wholesale societies into a National Cooperative Wholesale, and which seem to be on the eve of a great growth. Ten years ago the department stores were frightening the smaller city retailers into hysteria, but

139

now [in 1919] they are only a minor element in the encroachments upon ordinary retail trade.

These facts, however, give only a part of the story, for, to an ever-growing extent, the retailer's independence is affected by requirements and limitations imposed on him from without. He sells largely fixed-price articles, many of them under a system of fixed trade discounts, and for these he is merely a warehouseman, his one merchandising function being to sell as much of them as he can. He sells goods for which the consumers' demand is built up and controlled through suggestive and compulsive advertising, provided and maintained by [the] manufacturer or main distributor.

In certain lines, such as drugs, he does much of his buying through central agencies which lend him a trade name and have a superficial cooperative appearance, though not an actual profit-sharing arrangement. In other lines he is under such direct and continuous supervision from branch houses, "block men," and other district agents of the manufacturers, that he becomes to [a] great extent a manufacturers' agent himself. In meats and staple foods, the distributive organization of the Big Five packers is progressing so rapidly that Chairman Colver of the Federal Trade Commission has repeatedly asserted that within ten years, or possibly five, not merely the wholesale grocery business of the country, but the retail business as well, will lie within these packers' hands to do with . . . [as they please].[2]

A few years ago we used to think of the retailer as unfortunately and wastefully struggling to survive among the insecurities of his business environment. Today we must think of him as not merely the prey of all these insecurities, so far as he remains an independent operator, but more important still, as already half-engorged [swallowed] in a great, developing organization that ties him into it and makes him in many respects more its agent than an outsider with whom it deals; and that tends ever more to replace him with its own direct agents. An organization, we may say—although what the retailer now is facing is rather a nexus of many organizations jointly operating to a common end—and ever more susceptible of fusion under changing conditions.

So far as the general nature of this development is concerned, it is useless to apply the words "good" or "bad." The thing is inevitable, and [in the future] to an extent vastly greater than has today been attained. "Good" or "bad" will be dependent in the outcome, on the extent to which the organization becomes devoted to public service; or, in contrast, on the extent to which its control remains under the test of massed profits. The answer to that is one for the nation to give.

But even at the present time there is a very clear question of good or bad, measurable unequivocally in dollars: the question of costs. That many of these organizations make great savings in costs, in some part of which the consumer gets the benefit, is unquestionably true, just as it is true that many of them give the consumer trade facilities which he would otherwise have difficulty in getting. But it is also true that their methods of controlling their business involves another range of costs, which cannot be adjudged as anything but pure wastes when looked at from the standpoint of the nation supplying . . . its [own] needs. These costs are aggressive costs, business-compelling costs, which have the advantage of being cleverer costs—as contrasted with the old, scattered, and, so to speak, stupid costs; and which are successful for the appropriate purposes of the organizers, although clearly and strikingly wasteful for the purposes of the consumer. Only to such an extent as consumers are envisaged as flocks of sheep, to be tolled [lured] or driven through this or that gate, are [these costs] defensible. For the consumer, envisaged as a human being with abilities corresponding to his desires, they are, in a sense, his shame. This is true—directly and immediately—of the advertising, price-fixing, discount-fixing, and inspection-fixing systems; and it is true indirectly of the capitalizations of good will, such as Woolworths' fifty millions (already described), and of the permanent dividends that must be paid upon them while their system successfully stands.

This whole organization has more far-reaching effects upon the retailer personally than in the mere narrowing of his field of activities and the narrowing of his independence within that field. Sometimes it seems, indeed, to give new opportunities of its own for retail enterprise, but these opportunities are usually deceptive. For as fast as the system lures new men to . . . [it], it reduces the earnings of these men, changing them from possible "profits" to "costs," and thus takes away from them with one hand what it seems to offer with the other.

Observe this in a business in which retail prices are fixed by the manufacturers. The rate of profits is fixed as well as the price; the margin is good; the dealer pushes sales; he begins to be very well satisfied. But no sooner has he reached this position than a new dealer appears with a similar line of goods, also with his fixed prices and fixed profits. Now the trade must be fought for by the two men. They must seek "prospects" and follow them up. Two men spend their time and gasoline doing what one man could have done. Each man works harder to sell less. Neither man can make very much because as soon as he prospers, a new dealer appears and introduces new "costs" to eat up the margin of profit. We have just the reverse of that old theoretical competitive process assured to wipe out exceptional profits; we have a fixed amount set aside by the trade for costs, and we have a struggle among the dealers which absorbs this amount. The community offers a sort of receptacle to fill up; and, under existing conditions, it fills up largely with duplications, business friction, and waste motion, instead of with productive motions.[3] The community pays the bill.

Rising costs are typical of all retail trade. [Wheeler R. Sammons'] *Keeping Up With Rising Costs* [Chicago: A. W. Shaw Company, 1915] was the very significant title of a recent statistical work on retail trade . . . . The above illustration, and the following ones, indicate . . . the [real] nature of these costs . . . .

What is true of stores handling exclusively fixed-price goods is also true of special lines or special articles within a store. The grocer has a large number of fixed-price package-goods. His profits on them are fixed; and the more he makes out of them, the more other grocers are tempted into the field to sop up the profits and increase the costs of the trade for the community as a whole.

The illegality of fixed prices and restrictions on retail freedom makes little or no difference in actual trade conditions.* The re-

* Bentley's "fixed price" system is apparently resale price maintenance or "fair trade." This refers to stipulations, by manufacturers or other sellers, of minimum prices below which their branded goods may not be resold. Such arrangements were commonly held illegal by the courts at the time Bentley was writing. In the intervening period, Congress has twice passed enabling legislation exempting

tailer is not bound to the prices; he simply has to live up to them if he wishes to get stock and do business. After the war, a large phonograph company which once was protected by its patents but now is protected just as fully by [a] trade organization without patents, announced that it would establish no more agencies for several years. The existing agencies were profitable and valuable. For an agent to cut prices on any article meant that while his orders might be accepted, he would certainly not get deliveries. Furthermore, he was required to carry a fixed amount of stock and have a certain approved equipment, or he could not get deliveries. The expense, all coming out of the consumer, was an enormous percentage of [the sales] price, but the profits margin was maintained for the company and the dealer, and that was all that was sought.[4]

Such fixed-price articles are, of course, in [the] great minority among [all] articles sold, but nevertheless they typify the whole manufacturing-jobbing-retailing nexus of trade. They merely bring out in written form—in the form of command and obedience— what is implicit in most other transactions. Consider the way a manufacturer . . . of canned goods organizes his prices when he is putting a new article on the market. He first considers the possibilities of sales at 10 cents, at two for 25 cents, at 15 cents; then he figures out the margins which each dealer or jobber along the line must have, thus finding out what he can get himself; and finally he debates the question as to what quantity and quality he can provide. At a food hearing in Chicago, three wholesale grocers testified in succession that when they bought army supplies at $1 per case, they sold them at $1.35, making a 35 per cent profit; because in that way they best fitted the "two-for-a-quarter trade," leaving the retailer enough profit to tempt him to buy of them.[5]

The retailer too can take a hand in the fixed-price system. A small town was observed recently in which the retailers understood each other so well that they got 7 cents . . . for advertised 5-cent

resale price maintenance from the federal antitrust laws (Miller-Tydings Act amending the Sherman Act, 1937; and McGuire-Keogh Act amending Federal Trade Commission Act, 1952). By 1964, however, 23 of 46 existing *state* fair trade statutes had been held fully or partially illegal by state courts. Bentley is probably correct in maintaining that fair trade is practiced even when and where illegal; but incorrect in stating that legality makes "little or no difference." Certainly in recent years the volume of trade affected by resale price maintanance has declined with the decline in legality.

drinks which were still bringing the regular price in neighboring towns; and . . . many other articles in restaurants were similarly handled. It is hardly necessary to add that there were three times as many stores of these types in that town as were needed. All the way from the first stage in the manufacturing to the last in selling we find these duplications, wastes, high costs, fixed margins of profit; and we find more duplications, more high costs, and more margins building themselves up. Under the profiteering frenzy of the summer of . . . [1918] even . . . standard sugar, the regular grocers' "leader" normally sold on a "warehousing" rather than "high cost and overhead" margin, was pushed up in many stores in Chicago and other cities to 16 cents a pound at a time when the Food Administration said 11 cents was ample.

Here is an illustration of what the system of fixed prices costs us. On the ordinary cheap safety-razor, the retailer gets 25 per cent and the jobber about 15 per cent [profit margin]. For the manufacturer who owns the trade-names, capitalizes the advertising, and sets terms for jobber and retailer, it works out this way:

Plant Investment	$ 800,000
Current Assets	3,300,000
Good will & Trade-Marks	8,600,000
Stock Issues—par	20,000,000
Stock Issues—carried on books	10,800,000
Estimated 1920 Earnings	2,000,000
Estimated 1920 Sales:	
2,000,000 Razors	
105,000,000 Blades	

These are the figures of September 10, 1919, for the newly organized American Safety Razor corporation, consolidating the Star, Gem, and Ever Ready razors. Good will, which is more than double the [current] assets, indicates the present capitalized value of [corporate] power. Par of capitalization indicates the confidently foreseen value of power in the near future. The excessive costs . . . [to] the little retailer [who is] bound to the chariot wheel of such enterprises are to be added in figuring what we, as a nation, do not get for what we pay.[6]

. . . [These three points we wish to emphasize]: that our retail trade, both in its action and in its policy, is being carried largely in the hands of the complicated manufacturing-advertising-distributing system behind it;[7] that where this system cuts costs, it capitalizes a great part of its savings and re-establishes all the costs it may on a new basis; and finally, that under these conditions, our retail trade takes on more and more [of] a warehousing character, though one that is unnecessarily expensive to [an] almost incredible degree.

The first two points show the evils under which we suffer. The third point is one from which the way may lead either to the elimination of these evils [and] their huge costs and wastes, or towards their consolidation and tightening into a permanent incubus upon us. Such a permanent . . . [burden] is . . . [assured] if we let the system work itself out on its present lines of mastery. But elimination of the evils will certainly be attained if we assume the guidance ourselves, as a people with deliberate purpose, based on clear understanding of what is going on; a guidance we have a right to assume if we have any right at all to care as a people for our own welfare.

Without offering any cure-all plan for these evils, and without even implying any particular steps in reform, it may nevertheless be confidently said that this existing system, considering all its elements including the achievements of the chain [stores] and mail-order houses, has reached a point where thorough reorganization on a public-service basis is practicable. Indeed . . . about all that will be necessary to bring this about when the time is ripe is a kaleidoscopic jar which will let the pieces fly around and reassemble. Certainly this is true of the staple lines; not only the great staples, but the many standardized staples. For the minor novelties and specialties we need express no opinion, and we may indeed assume that here will always be a field for a peculiar type of adventuring; one, however, which we may hope will be much less costly to us in effort than the present.

These considerations are strengthened by noting how far standardization of products has actually gone in this country, a standardization which, though obscured and concealed in many ways, is nevertheless actual. Long ago there were days when primitive custom ruled, and different communities desired different commodities and different styles; customs which still persist to [a] large degree in Europe.[8] Then came the whirlwind of inventions and innovations, and finally the standardizations of today for the whole nation. Our great needs are regular in quantity, and the supplies for them must come, on the whole, quite as regularly; whether we think in terms of the nation, of some section of it, or [of] a particular community. Labels and advertising campaigns obscure the actual standardizations, but they are nevertheless there. It is not the product that is different in most cases, but the trade name, the slogan, the picture on the wrapper.[9] Advertising strains itself day by day to develop clues to differences with which to attract attention and capture custom. More and more, a good trade name becomes an important part of capital; . . . advertising firms become the backers and part-owners, or even whole-owners, of what purport to be real manufacturing industries.

Under such conditions, one may readily believe that trade—and especially trade in the great staples—could be made the most automatic and economical of all the great activities of the nation at work, instead of the special field for profiteering which it now is. In place of attracting the talents of appropriators, it might become attractive in its main lines to a special branch of engineering ability, which would welcome the opportunity for developing specialized organizations for its needs.

Thomas A. Edison has said:

Selling and distribution are simply machines for getting products to consumers. And like all machines they can be improved with great resulting economy.

But it is the plain truth that these machines for distribution have made the least progress of all machines. They are the same in many instances that they were forty and fifty years ago. They are imitations of each other, and manufacturers follow each other like sheep in the matter of selling and distribution, the very same manufacturers, ofttimes, who are tremendously keen to secure the benefits of new invention in their factories.

As a result selling cost is outrageously high—manufacturing cost is often small beside it. Now, why not put more inventive genius to work upon the big problem of distribution? At this time of general lamentation over high prices it is peculiarly desirable. The average selling machine has become unwieldy and ancient. Did you ever see the Jacquard loom?

It is marvelous how perfectly and simply it performs complicated weaving of patterns. That perfect the selling machine should be—getting goods quickly, economically and satisfactorily to those who want them.[10]

Back of such an engineering control of trade, of course, would have to be centralized information and judgment. Crops from huckleberries to wheat have their variations in quantity from year to year. Estimates of demand and supply and transportation would need to be made. But the [national] government took this matter in hand during the war and worked it well, and that under the most unfavorable conditions for success; the lesser of which rose out of war necessities and supply shortages, the greater by far coming from [the] resistance of the present cost-and-profit specialists.

We can conceive as easily of our retail merchants fitting into such a new system as we can of leaders being found for it. There already are towns which have gone a long way upon the road by their own efforts. There are English towns in which not a single private store exists, the whole trade being cooperative. The tendency would merely be to greater prominence and greater opportunity for the warehousing and organizing and distributing type of ability, and to lesser prominence for the technically trading, appropriating type. Inside a family, it is the exception for the members to be always tricking and deluding and playing upon each other for advantage. Inside a store, it would be a poor proprietor who would permit a continual round of wasteful effort among the clerks to [gain] advantage one over the other. Inside a community, if once the heart of the appropriative struggle is struck at, the same possibilities of harmonized effort exist.

We can . . . easily conceive of the great majority of even the present independent merchants welcoming such a tendency of change, for the majority of them are none too happy as it is. And, further, they have their interests as consumers of other peoples' goods, even stronger at times than their interests as sellers. Their present arrangement is one of "you tickle me, and I tickle you"; "you take a profit from me, and I take a profit from you"; "you take a bite out of me, and I take a bite out of you." It is all very well for the most successful of the reciprocal profiteers; they can pay out with a free hand, if with pursed eyes, to others in like position. But the method is not at all pleasant for those without profit schemes of their own. And it can often go too far even for the minor profiteers themselves.

Such a development as is suggested, does not posit turning all storekeepers into clerks or managers. It is in no way hostile to arrangements that permit the head of a business or department to secure earnings on the basis of his ability and the results he produces. It is hostile only to appropriative profits and, much worse than appropriative profits, appropriative costs. It is hostile to the "fishy eye," the "hard-boiled" trader, the dispenser of too much "blue-sky" from his shelves. It does not dream of wholly eliminating these articles from the world. It would remove their easy opportunities. It would decrease their present respectability, transferring them gradually to association with their cruder fellows, the highway robber, the burglar, the forger, and the confidence man. It would give the opportunities society now offers them to men with [a] keener instinct for productive service.

Notes

1. Appendix K [unpublished because similar data are presented in Harold Barger, *Distribution's Place in the American Economy Since 1869* (Princeton: Princeton University Press, 1955)].
2. The Big Five have already (August, 1919) over 1,000 retail meat markets in Great Britain, where they have developed this part of their organization faster than here. The transfer of the packers' grocery business to separate corporations under the [Attorney-General] Palmer-Packers' compromise is evidently one more of surface appearance than of business fact.
3. Similarly, in the meat industry we have seen the Big Five setting price levels and limitations of field activity, while the admittedly more efficient independent packers hold themselves within limits and content themselves with the higher profits in smaller business, rather than with the lower profit rates on larger business which they could secure on a basis of efficiency if given a fighting chance.
4. The writer has in mind a small city store in a large city that had such an agency. It was compelled to put in about $8,000 of special fixtures, and [to] keep an investment, including stock, of between $15,000 [and] $20,000 before it could get its orders filled. Yet for its particular class of trade it could probably do just as large a business without this investment; and what it could do if phonographs sold at a reasonable margin above manufacturing cost—to cover warehousing, delivery, and retail profit—would be many times as great as it can ever hope to do under present conditions.
5. *Chicago Tribune*, September 12, 1919.

6. Figures from *Chicago Tribune,* September 20, 1919.

7. Consider the following: (*Louisville Courier-Journal,* April 8, 1919) "The Retail Grocers Association appointed a committee of twelve to arrange with the Big Five packers measures for preventing consumers buying at wholesale. The association wished even to shut out wholesale purchases by restaurants. W. A. Fisher, manager of the Swift branch, told the meeting of his firm's past and present efforts to shut out the consumers' buying and promised for the future even to refuse to sell to his own employees if the Retail Grocers formally requested it. A. H. Thomas, manager of the Armour branch, thanked the association for calling his attention to the 'abuses' of sales to consumers."

8. Of course, we have some of them still in minor matters, as for example, the different cuts of beef and different housewives' names for cuts which characterize our eastern cities, or the preference for white eggs in New York and for brown eggs in Boston.

9. At the Chicago hearing referred to, the manager of the canned goods department of Sprague, Warner and Co. stated that his firm had changed the labels of beans bought of the government from those of the Arcadia Canning Company to [those of] his own firm. "Why?" he was asked. "To meet the demand of our customers for Sprague, Warner and Company's goods," he replied.

10. Quoted from *Printer's Ink* by Emerson P. Harris, *Cooperation: The Hope of the Consumer* (New York: Macmillan, 1918), p. 45.

XIV

The High Cost of Living

Fundamentally, the problem of the high cost of living is the problem of national waste. If we produce only one-third as much as we might produce with the same effort, it is clear that what we get is costing us three times what it ought to cost. If our system of production is shot through with elements that make for rising costs, then things are becoming worse instead of better; our living is costing us always more. These are indeed the facts. The great drafts which we have been able to make upon our bounteous natural resources have kept us from feeling the pinch in the past; indeed, the very possibility of such drafts has given favorable soil for the development of a profiteering system which makes use of high costs. But now the great yearly increments from fresh resources have lost their relative importance, while the high and ever higher costs are still with us. Now [in 1919–20] we are beginning really to feel the pinch; we are beginning to feel it sharply, and we face the prospect of being compelled to pay for the past as well as for the present.

Superficially, rather than fundamentally, the problem of the high cost of living has to do with the increase of money prices faster than [most people's] money incomes.* Superficially, therefore, it is the problem of people with relatively definite incomes who can

* Bentley seems, throughout this chapter and elsewhere, to be mingling two closely related but distinct problems: (1) the *rising* cost of living, which is what he is most concerned about above; and the *high* cost of living, a more static concept referring to the wastes and production limitations of the system, which serve to restrict supplies of goods, and result in a higher price level than would exist in freer circumstances.

but slowly increase them to correspond to rising prices. These include the people with fixed-dollar incomes from invested money, especially those with small incomes . . . who cannot mobilize their capital readily for better investments. They include the wage-earners, clerks, teachers, and salaried people; the relative suffering being modified for each class and within each class by special elements of economic power—how badly their services are needed at any given time, and for any special profiteering operation, and how much organized force they may have to compel attention to their demands.

We have next to see how this superficial problem of the high cost of living is tied in with the fundamental problem of national waste. The very methods and system which make for the permanent high costs are those which work most hurtfully in a period of [a] rapidly changing burden of costs. We must remember that we are dealing not merely with an economic matter, but with the very substance of the political transformations of the future, for which the temporary problems of the high cost of living are but an immediate ferment.

The high prices of war days and after are attributed to many causes. President Wilson's address to Congress on this subject [on August 8, 1919] did not attempt to search into the matter, but confined itself mainly to suggesting remedies for prices "artificially and deliberately created by vicious practices" which ought immediately to be checked by law.[1] It was followed quickly by two official or semi-official statements, one from the governor of the Federal Reserve Board, and the other from the Council of National Defense.

The common argument is to refer [attribute] heightened prices to increased quantity of currency in circulation. This [quantity] theory the Federal Reserve Board has attacked through an analysis of the quantity and use of cash and credit items in the country before, during, and after the war [World War I], and with a showing of the way these items react to prices rather than determine them.[2] The Board[3] holds that high prices during the war were due to the urgent needs of the Allied governments for goods and for quick deliveries, while for high prices since the war [after November 1918] it lists as causes:

1. General relaxation of the wartime reign of personal economy [i.e., increased personal consumption expenditure].

2. Increased demand for [American] commodities by individuals who restricted their purchases during the war, but who are now [1919] buying in competition with export demand [from abroad].

3. Accrued incomes and increased wages leading to heavy demands for commodities not of prime necessity, which have resulted in diverting labor and material from essentials to nonessentials.

The Council of National Defense has gone deeper than this. Its analysis listed [as causes of postwar high prices]:[4]

1. Curtailment in the production of nearly all articles except raw food products.

2. Hoarding of storage food products.

3. Profiteering, conscious and unconscious.

4. Inflation of circulating credits.

It drew a sharp distinction between the kind of profiteering which consists in producing a large crop and selling it at abnormally high prices; and "that other species of profiteering which deliberately reduces output in the expectation that the extortionate prices which the reduced product will command, may more than make up to the producer or the speculator for the portion of production withheld or the portion of hoarded goods condemned to spoil and be lost to the nation." Among its recommendations are the "improvement and standardization of methods and facilities for distributing and marketing goods," and "the perfecting of means of keeping the nation frequently, properly and adequately informed regarding probable material requirements and of current production of stocks of the more important commodities."

Without being hypercritical, and while recognizing fully that there are many truths which it would be impolitic to introduce into an official report—that, indeed, to introduce them might defeat the useful immediate purpose of the report—we may nevertheless glance at these reasons and see what kind of meaning they have. With regard to the currency theory, it is apparent that just as the high price of commodities leads us to consider the low price of the medium of circulation, so the latter leads us back to the high commodity price. Here is no question of increase in quantity of gold or silver coin, but of the increase of other instruments of exchange, themselves dependent for appearance upon the exchange process. And even without that consideration, if we tried to use the currency theory directly, our study of the actual technique of rising prices would take us into the whole existing system of industry; and all the interesting problems raised would show themselves involved in the relationships existing under that system.

We are in no better case with the Federal Reserve Board's complaints about relaxation of economy and about increased purchases and the effects of higher wages. Money wages are higher, but real wages, in terms of purchasing power for labor as a whole, are lower than formerly. Wage-earners as a whole cannot possibly be buying more commodities than they formerly did. Further than that, all commodities are made to be consumed; directly or indirectly, that is . . . [the] purpose of production; to produce and not to consume, would throw all industry into convulsions. The actual savings of physical capital goods in the nation have become very slight, proportionately; most so-called "savings" today being in reality increments of liability—claims against the future. It does not help this argument any to assume the temporary abandonment of a type of saving that has long since, and for deeper causes, tended to decline. With demands for luxuries and semi-luxuries the Board has a better case, but here again we have an evil that is really an incident to our productive system and means nothing unless interpreted in terms of that system. To talk of luxuries and [to] appeal to man's morals and good sense and stop there, gets nowhere. One must go back to the conditions and opportunities of this massed luxury-expenditure to get conclusions of any value.

The Council of National Defense gives us much [more] solid ground. Curtailment of production, hoarding and profiteering, and the consequent decreased production, are vital things. But they, too, must be discussed in terms of the whole system if they are to have a real meaning. This is clear enough from the very positive assertion of the Council that while other production has decreased, food production has improved. For we at once note that, while other production is directly in the hands of those who throttle it for profit, food production is only indirectly throttled under normal conditions, and was therefore better and longer responsive to the government's war and postwar appeals. One dare not stop upon the surface of these questions. In emphasizing standardized methods and facilities for distribution, and perfected government information service, the Council does indeed go below the surface with its recommendations; but even here it does not attempt to trace the story back to the vital . . . [parts] of the industrial process.

Briefly, the changes in the cost of living in the last twenty years have been as follows. In the first third of that period, down to 1907, there was a steady yearly increase which gave us . . . , prices 25 per cent higher (both wholesale and retail) than the average for the decade 1890–1899. Between 1907 and 1914 we had something like a 10 per cent increase in wholesale prices over the 1907 figures, something like a 20 per cent increase in retail prices, and something like an 8 per cent increase in wages. Between 1914 and 1918, the war years, the wholesale prices almost doubled, retail prices advanced two-thirds to three-quarters, and wages increased something like one-third. Since then, retail prices and wages have both been increasing more rapidly and, in part at least, catching up with the wholesale advances. The phenomena are at once, therefore, put before us; not primarily as war phenomena, but as facts concurrent with the centralizing organization phases of our autocratic industrial government.

The year 1914 was one of bad omen. In 1913 a record had been made for business failures, not only in total number, but also in total amount of liabilities and in average amount of liabilities. In 1914, the total liabilities of failures increased 20 per cent, and the number of failures and average liabilities increased about 15 per cent. After war [World War I] began in Europe, the *number* of failures continued large, and indeed, increased through 1915, but the average size of failures fell off even in the last half of 1914 as compared with the first half.

The war changed these evil prognostications by providing a tremendous demand for supplies, first in special lines and later in almost all lines, so as to keep all plants and workers busy. Prices were bid up; enormous profits were [first] made in the great speculative markets, then in special manufacturing lines; and later, the ultimate beneficiaries of practically all industries, the master manipulators and the holders of common stock, heaped up their gains.

The common stocks are the ones which, by and large, rest in the most concentrated holdings. The master adventurers of the world, now no longer adventurers, but rather master appropriators, won.

But the "safe" people of the world lost: the men and women who directly . . . or indirectly—through savings, bank deposits, and insurance policies—owned the more widely distributed bonds, . . . preferred stocks, . . . mortgages, and other fixed investments. With doubled prices, they found their very safety had taken from them half of what they had formerly had in real value, leaving them a wealth which, while equal in dollars, was nevertheless available to them only in half-price dollars. Along with them, the fixed-salary people suffered in somewhat similar degree, and the wage-earners also, except as these latter were specially needed by war profiteers or were especially strong in organizing to compel attention to their demands.

Every person who has lived through these times knows the vicious circles that began to show themselves. Flour, fats, and sugar increased enormously in price; and then wool, leather, and cotton. The pinch was felt, wage increases began, heightened wage figures made [for] higher dollar demand and pushed upwards on prices. Organized systems for speculatively anticipating the heightened demand were in action, and, by their manipulations and profits, increased the prices. Came more wage increases, more dollar demand, more speculation, more upward pressure, and so apparently ad infinitum, ad infinitum—that is, barring catastrophe.[5]

To state this wheel of evil in terms of wages and prices, however, is deliberately to leave out the worst of the influences. Wage increases meant a painful upward pressure from seekers for necessities; but far more important still was the devil-may-care upward pressure from specially favored beneficiaries of profiteering, gluttonous for display, regardless [heedless] as to cost, dispensing hurtfully that which had so painlessly come to them. The wage recipients, except in a few specially benefited classes, struggled merely to catch up. The profiteers led in [this] debauch; what they could during war, wildly after war. Many new fortunes were in the hands of the adventurers on "shoestrings," and many enormously increased fortunes [were] in the hands of old fortune owners.

But again it was not the display expenditures of the profiteers that was the worst result of their fortune. It was their power to use their funds recklessly for new upward pressures through speculations and manipulations. And this power, which despite its curtailing through Liberty Loan investments has already shown its evil effects in that comparatively minor matter of our immediate living expenses, remains over, for no one knows what more terrific effects [may occur] in those more important matters—the permanent status of our industry, and our relations with other lands, new and old, upon which our adventurers are moving.

Nor is this all. The possibilities of profiteering passed on to the retail trade, developing a wild hysteria. The old landmarks were gone. Anything seemed possible to those who had the power. The limits of consumers' endurance were not apparent; consumers were indeed dazed as to where they could rightfully break in for their defense. It was again, at bottom, the organized trading system that made itself felt; those elements of rising costs, wasteful absorptions of energy and ability, strongly maintained margins of profit, and all that technique, already discussed, by which retail trade is partly knit into the organized system and partly trailed along with it. Retail prices, as the government price indices show, came back finally to large extent into their own—into, that is, . . . what will be their own—until we, by positive action, prevent it. Local dealers in articles of doubled prices took not only their old percentage of profit on these new prices, but they [also] took higher margins, higher rates of mark-up. Sales fell off sharply, but the dealer was cared for richly.

Shoes tell the story fully. With a 37-cent labor cost [average hourly wage] for welt lace shoes as of 1914,[6] increased to not over 50 cents in 1917, and probably not over 75 cents at the highest later; with a leather cost formerly around $1.50 at the outside for substantial shoes—somewhat less than doubled in December 1918, and showing, under hoarding and speculation, a prospect of tripled cost in the spring of 1919 for future production—[with all this] $8, $10 and $12 was the rule for substantial shoes at the stores, with . . . up to $25 and more charged for special styles. "Extreme curtailment" in production, such as the Council of Defense recites

(60 per cent less in the first quarter of 1919 than in the last quarter of 1918), was of course a result.*

The war [World War I] facts and the postwar facts of prices and of profiteering, as we had them and endured them, are not primarily war facts. They are primarily facts of organized trade, writ large against the war sky. Trouble enough we would have had . . . to make up for our war waste—our huge destruction of our products calling upon us for extra labor to replace them in future years. But it is nothing as compared with the trouble that was brewing underneath in peace, and that magnified itself so hugely in war in proportion to the enlarged opportunities that were offered. And the trouble of today is nothing as compared with the troubles of the morrow. The high cost of living, attack it as one may at this surface point or that, is with us till we attack it at its source, till we master the wasters, and cease to permit their waste and their power to master us.

The bright spot is what the [national] government itself achieved [under the guidance of Wilson, Baruch, Hoover, and McAdoo] to increase production, to prevent the worst manifestations of profiteering during the war [World War I]. Its machinery, [e.g., War Industries Board, Food Administration, Fuel Administration] thrown into the discard [with] the Armistice [of November 11, 1918] . . . and called back in part by bitter necessity before a year had gone by, remains to prove what can be done, as well as to point the way to what must be done more completely and more radically before relief is gained.

Notes

1. *New York Times*, August 9, 1919.
2. For the quantity theory in its latest form [as of 1919–20] as applied to existing conditions, see Professor Irving Fisher's address "The New Price Revolution," read to the Conference of Governors and Mayors at the White House, March 3–5, 1919, published by [the] U.S. Department of Labor (Washington,

* Cf., Federal Trade Commission Report on Shoe Costs, 1914 to 1918, *New York Times,* August 7, 1919; and the FTC *Report . . . on Shoes and Leather Costs and Prices* (Washington: Government Printing Office, 1921).

Government Printing Office, March, 1919). For a survey of the whole subject see J. Laurence Laughlin, *Money and Prices* (New York: C. Scribner's Sons, 1919).

3. Letter from Governor William P. G. Harding to Senator George P. McLean, chairman of the Senate Committee on Banking and Currency, *New York Times,* August 11, 1919. [For new light on and criticism of Harding's policies, see Milton Friedman and Anna J. Schwartz, *A Monetary History of the United States 1867–1960* (Princeton: Princeton University Press, 1963), pp. 224–31.]

4. *New York Times,* August 31, 1919.

5. For official recognition of the effects of speculation in increasing, rather than lowering prices, we have not only the Council of National Defense's discussion of hoarding and profiteering, but [also] President Wilson's address to Congress on this subject; and an interview in the cable dispatches [of *New York Times*] September 4, 1919, from the man who is certainly most competent to give authoritative opinion on such a subject: Herbert Hoover. [For an analysis of competitive v. monopolistic speculation, see Abba P. Lerner, *The Economics of Control* (New York: Macmillan, 1944), pp. 88–95.]

6. U.S. Department of Labor Bulletin No. 232 (Washington: Government Printing Office, May, 1918). *Wages and Hours of Labor in the Boot and Shoe Industry 1907 to 1916.*

XV

The Nation's Peril:
Crises and Revolution

A nation's welfare is just as much dependent on certain factors of good sense in the adjustment of expenditures to resources as is the welfare of an individual merchant.

A merchant can let the departments of his business run loosely and contentiously; he can let his till stand freely open to the members of his family who run to it whenever they have need; he can live up to his income and to his prospects of coming income, borrowing against his expanding business so heavily that what he has anticipated from the future must always be provided to the last dollar by the future. He can do these things, but he must pay hard in the end.

And so with a nation. It can live up to its income. It can dispense with a free hand. It can capitalize the future so long as things go right. But if the open and easy fields for its winnings cease, if it finds itself with too many idle or wasteful hands to feed, then may come catastrophe. And the catastrophe that comes may be very much worse for the nation than bankruptcy is for the individual. The nation may not so readily find a new opening for its energies and efforts when once it has reached catastrophic distortion.[1]

We have had a number of business crises since the beginning of the development of modern industrial organization. Fortunately, one does not need to be the possessor of a thorough-going theory of crises to be permitted to speak on this subject. A recent writer . . . has listed a dozen theories which attribute crises respectively to "industrial competition," "disproportion between wages and productivity," "over-saving," "diminishing marginal utility of an increasing supply of commodities," "over-capitalization," "over-production of industrial equipment and under production of complementary goods," "high costs of construction," "declining prospects of profits," "discrepancy between anticipated profits and current capitalization," "unlike rhythm of production in the organic and inorganic realm," "dissimilar price fluctuations of producers and consumers goods," and "slowness with which interest rates are adjusted to changes in price level."[2]

It is of course plain that all of the theories thus summarized have to do with the distortion of industry under the present system of controls based on the appropriative use of private property. It is equally plain that all of them in one way or another involve a maladjustment of spending power. And insofar as all crises involve wastes of the nation's productive power and often of its physical resources, they are all theories of certain wasteful tendencies in our industrial organization.

We recall, of course, the period of optimism after the formation in . . . [the early 1900's] of the United States Steel Corporation and other great trusts, and the belief that a way had been found to keep a strong hand on industry and [to] prevent its periodic distortions. Nevertheless, in 1907 we had a bad moment, though the trouble was confined to the field of credit and did not bite deep into industry; a panic rather than an economic crisis.[3] In 1914 we seemed again to be on the verge of disaster (the failure figures of the year have already been cited) but the war intervened, giving its peculiar type of business prosperity, and the disaster . . . did not come.

The Morgan creed, the creed of the trust-promoter, was optimism —a solid confidence in the future of America. That is to say, a solid confidence that no matter what claims we might place upon the future production of the country, and no matter who might hold those claims, the country could and would cash them in at their face value. Hence, for example, the payment to Andrew Carnegie of securities of a face value of $492 million and a market value of $447 million for assets to which Mr. Carnegie had given a sworn value of $76 million [only] . . . sixteen months before, and which his companies had carried at a book value of $101 million twelve months before.[4] Since then, this capitalization of the future has gone on as merrily as ever; not always estimated at the full face value of its claims by the market, but always, in both face totals and market totals, heaping upwards into greater amounts.

Meantime, two developments [have occurred]. While the capitalizations and claims have been heaping up so fast, actual national savings of the real goods we use to aid us in producing other goods, seem, according to the best estimates we can get, to have fallen off strikingly in percentage. And further, the confidence in our boasted national efficiency has received many serious setbacks. Carnegie was retired because of the very fact of his efficiency. He and his organization of partners could not be permitted by the Steel Corporation to go ahead in rivalry to it. Carnegie himself has said: "The best corporations that ever were formed will be beaten by such an organization as we had in the Carnegie Steel Company."[5] Henry O. Havemeyer told the Industrial Commission that the chief advantage the Sugar Trust had was in buying up refineries and shutting them down.[6] And Brandeis in the essay just referred to comes to the following conclusions:

No conspicuous American trust owes its existence to the desire for increased efficiency. . . . On the contrary, the purpose has often been to curb efficiency or to promote inefficiency. . . .

No conspicuously profitable trust owed its profits largely to superior efficiency. . . .

No conspicuous trust has been efficient enough to maintain long, as against the independents, its proportion of the business without continuing to buy up from time to time its successful competitors. . . .

Most of the trusts which did not secure monopolistic positions have failed to show marked success in efficiency as compared with independent competing concerns.[7]

We have a clear case of huge claims without a clear case of assured production to justify them. We have a provisional case for the successful control of minor crises without any case at all for the control of a great crisis [such as was to occur in 1929]. We have a clear showing of a nexus of industry so huge that we cannot help fearing that the crisis, when and if it does break through, will go to the very heart of our industrial life with rending force.

What is the great crisis? What is the crisis that breaks through with rending force? It is nothing less than revolution. The barons at Runnymede were assembled on an economic basis. The French Revolution was a huge industrial crisis, based on an appropriative system which had suppressed production, which had resulted in huge wastes, and which had been held down under heavy bonds until the pent-up forces released themselves with unheard-of violence. The Russian Revolution is the ultimate crisis of Russian agriculture and Russian industry under war burdens.

The relation between crisis and revolution is not a mere analogy, not an illustration of the one from the other. The two are the same thing, first in little, then in big. For a country organized industrially like ours, it is the wage system that furnishes the first cleavage for revolution. The group that is shut out of control—that gets only what it fights for, and gets that only in partial extent and for only part of its members—will find among its less successful elements deliberate leaders of revolution. But this is not by any means the only line of cleavage. Another is implied in the cutting in two of fixed incomes at the very time when the more favored of the active appropriators are securing the hugest of present gains and establishing still huger claims upon the industry of the future. Not only all holders of fixed-dollar incomes, but also all men whose interests as consumers of products predominate over their other interests, are involved. And the wage-earner enters into this new cleavage himself on a new basis, with interests broader than those of his old established economic class-consciousness.

A crisis may not have its advance philosophers and its loud agitators like a revolution. But a crisis very often has its group of manipulators working behind the scenes, fostering and guiding it and reaping their profits from it. Moreover, the philosophers and the loud talkers are far from being the revolution. The revolution itself may come, and sometimes does come, as spontaneously, as inevitably, up from the ground as come the upheavals and wreckages of any of our crises.

Crises and revolutions are alike in that both work great destructions of claims. They wipe out the liabilities that cannot or will not be carried further. They may incidentally destroy physical property or take the value out of physical property, but their great working, their great liquidation, is in claims upon income; while the other destruction is rather an incident to the methods of procedure than an essential element in what is happening.

To get a thorough understanding of our situation with reference to such an ultimate crisis, we must examine more carefully the nation's balance sheet and its income. Regarding the nation's whole business as one great enterprise, we must consider property, income, and claims in their respective proportions, so as to see how the possible ultimate crisis will affect them.

We talk very largely of the huge wealth that we have accumulated and of our deep dependence on it for production. And in its aggregate, of course, it is huge as looked at from the standpoint of an individual. But when we measure it by our total population, it does not seem so large. And when further we seek out the part of this aggregate wealth which is serviceable property, and separate from it the elements which are rather private claims upon income, the exhibit of wealth loses some of its supposed glamor.

The truth is that in our current discussions and judgments we rarely recognize how lightly we touch the surface of our universe with our tools and equipment, and how very slight that equipment is when viewed in terms of our working power—in terms of our productive capacity. We [i.e., society] suffer from something of an idolatry of equipment, of capital, of wealth; [an idolatry] over and above that individual worship of wealth, in a different sense of the word "wealth," with which many of us as individuals can be charged. We think of our stored-up capital goods as the achievement of the ages, when actually those goods are merely the achievement of a year or two. We think of ourselves as working in a huge permanent physical structure of our society when actually we are working with but a few slight tools in our hands. Knowledge and technique are indeed of the ages, but accumulated goods are almost of the day.

[Facts have been cited earlier, in Chapter 2] . . . which showed [that] in 1912, the amount of capital per worker invested in mining and manufacturing was around $2,200, ranging for other occupations up to $11,000 with an average of about $3,200. Per . . . [capita], the investment would be about 40 per cent of these figures, or between $1,250 and $1,300. However, this is a statement of the capital employed collectively in business enterprises as such. It includes the land values used in agriculture, trade, and industry; but it does not include either the homes which the workers need for their shelter, or the stocks of commodities they keep in their own hands for current uses . . . which are necessary to them, and therefore to the nation, to keep the wheels of industry turning.

From the national point of view, which regards the country as a going concern, engaged in producing the livings of its entire population, we need a different kind of statement if we are to envisage correctly the quantity of our capital goods, and [if we are] to measure them in terms of the length of time it takes us to replace them. We must include the necessary housing and the home and household supplies, and we must exclude that part of real-estate values which is clear capitalization of claims against future income, fluctuating in value, not in its character of productive property but with conditions favorable or unfavorable for realization on its claims.

Equipment and products in stock on the farms, in factories, and in trade, together with all coin and with all necessary goods in consumers' hands, amounted in 1912 to $43 billions or about $450 per capita.* Adding about $15 billions for the equipment of railroads and public utilities, as distinct from their land values, we raise the figure to $600 per capita.

[There] remains public and private real estate to consider. There are some elements in building values which should be excluded, and some elements in land values which should be included. On the basis of the facts, we shall probably not be far wrong if we include all private buildings of whatsoever description and exclude all land values. Part of this exclusion is due not to consideration of capitalization, but to the fact that much of land improvement apart from buildings has become a modification of the physical environment, paid for by the public and now held as common property for the general welfare. Not only are river improvement, canals, [and] drainage and irrigation systems of this nature, but many elements of right-of-ways and of public facilities for city life.

---

* See Chapter II for some of the figures for this and the following estimates. Deviation from these earlier figures in the text occur where Bentley excluded certain types of property he did not regard as genuine capital from the standpoint of the population.

Adding $41 billions more for all private buildings we get a total of $100 billions, or, let us say, roughly between $1,000 and $1,100 per capita. If other elements of land values ought properly to be included, the figure would only be slightly raised, and as it stands it includes 40 per cent of all real-estate values. This $1,000 or $1,100 per capita is the value of actual goods which we have accumulated to keep up our industrial life, and which we must keep in existence in order to continue that life on its present standard of production.

The way to measure that value, in terms of its meaning to us as producers, is by comparison with our annual income. It is a question of proportions, and all that is necessary is to get our annual income computed on a somewhat similar basis.[8] The product of the nation per capita may be put at around $350 a year.[9] With capital accumulations, [then] not [exceeding] three years' product, we are doing our usual work.[10] And when we remember that very conservative estimates, based on measures which ought to be thoroughly practicable for us to undertake, show that we could readily triple our national income (measured in welfare goods), it would appear that with the aid of one year's practicable product, employed with the knowledge and skill the race has acquired, we could provide the supplies and equipment for as much income as we now have or ever have had. Indeed, in all probability, for several times as much.

If this is probable for today, what . . . might not be possible for the future, when we have our powers fully in hand?

This now puts a very different face on the problems growing out of the national status of our capitalizations, and our relations to nature for productive purposes. It gives us light, for example, on certain great aspects of war economics and finance which often seem so surprising. Everyone thought before the war that the cost of modern military operations was too . . . [enormous] for any nation to carry for more than a few months. [Lord] Kitchener, [British War Secretary] thinking in terms of war endurance rather than of national resources, predicted three years [as the limit]; but it is certain that even the Germans never calculated in advance on so prolonged a strain. The error rose out of a confused sense of the relations of national capital, national income, and national capitalizations. As a matter of fact, the nations rode through four years; and counting the demobilization strains, which were almost of war weight, through five years of waste.

So far as their actual physical resources were concerned, they came through in very good shape. Heightened speed of production under war emergency, shifting of lines of production, elimination of some of the worst of peace wastes, did the work. Real world capital was so little ahead of annual world income in quantity that it was not difficult to keep the balance. Of course there was a real destruction of capital, and it is affecting us and will continue to affect us seriously. Not to speak of the ravaged lands—cities, homes, factories, equipment, even soil fertility gone—there is all the ammunition, the specialized war implements and vessels, the food and clothing, the transportation of the soldiers, which has been thrown away leaving no equivalent behind. Victory we won, victory worth more than all of these things—but that victory has become part of our common immaterial wealth, in the class with air and climate and unappropriated technology. For the lost goods, for them at least so far as they were not excess products that we would not otherwise have had, we must pay by our future labor; and we must bear the burden while paying.

How small, however, is this part of our payment compared with the payment we actually have to make; the payment, not in terms of real capital, but of the capitalizations of all of the appropriators' claims upon our future? How small is the effect upon our present welfare, upon the present high cost of living arising directly out of the war losses, compared with the effects arising out of the manipulation of the situation by the masters who control it? The examination brings us again into the technical procedure involved in the heightened costs, and leads us to a completion of the discussion left unfinished at the end of the preceding chapter.

For the goods and services produced and destroyed, we paid in part through taxes, in much larger part through the issue of securities. So far as we paid by taxes, the amount of those taxes entered directly into prices* to heighten them; modified of course by gains

* If Bentley's implication is that the tax increases were financed through price increases, with the burden thus borne exclusively by consumers, it is incorrect. The question whether the price increases forced the consumers to bear the major

from higher efficiency, and by eliminations of waste consumption, so far as these were equally distributed. In substance the situation was this: Out of the 100 per cent of our production, the part we took for war and paid for by taxes was perhaps 10 per cent. The remaining 90 per cent of commodities had to go 'round among the 100 per cent of consumers. Price adjustments, including taxes, distributed the total prices of all the commodities over the remaining 90 per cent and raised them somewhat in proportion. . . .

But this was only part of the procedure. The government took another great part of our produce, 10 per cent or 20 per cent or 30 per cent more, and paid for it by securities—promises to pay in the future—claims against the future product and income of the nation; claims with nothing left behind in existence to represent them. Nothing, indeed, except the great test of all things, national life and existence. But that national life and existence is the common weal—the claims are personal and private.

. . . This creation of claims also entered into our prices at once and heightened them. The war goods disappeared, just as in the first case of those that were paid for by taxes. The workers who produced them had to live off . . . the products of the other workers, and prices had to make the adjustment. The government securities went largely in[to] concentrated holdings in the hands of the profiteers, the great owners of the common stock of the corporations with tripled war earnings, there to be used for further profiteering. They became the basis of credits.[11] Interest charges began to accumulate and the funds to cover these had to come out of product. Anticipation of future requirements for repayment, the speculative readjustment, began at once.

Here now remain these huge claims to be met in the future; claims based not on product as we usually assume [it] to be measured—not even based solely on real product devoured by war and required to be replaced—but claims based largely on strategic

tax or substitute tax burden is a complicated one, depending on the structure of the new taxes. John M. Clark, *The Costs of the World War to the American People*, pp. 137–38, gives this verdict: "Out of some 31 billions of national resources devoted to war . . . 1917–19, possibly 18 billions came out of decreased consumption as compared to the 1915 rate per capita, some 5.75 billions came out of increased personal real income beyond the 1915 per capita level, which leaves 7.25 billions to come out of increased productive effort represented in undivided corporate income, either borrowed or taken in taxes."

position, on the opportunity to profiteer, on the crude power to write themselves upon the books. Claims reposing now in large measure in the safe lair of government securities, while waiting the opening of new opportunities to increase and multiply abroad and at home. The over-capitalization before the war, as measured on business returns and census reports, and the greater over-capitalization shown in the more careful analysis that has just been completed, were nothing as compared with our postwar situation.

This may all be very well; or it may seem so at least, so long as the opportunities to expand—to realize in the future the claims established in the present—continue to offer themselves. When the home field closes, as it did long ago for England, there is the foreign field; there is imperialism. So long as we can prey upon the rest of the world, cash in from the rest of the world the claims that the homeland can no longer meet, we can stave off the reckoning. When that power comes to an end—it is the end. From the train of little shocks we arrive finally at the great shock.

In Europe, of course, the situation is in certain respects, so far as immediate prospects are concerned, far worse than it is here. The menace of revolution is closer. But also we are most intimately bound up with Europe in all that the realization on our claims requires. Merely in the one phase of national finance proper, the finances of the government as separate from the whole state of industry, bankruptcies among European governments are threatening to such [an] extent that at times revolutions seem to be staying their hands to permit bankruptcies to do their work for them. But even this is but the surface of Europe's trouble. Below is the deeper abyss.

Frank A. Vanderlip bears witness to the facts.[12] He went abroad to study national finances, and . . . national bankruptcies. He remained to study the frightful "distortion and paralysis of industrial production" beside which the financial condition of the governments seemed to him to shrink to lesser importance. He deliberately concluded that such destruction of capital as France has had in its war zone—its lost factories and machinery, its ruined coal and iron mines—was not the real seat of the trouble. The breakdown of domestic transportation, the lack of ocean tonnage, and labor shortages and unrest were greater obstacles; but they could be surmounted. Raw materials were lacking, but they could be obtained. The vital need was credit, and the resulting situation was one "where the need of goods is practically without limit, but the difficulties surrounding their production and marketing are so great that up to the present time there is a condition of idleness unprecedented in industrial history."[13] The credit system, with all its reliances and resources used by the existing industrial organization, was in collapse.

"Not only is Europe enormously rich" says Mr. Vanderlip, "but there is inherent in the present situation a power of rapid recovery if the tangle only can be straightened out, which will set the continent in the direction of recovery." But with credit "so delicate a thing that it is dangerous to talk about it . . . there is not a credit in Europe today that does not need to be weighed and its chance of repayment carefully appraised."[14]

In other words (and here we do not wish to commit Mr. Vanderlip), the burden of the whole system of claims upon industry—old and new, private and public—has broken the camel's back. The load is too big. The machine cannot pick it up.

Mr. Vanderlip's solution is to segregate the most assured power of income-appropriation that can be located in this world for the future, namely national customs, and make out of it a basis of credit for the immediate needs of industry. He goes clear to the extreme of [capitalist, national] security, assuming present governments to survive, in order to get credit for what would normally be the most momentary needs. And [even] with that, he does not believe that one nation alone can win out. He believes that all the European nations must pool their credit, and place it in the hands of the most solvent nation, the United States, if they are to survive. The United States must administer a receivership of them for their benefit.

How desperate is this remedy may be seen from the fact that if, through it, credit is restored and industry survives, it will be merely to undertake the Sisyphian labor of wiping out the claims recorded against it. The burden will remain for generations upon the shoulders of those who must ultimately do the day's work and pay the bill out of the proceeds. A burden that would mean no more than a year or two of somewhat increased effort measured in actual capital goods, becomes the struggle of generations under our established system of wastes and liabilities.

Notes

1. Recall the very concrete statement of Prime Minister Lloyd George in addressing the House of Commons, August 18, 1919. "We shall never improve matters until we increase production, or we will be driven later to reduce even lower the standard of living in this country. There is no alternative except quitting the country for which we fought for four years." [Cf., *New York Times*, August 19, 1919.]

2. Professor Wesley C. Mitchell in Melvin T. Copeland (ed.), *Business Statistics* (Cambridge: Harvard University Press, 1917). The theories are, in order, those of: Beveridge, May, Hobson, Aftalion, Bouniatian, Spiethoff, Hull, Lescure, Veblen, Sombart, Carver, and Fisher.

3. The new currency and credit system under the Federal Reserve was established to better coordinate and safeguard the credit agencies, but its remedial measures did not reach into the deeper sources of the trouble.

4. Justice Louis D. Brandeis, "Trusts and Efficiency" in the volume *Business—A Profession* (Boston: Small, Maynard & Co., 1914), p. 203. He quotes the Stanley Committee's finding that this was "not the purchase of a mill but the retirement of a man," and mentions also the Morgan promotion fees on the deal as [being] $62,500,000 (p. 205).

5. Testimony before Stanley Committee, quoted in Amos R. E. Pinchot, "The Costs of Private Monopoly to Public and Wage Earner," *Annals,* American Academy of Political and Social Science, Vol. XLVIII (July 1913), pp. 164–88, esp. p. 168.

6. Quoted in *ibid.*, p. 167.

7. Brandeis, *op. cit.*, pp. 200–201.

8. While prices have advanced, there is no ground to think that actual stocks of capital goods have increased since 1912. Indeed, the result of the war may have been a decrease even for the United States. The Council of National Defense seems to incline to this view, for the year 1919 at least. See report, *Analysis of the High Cost of Living Problem*, August 1919, pp. 7, 18.

9. Compare Chapter II. Professor B. M. Anderson's estimate of our 1912 [net] income was $33.8 billions. *Annalist,* Vol. XIII, No. 312 (Jan. 6, 1919), pp. 5, 6, 61.

10. The situation today may be stated . . . as follows: Nation's annual income—1 unit; Real capital used—3 units; Income to workers—½ unit; Income to title holders—½ unit; Private capitalizations at 6 per cent to 8 per cent on incomes—7 or 8 units.

The writer is entirely aware that psychic goods and claims secure their values on the basis of the same economic procedure, and that the distinction here can be obliterated by the logomachies of logic. What are at question are the facts— definitely differentiated facts on the big scale in industrial society. As for the process, that is the very heart of the whole trouble, not a court of appeal for interpreting away the facts.

11. The Federal Reserve Board, in its letter on currency inflation previously discussed, recognizes a clear case of inflation in the use of war bonds as a basis for credit.

12. Frank A. Vanderlip, *What Happened to Europe* (New York: Macmillan, 1919).

13. In England, 1 million workers were receiving over £1.25 million a week in unemployment wages; and in addition, a further aid through the sale of wheat below cost at an expense to the nation of £50 million a year. In Belgium, 800,000 workers were receiving unemployment wages. *Ibid.*, pp. 115–16.

14. *Ibid.*, pp. 98, 106.

XVI

Labor and Revolution

In the two preceding chapters, attention has been given to certain aspects of national income and claims against it; of crises and revolutions; of war and prices; and the attempt has been made to bring them into relation. Crises have been observed as maladjustments of industry, associated with wastes and involving claims against future industry which cannot, or seemingly cannot, be met. The effects of the [First] World War in enormously increasing the quantity of such claims have been noted. The method has been traced by which doubled prices, manipulated in the service of profiteering, further this tendency and operate to lower the economic status not only of producers, but of all consumers with relatively fixed incomes. The signs have been observed of the approach of that maximum maladjustment of industry which carries with it the threat of the ultimate crisis: industrial revolution. The lines of cleavage in this maladjustment have been indicated.

The first great line of cleavage which opens itself is that of wage-labor, of the proletariat. Mr. [Frank A.] Vanderlip states that in England both conservatives and radicals estimate that, at the very least, between 10 per cent and 15 per cent of organized laborers are industrial revolutionists. Organized laborers are 85 per cent of the industrial workers, which would make the extremists' number 9 to 12 per cent of the working population. He extends the same estimate to other European countries.[1] A similar percentage of all the workers under our factory wage-labor system in this country (excluding agricultural, trade, domestic, and independent artisan-labor) would [amount to] a million men; no inconsiderable power, but still not a power that would be apt to endanger the country

172

immediately to any extent. Whether the number is so great or not we have no means of knowing.[2] The dangers of revolution, however, manifestly rest not in the revolutionary forces now existing, but in the accessions which they may presumably receive to their numbers; and such accessions again depend on what the future conditions of living are to be, not only among the wage-earners, but among other elements of the population; and upon the judgment which all of these elements of the population may make upon the relation of their production and their reward to their deserts. It will not be so much a question of the accuracy of these judgments as of their plausibility, and the tests of plausibility do not come out of the thin air. They are not drawn from some ready reservoir of ignorance or evil, but arise out of the very industrial organization itself in which the men live and work.[3]

In casting a glance over the revolutionary tendencies of the country, we may discard the anarchies altogether. The more generalized a protest is against everything, the narrower will be its circle of adherents, and the less effective its work. The anarchies, [through] their unbalanced followers, may throw an occasional bomb—or may have an occasional bomb thrown in their name—but that is about all; and that is far from being our most vital social problem.[4]

Nor have we much more need of giving attention to socialism as it has developed historically in the last two or three generations . . . European socialism has developed into a political force and modified itself so that, in the case of Germany, its official program is little more than the establishment of representative political government, and its platform is little more than moderatively progressive. [Meanwhile] socialism in the United States has insisted on an orthodoxy and a bigotry that has driven out of its ranks most of its ablest leaders, and [has] led it to such a splitting of its forces as to make it in most ways insignificant. One cannot even seek from socialism itself a definition of what it is. The old State Socialism is no longer [in 1920] a living creed [in Western Europe and America, excepting Soviet Russia] and many Socialist writers regard programs of its type as offering rather an objectionable State Capitalism than any true form of socialism[5] (though men like Nicholas Murray Butler [the conservative President of Columbia University] still [in 1920] portray the rigid horrors of such socialism as though it were the enemy to be feared, and contrast them with the blessings of our present unlimited prosperity and freedom, the praises of which they intone.[6] In common understanding, socialism is somehow supposed to be the program of class-conscious wage-labor; but, despite the fact that the Marxian socialism has dealt much with the proletariat in contrast with all other elements of the population, it is clear enough that any such identification of wage-labor generally with socialism, as a political or industrial fact of America today [1920], is far from the truth.

Wage-labor, in its attitude toward industrial reconstruction, ranges all the way from the extreme conservatism of the [Samuel] Gompers group in control of the American Federation of Labor, through various elements of growing strength presenting progressive political programs, to two groups of revolutionists professing "direct action" in the industrial field as their only solution. The Gompers policy, as we have seen, rests deliberately on an organization for appropriating as much of the product as it can; imitating, though with its own special tools, the appropriative principles of the masters of large property, and developing, wherever it is especially successful, a marked cooperative feeling towards the great appropriative business powers as against any projects of revolution which would entirely change the basis of its action. "More" is the motto of the Gompers group, just as it is the motto of the investment bankers; and this "more" is, primarily, a "more" of seizure, not of production.

The two revolutionary groups among laborers are the Communist or Extreme Left group of socialism, and the Industrial Workers of the World, the IWW. The former is constructing itself largely on the basis of inspiration from the Russian Revolution, and shows itself rather as a gathering of extremists and would-be leaders than as an actual organization of the rank-and-file.[7] The latter is a native product, though with some borrowings from French syndicalism, and rallies to itself in very large numbers the worst paid, worst treated, and generally most neglected elements among labor.

The American Federation of Labor and affiliated trade unions in 1913–14 were computed to have 2,674,400 members, or about 7 per cent of all the occupied classes.[8] This number has now increased [1920] to 4,500,000, or 12 per cent, but after excluding agricultural occupations and various groups not susceptible of organization, it is estimated to be 50 per cent of all wage-earners who can be organized.[9] The IWW cannot be so readily estimated as to size, for it [is] very loosely organized. For example, it has no president or chairman, but functions through a general secretary and general executive board. To confiscate its records and offices and put its leaders in jail merely means that other leaders slide into the vacant places. Its organizers earn their way by working at what jobs they can find; and seek not so much at present to found permanent branches, as to take advantage of any temporary trade struggles that may develop among the unorganized and organized workers, and lead them forward in "direct action." Despite all this looseness of structure, it [the IWW] has a much more clearly defined program for the future than any other extremist group in the country; a program for the organization of all national industry in great industrial branches, as distinct from trade; each branch controlled by the workers within it, and all federated together for the necessary processes of adjustment and compromise at the top. It would substitute for the present political government another government of what is loosely called a "Soviet" type, organized . . . out of industrial [labor] elements.[10]

There was a time in the early part of 1919 when it seemed as though some one or other form of revolutionary leadership might spread so rapidly as to be of vital immediate importance to the nation; that seeming, of course, had to do with the uncertainties attending the coming home [of men] from the war [World War I] and the readjustment to a state of peace. That was at a time when unprecedented unemployment or unprecedented demand for workers seemed equally probable; when the country fluctuated from day to day between opinions as to whether immigration or emigration would be the most pronounced postwar tendency. But things do not go so fast as it seems they may in hectic moments; and the settling down, such as it has been (even though manifested in an unusually complete Gompers control of the American Federation of Labor at its 1919 convention), does not indicate that the struggle is over, but rather that it is deeply preparing itself.

With this much of statement of the surface facts, let us see what the possibilities and prospects of proletarian revolution are in this country—a revolution that would originate among, and work itself through . . . the ranks of people who pursue their daily occupations under the established factory wage system without the use of their own capital. It would be a revolution industrial in origins, industrial in its methods, bursting in upon political institutions as if from without, and transforming them for its own purposes. The possibilities of such revolution must inevitably be discussed in terms of those industrial conditions which, through their continued working, bring the rank-and-file [of industrial workers] into action, following the leaders who already believe the conditions call for it. Not the leaders, but the conditions will bring it about.

It will be useless to try to discuss these possibilities with persons who regard revolution as some kind of a germ-disease of words, an infection which spreads through the body politic and which can be cured by surgical operations on the words and the users of the words. Words, and theories which are made up of words, slogans, and "isms" alike, may dance across the country in trifles, in amusements and fads, playing their little part and gone. But the deeper things (the actual programs and actions and political and industrial developments) go their way, making use of what convenient words and "isms" they find, or creating new ones to suit their needs. Let us throw aside, to start with, all superstitious fear of theories or men, of socialisms, syndicalisms or communisms, of Lenins or Trotskys or Bill Haywoods.

What are now the possibilities that the three-quarters of the occupied population [in the United States] who work for pay without direct use of their own capital will become involved in proletariat revolution? [These comprise] the 10 million workers under the wage system, the 13 million other laborers, the 4 million clerks and salespeople.[11] What . . . kind of revolution . . . [could they] produce?

In the first place, we may readily admit that the greater part of these [workers] will not be active revolutionists. It will be enough if their apathetic endurance of present conditions [relations of workers to employers] shifts [to] an equally apathetic acquiescence in violent reconstruction [of society]. Always, in social life, the great majority of the people are in the gallery; at most, vociferously registering their presence. It will be enough if a quarter, or even perhaps a tenth, become actively interested; for given the condition [needed] to make the little shift in type [degree] of apathy, the transformation, or at least the great disturbance, can take place.

[Other] factors to consider are not merely the industrial conditions, but the way they are known and understood (the relative degree of ignorance and information) and the way power arising from them is utilized; the kind of force exerted from or upon the political government. A word first as to these subsidiary aspects.

Deep as is the ignorance [about the power-structure of the American economy] among all classes of people, it is in one sense much less among the laboring groups than among other parts of the population. Ignorance of [economic] theories—the kind of theories that once answered to economic conditions and are still religiously held by all who benefit from such conditions—may of course be imputed to them; and where their ignorance has broken down, that thing worse than ignorance in the mind of the believer, namely disbelief, may be imputed. But there is another question as to ignorance—by far the greater question—that concerning not arguments or theories, but facts: the whole question of information. And here the situation is probably the other way around. The great masters of industry have, of course, their very complete information and understanding based upon private systems of investigation needful to their affairs. They do not depend upon the daily press; on the contrary, they use it to spread such kinds of information or misinformation as they wish. The laboring classes in their various branches have available, in part at least, their own agencies of information; their own publishing houses, their own press, their own pamphlets. The middle classes, on the contrary (including all classes who depend almost entirely for facts upon the daily and weekly press and upon the journalistic type of magazine), are shut off from the facts in a very peculiar way. They probably know less than any other people, for example, about such facts as have been developed by the Federal Commission [on] Industrial [Relations] and the Federal Trade Commission in the last decade. Not securing or using such material for their own purposes, they [the middle classes] are idly letting it percolate into the rank-and-file of labor for use for its purposes.

Next, [something may be said] in regard to force and, first, the kind of [police and military] force that has always been exerted by masters [of business and industry] when their mastery is threatened. We have already seen such force exerted in our country in aggressive forms a hundred fold, perhaps many hundred fold, greater than aggressive force from all the anarchists and revolters and agents of strike violence combined. Some description of this as we have it today will be given in a later chapter. The case of [Tom] Mooney,* universally assumed guilty among middle-class people—but against whom no credible evidence has been brought in court or outside of court, and who nevertheless remains in prison and who cannot get a rehearing even at the repeated suggestion of the President of the United States—will serve for an illustration. Such exercise of force, given our present degree of education and information among the victims, is most clearly pressing, not away from but toward revolution; heightening and deepening conviction, destroying willingness for compromise and mutual understanding, [and] developing fanaticism.

The other abuses of force, those coming from the opposite side and working not through political forms but against them, are equally unpleasant to contemplate. There is a world of new technique and appliance for devilish destruction, the result of war [World War I] experiences; and while for organized use, the opponents of revolution would have all the advantages at the start, it must not be forgotten that the revolutionists would include great numbers of men who have been thoroughly trained not only in methods of use [of these techniques], but in ruthlessness of use. And the worst of it is that they might think that their greatest chance of success would be dependent on the extreme of ruthlessness at the very start.

We cannot here rely on any meekness or mildness in American character. Not to refer again to the effects of war experience, we have had only too many riots and lynchings to indicate what excesses our American-born people are capable of; and our hard-

---

* Sentenced to death in February, 1917, for alleged involvement in a bomb explosion at a Preparedness Day parade in San Francisco in July, 1916, President Wilson commuted the sentence to life-imprisonment. Mooney was eventually pardoned and released from jail in 1939.

boiled prison camps and our treatment of conscientious objectors [during World War I] point the same way. Nor would the prospect appear any better in the event of possible success of a revolutionary movement of this kind. Whatever good resolutions may have been made by this leader or by that leader, it is only too common an experience in such matters that the good resolutions disappear; or, if they do not, that the makers of the good resolutions themselves disappear, and that ruthlessness modelled on the old official patterns, but more extreme in application, comes into the saddle.

Here now are the conditions out of which the future will create itself, subject to the various factors of information and force:

1. A quarter of the working population, comprising a third (at least) of all wage-earners, with incomes below what is known to be necessary for the maintenance of healthful family efficiency.

2. Those people, not so low as to be sodden or hopeless, but possessing sources of information that keep them informed as to their relative position under the present industrial organization.

3. Wage scales which, for the present at least, and excepting certain specially strong and favored working groups, have not kept up with the advancing cost of living.

4. Income possibilities, resting on fortified strategic positions in production and trade, increasing rapidly,

a) In land ownership where the capitalized values, though showing a very strong upward trend, do not show any such concentration of titles as to shut the door of opportunity to men who can get far enough ahead to take advantage of them;

b) In organized industry where there is an even greater increase in position values, combined with a centralized control that is ever more strongly marked in power.

5. Enormous increases in claims upon the national product of the future, showing itself especially,

a) In the capitalizations of the great war-profiteering corporations with their tripled dividends and surplus increments, which not only add directly to their capital, but permit, if they can be maintained, new high levels of manipulated capitalization;

b) In government war debts.

6. Systematic depression of production by the masters for profiteering purposes.

7. Systematic sabotage by the workers, similarly depressing production, and producing higher costs of living.

8. The growing wastes of the trading system, indicated by rising costs and higher rates of mark-up, again involving decreased production and increases in the cost of living.

9. And finally, we may add, outside our own land: threatening bankruptcy, both of European governments as such and of European industry generally, with which we will be certainly involved to the extent of the heaviest of shocks—not merely because of our present interrelations, but because the holders of our large surpluses for investment are looking abroad and cannot help looking abroad for fresh fields and for fresh profits, which they cannot possibly secure without taking the risks of involving us all more deeply than ever in European political affairs.

These facts stand, not as an argument of the possibility of revolution today, but as an evidence that when the shock comes, arising out of the enormously excessive claims in the future upon the possible limit of product, all the conditions exist to turn us from mere crisis of business under its old plan of organization into revolution which shatters that plan of organization itself.

Now, the attitude of the revolutionist among wage-earners is not fundamentally so different from the attitude of the successful capitalist appropriator, or from that of the more successful of the trade-union appropriators, those of the [Samuel] Gompers [AFL] leadership. All three of them see a product as "there" in front of them and seek to appropriate it. The capitalist, to use . . . labor's manner of speech, has traditionally seen the labor supply as something existing on hand, ready for his purposes, and he has appropriated all of its product except the minimum he was compelled to return to it. The appropriative trade union of the stronger type has seen the product in terms of dollars in the hands of the capitalist, and has got of it, step by step, as much as its power would [allow], as notably instanced by the railroad unions in our war [World War I] emergency. The revolutionary wage-earner now similarly starts out for [his] opportunities, but in contrast to the methods of the others, he starts out to appropriate the whole thing, all at once, if he can [only] get it.

The trouble with the revolutionary element in proletariat leadership is not that it is different from the old organization, but too much that it is fundamentally the same thing. The wage-earner, divorced from personal ownership of his own instruments of production, regards all production and industry from the point of view of the divorce. He regards himself as a man out to get something, not as a man with a tool in his hand out to produce something. This is far from blaming or criticizing him for that point of view. He is only following his most successful examples, his most orthodox and most solidly established examples.

Yet the fact remains that the nation at work is simply the mass of men with tools in their hands. This is true, no matter whether labor is looked upon as a commodity, no matter to what extent or whether the tools are protected by law in private ownership of men other than the laborer. The real thing, the fundamental fact, is the man with the tool. The real industrial nation is all the men with all of their tools. It seems a banality to say it, and yet none of the opposed elements actually like to look at it that way in practice.

And so the danger of proletarian revolution, the very thing that makes it revolution in the feared sense of the term, is this segregated position as wage-receivers rather than as equipped producers, into which so large a proportion of our workers have been driven by our system of organization. It is that which carries with it the possibility, not merely of reorganization, not merely of some slight title rearrangement, but of radical destructiveness if the issue is forced to a finish upon such lines.

We must not be deceived by the temporary reactionary temper of the American Federation of Labor. That is the expression of a typical [political] "machine" in full power over its rank-and-file; and as such, no matter how significant it is for today, it is no evidence of what the temper of the rank-and-file will be a year, or two years, hence. More significant is the trend towards syndicalism in one or the other form in other nations. In Canada, the splitting away of the trade unions from our American Federation of Labor, and the formation of The One Big Union, sympathetic in many respects with our IWW or, better, with what our IWW would be if it was less of an outcast in feeling and in treatment, seems well advanced. In Seattle during the [mass] strikes [of February 1919] there was a considerable fusion of trade-union members with the

IWW, as evidenced by the men who carried cards in both organizations. [More than four million workers were on strike in 1919, from one end of the United States to the other.] The situation [the conditions making for revolution] even in the strongholds of trade unionism, has the possibilities of kaleidoscopic change, of sudden crystallization, into a very different form. [The Bolshevik Revolution of October, 1917, was an epoch-making example of a swift seizure of power that stimulated some discontented groups in other countries, e.g., Hungary, to similar action.]

Nor may we permit ourselves to be misled in our attitude by any attack on all property from the side of the proletariat revolutionists, or by any apotheosis of property from the side of the great [business] appropriators. The property of which the masters of industry so loudly sing the praises is not the common goods and tools and securities of daily life, but their power of appropriating to themselves the nation's income of the future. The property which the proletariat leaders really attack is also this power of appropriation. Confused thought and confused use of terms on the latter side is no worse, no more dangerous, than deliberate mystification by the same confusion of terms on the former side. It is for the man in the middle not to permit himself to be misled, not to permit himself to be made the victim of either side.

Notes

1. Frank A. Vanderlip, *What Happened to Europe,* pp. 34, 155.
2. The highest Socialist vote thus far in this country has been 900,000; but that is no criterion, owing to the many non-socialists who in that year [1920] sought a form of protest against both parties.
3. The Seattle mayoralty election [of] February, 1920, where the most radical issue ever fought out in American politics appeared, showed a 40 per cent vote for the Radical candidate; this number being about 36 per cent of the entire registration.
4. How little we need be alarmed about them will be evident from their insignificance even in revolutionary Russia [of 1917–20].
5. See John Spargo, *Social Democracy Explained* (New York and London: Harper & Brothers, 1918), p. 48.
6. See Butler's address, "Is America Worth Saving—Republic or Socialistic Autocracy?" before the Commercial Club of Cincinnati, April 19, 1919, reprinted in *Is America Worth Saving?* (New York: Scribner's, 1920), pp. 1–25.
7. This group appears in two branches: the Communist Party of America,

representing largely foreign nationalities; and the Communist Labor Party, the extreme left of the American-born Socialists. These two groups held conventions in Chicago for organization purposes in September, 1919, concurrently with the convention of the Orthodox Socialists. [Cf., Donald Drew Egbert and Stow Persons, eds., *Socialism and American Life*, 2 vols. (Princeton: Princeton University Press, 1952), Vol. I, pp. 318ff.]

8. See W. Jett Lauck and Edgar Sydenstricker, *Conditions of Labor in American Industries* (New York and London: Funk & Wagnalls Co., 1917), pp. 12, 18ff.

9. [Unsigned article] Ralph M. Easley [editor], *National Civic Federation Review*, Vol. V (January, 1920), p. 10.

10. . . . [See] Paul F. Brissenden, *The I. W. W., A Study of American Syndicalism* (New York: Columbia University, 1919, reprinted, New York: Russell & Russell, 1957).

11. See Chapter II [and U.S. Bureau of Census, *Historical Statistics of the United States, Colonial Time to 1957* (Washington, D.C.: Government Printing Office, 1960), pp. 74ff.]

XVII

A Middle-Class Counter-Revolution

Although socialism has now proved itself with rivers of blood and suffering to be an economic and spiritual fallacy and to have wrecked itself on the rock of production, I believe it was necessary for the world to have had this demonstration. It is not necessary, however, that we of the United States, now that we have witnessed these results, should plunge our own population into these miseries and into a laboratory for experiment in foreign social diseases.

The paramount business of every American today is this business of finding a solution to these issues, but this solution must be found by Americans in a practical American way, based upon American ideas, on American philosophy of life. A definite American substitute is needed for these disintegrating theories of Europe. It must be founded on our national instincts and upon the normal development of our national institutions.

Herbert Hoover.   Address at New York City,
September 16, 1919.

We have been speaking of revolution with some of the overtones of horror with which King George III thought of his Americans, or with which the Russian aristocracy thinks of its Lenin and its proletariat. We should, nevertheless, remember that some revolutions are eminently respectable in the minds of their successful beneficiaries and their descendants, and that one at least, our own, was presided over by perhaps the most austerely minded and Olympian figure in the world's political history.[1] We should remember further that not all revolutions are bloody and spectacular, but that some are slow and insidious. Not all are risings of the masses against power, but some are seizures of power from the masses. Revolu-
184

tions may have their counter-revolutions, and these again may be reactions against slow, insidious seizures or against violent convulsions.

If we of America are to avoid convulsive revolution—if we are to avoid the final bloody issue of a cleavage between labor and its masters; if we are to find that "definite American substitute" for such a bloody issue, which Herbert Hoover hopes—we must put our knife to the roots of the trouble. The day for triflings and palliatives has passed. It is the middle classes who alone can find this substitute, who alone can go to the roots of the trouble—the middle classes, illuminated as to where they themselves stand, as to how their own interests are at stake. Far as it is from a certainty that they will so act, there is just as certainly a hope.

Will such radical middle-class intervention be revolution or counter-revolution? The answer depends on how one envisages the facts of the time. If one takes blindly the conditions [the economic and political power-structures] as they now exist, attributing to them full desirability and permanence, and falls into horrors over any prospect of change, intervention will be revolution. If one judges the facts of the time by the conditions of even one generation ago [from] which they have sprung; if one makes those conditions of a generation ago—or something corresponding to them under the industrial organization and technology of today—his standard and test, then our existing concentrated control of industry is itself the [product and agency of] revolution, and the restorative intervention will be not revolutionary but counter-revolutionary.

Let us take as a standpoint a nation with a functioning representative government: [all] its citizens showing some practical participation in its control, [all] its workers having . . . opportunity to direct or control or own some individualized part of its industry; a society of laissez faire, of competition and the benefits of competition, and of individual freedom. Such a society would be a political democracy, and while not an industrial democracy in a consciously developed or organized form, it would at least assume tacitly the makings of industrial democracy. It is just such a society as we [Americans] had, or assumed we had, or at least assumed we were building, through almost the whole course of the nineteenth century. It is the type of society from which many people today evolve standards which they believe apply, or can be made to apply, to our present and coming national life.

Without mincing words, I think we can positively assert that from such . . . a standpoint, the facts of today show that we are already far advanced in revolution. And, further, that that revolution is not a peaceable one but one of force, of compulsion, even though the exercise of force has been not in huge spectacular forms but in the cumulative effect of detailed oppressions; some of man against man or of corporation against corporation, some of corporation against local government, and some under cover of, or by protection of legal forms. In short, our industrial government (as it has been described in Chapter III, as it has been studied in following chapters in its various strategic strongholds on the highways, and with its technique of confiscations and persecutions) is itself a revolution. It is a revolution not fully perfected; one keeping its central powers as well under cover as practicable. It is a revolution which at this time shows no tendency to dissipate itself, but rather to concentrate and perpetuate itself.

Middle-class intervention, no matter how radical, must then be regarded more as counter-revolution than as revolution. Barring its intervention, this concentrated direct control of industry [by the controllers of the giant corporations] and this related control of political government may, we may well believe, show a future development dependent in form on the strength of certain factors which already can clearly be described. Its masters will undoubtedly prefer the substance of power to the appearance. They will gladly let the representative political institutions stand as long as they can utilize them in their most important needs.

But suppose the revolutionary organizations of, the class-conscious proletariat steadily increase in strength till they form a standing menace to this control. Suppose the middle-class citizens, those of mixed interests, remain confused in mind and inactive in politics; indifferent to what happens through despair of effective intervention against such great forces and powers. Suppose the foreign trade and finance complications of the great investors and promoters [of business enterprise in the United States] become acute; [then] it may well be that these great investors and promoters will ultimately find it necessary to control the political government as directly as they now control the industrial government, and that they will substitute some form of political autocracy [or oligarchy] for the government we now have. This is not . . . [outside] the possibilities, no matter what we [Americans] may boast of our love of freedom and self-government. Englishmen have at times submitted themselves to arbitrary powers [e.g., under Cromwell]. Romans, despite all their developed popular government [under the Roman Republic], spent later centuries under a strong empire. We ourselves, under certain conditions, may surely surrender the appearance of freedom as readily as we have already, in many respects, surrendered the substance. I am far from predicting anything of this kind, but it is certainly among the possibilities.

Should such an autocratic development in the political field result in a flat conflict with opposed proletarian forces, the issue would be indeed doubtful. The brutal possibilities of [military] force, the catastrophic elements involved, have already been considered. But there is another type of control by which it might conceivably maintain itself, a policy of bread and . . . circuses; a Machiavellian mixture of force, of cunning, and of bribery. By an autocratic reduction of some of the wastes [necessary] to the protection of others, by a heavy levying of commercial tributes abroad (if indeed such continue to be possible), by a "benevolent" maintenance of a certain standard of comfort, a tempered use of force against rebellious spirits might long maintain a balance. Yet even today [1920], the persecutions of speech and thought which accompanied and followed the war have possibly stirred more people to definite plans of radical reform than anything else in our recent history. The ferment of [the] high cost of living may be expected to bite deeper [into the lives of the majority of people] but it has not yet as positively rallied its ranks. How the elements of power and resistance might arrange themselves no man can say, except that in the course of time they might well run the whole gamut of political experience [from right-wing to left-wing dictatorship].

Facing on one side the tendencies towards [Big Business] autocracy, and on the other the possibilities of proletarian revolution, is it possible to avoid them both by palliative measures of the kind with which we have dabbled in the past? [By] measures which would rub out some of the worst abuses here and there and temper some of the evil effects, without changing essential conditions or essential lines of development? The answer is, emphatically: No. There is hardly need of argument. The history of our railroad legislation suffices. We got rid of a mass of evils: injustices as between cities, as between trades, as between individual enterprises. We handled the general level of rates. But we did not attack the underlying appropriative purposes [of the major railroad-system promoters and controllers]. We merely limited certain of their opportunities and drove them to new methods. And the result of it all was that the railroads were hampered in service, they were incompetent to give us our necessary war transportation; we had to take them under provisional [national] government control, and we are left [in 1920] with the most serious problems of this industry in more acute form than ever before. Similarly, we have regulated our municipal utilities, but we are still suffering under colossal wastes in their administration, while at the same time they are three-quarters bankrupt. We have tried again and again to regulate the meat industry, and each time the masters of that industry have found new tools and new techniques as profitable for their purposes as what has been taken from them.

If the above exposition is even approximately true to the facts, if we [middle-class Americans] are at all in peril of class-conscious revolution of a destructive type on the one side; if we are at all in peril of [a] political autocracy [being] added to industrial autocracy on the other; if palliative pottering for thirty years has not in the slightest degree softened the sharpness of our approach to these possibilities; what then is the answer? Is it pessimism? Not at all. Middle-class intervention, we may repeat, far as it is from certain, is as certainly possible here.

We have, it is true, the most ignorant middle class in the world; but at the same time it is the most intelligent middle class. It is ignorant because the facts are hidden from it, not because it cannot comprehend and use the facts when it gets them. Its source of supply [of accurate information] in the dailies and weeklies and in the periodicals [of the United States] has become corrupted and biased to a degree that will be remembered in world history as among the worst of all developments of obscurantism. The great journals and periodicals are highly profitable, and [their owners] are of course dominated by motives of profit. They are knit up with all the great agencies of profit by advertising; at once the agencies of profit for the advertiser, and the direct source of profit to the publisher, and therefore the controlling influence on all news and editorial matter. In the era of profiteering, all of our sources of information beat heart-to-heart with the powers of profiteering. And if the suffering subscribers clamor for relief from the abuses of self-winding gas meters and un-illuminating gas, and from all the other varieties of [the] high cost of living (so that newspapers or magazine columns are filled with sensational copy touching on such troubles), it nevertheless remains true that all this is but the herring dragged across the trail, and that for our real enlightenment we must search in corners of financial and commercial pages and in obscure paragraphs dropped in by mistake, perhaps, in the rush of late hours before printing.[2]

Given its information, given knowledge of the digested and verified and well analyzed facts that have been accumulated by the government agencies (the Industrial Commissions, the [Federal] Trade Commission, the old Bureau of Corporations, the Internal Revenue Commission, the Department of Labor, the Department of Agriculture, and many Congressional committees), the middle class will be able to act. But if it does act, it cannot act through palliatives; it must act through a counter-revolution of its own—a middle-class reconstruction. One that is deliberate[ly] thought through; one that strikes through the superficial appearances of equity to the substantial underlying equities; one that avoids destruction and violence of whatsoever nature; one that is radical, not in attacking or destroying or assailing, but in searching out the heart of the trouble, and in guiding every step, slow or fast, so as best to reach that heart. The steps need not be radical, but the purpose—the direction of progress—inevitably must be radical if the end is to be attained.

This book is, in its way, an attempt to find the heart of the trouble as it may be seen by middle-class eyes. Its argument deals with [these problems:] the nature of mastery in our organized industrial society; the way in which that mastery is built up and utilized; the relation of the masters to the makers and users; the appropriative powers that are built upon the basis of property; the strategic positions that have been developed and occupied upon the highways of communication and intercourse and trade between man and man; the wastes that result, the larger part of them as the costs of [such Big Business] mastery, the smaller part of them as the misused rewards of [such] mastery; the throttling of production that results; the national losses of comforts and of life that result; the perils of violence from and to the masses of the people that result; the threat to all our organized producing and social living that results.

Middle-class eyes [do] not belong to some abstract man afloat in the universe, nor to some suffering man crushed by the universe, nor to some relentless man dominating his fellows at the call of his factions of power or of wealth. They belong to the man working in the world with his tools in his hand, playing the game with his fellows, adventuring his full[est] within the rules of the game, taking his ups and downs as skill and chance may give; but always a member of the great organization of makers and users, with some approach to sureness and safety and equality as a man among men.

The middle-class man is himself a maker of profits (corrupted, often, it is true, into a profiteer), but he is not the systematizer of appropriative powers, nor one of the great beneficiaries of such powers. And, however much he has become a retainer of the profiteering system, with minor profiteering values of his own, he is in perilous state in that capacity. He is the survival of the old era in which everybody was supposed to be like him or capable of becoming like him. He is not split off on the one side into the ranks of those forced to sell themselves and their product outright for a price, nor into the ranks of those others whose takings have been huge and whose taking powers remain huge or are becoming huger, whether through vested interests or through active profiteering.

The essential fact about the middle-class man, for the political purposes of the immediate future, is that his interests as a consumer have become superior to his interests as a producer or appropriator. It is these interests at which he must now begin to take a square look, and which will demand from him ever-increasing concentration of attention. It is the imperiling of these interests which will enable him to widen his political affiliations upwards and downwards as the scale of threatened income . . . [grows]; and outward, too, among the ranks of those who heretofore have thought of their interests as primarily those of producers. For example, the farmers are commencing ever more clearly to see that the high prices they pay are affecting their welfare as much as the large prices that are paid [to] them, and that it is the wastes of the present organization of industry that are robbing them of their earnings.

With farmers tending to emphasize their interests as consumers, with the tradesmen and clerks for the most part being given a harsh introduction to reality by high prices, with all persons of small fixed incomes clamorously helpless in the situation in which they find themselves, we may see the extension of this middle-class group as a political force into the higher level of fixed incomes; till we get to a point where spending power is great enough to make the price changes negligible. Certainly, it should extend to the level of family incomes of $5,000 as matters stand today; and, probably, we may safely add, to the level of family incomes of $10,000. We may see the same kind of extension of interest among the ranks of better paid wage-earners. Indeed, we have actually seen it in the [summer of 1919] demand of the railroad labor organizations to the President . . . that [the] cost of living be reduced, or wages raised; preferably the former. We may see it reach all the wage-earners who have reasonably adequate incomes, except those who by the existing system have been so violently thrown—in emotion and argument—into their detached outer world of the "proletariat" that they can see no way back except by appropriating, in their turn and comprehensively, what they have come to believe has been taken from them and from their class alone.

Our people are frequently exhorted to "produce more."[3] It is a most excellent and needed exhortation, but perfectly futile unless the producer can be assured of getting what he produces. They are exhorted to "save more." Again futile, unless they can be assured of being able to keep what they save. But when the vicious circles of prices and values under the exploitation of the great appropriators takes away from the consumers by indirect action (where it has not already taken it by direct action), most of what they get or save, and when the nature of the loss (if not its full technical process) is more clearly revealed by [the] very development [of such losses] in industry and trade, such an assurance of reward cannot be given with even a semblance of plausibility. It can only be on the basis of a full understanding [and elimination] of the existing wastes [and their deeper sources] that these exhortations to produce more and to save more can be made to produce results. . . .

But if the elimination of the wastes that have been described is to be the central work of the middle classes, then the radical nature of their work is apparent, as is the fact that it can be nothing less than a revolution that they are called upon to carry through—an aggressive but constructive and productive revolution, a peaceful political revolution—the cure for destructive or throttling revolutions from other quarters. Such a revolution must be aimed directly at the appropriative uses of property and at the powers that have grown out of such uses. It must be planned to give freer play to the productive uses of property in the hands of all of the people. It must be a revolution of property against [those with exploitative] powers over property. It must be a revolution that replaces, or, better said, that completes political democracy with industrial democracy.

To political democracy, which sets free the man as a person and gives him a reasonable measure of personal participation in the nation's political affairs, it must add industrial democracy, which sets free the man with his tools (the man with his working capital and supply of goods to maintain life) and gives him a reasonable power of productive control over them (himself and his equipment) in the nation's industrial life. In such a revolution the reality—income—not the symbol—wealth—must be kept to the fore.

To rally a force in this cause, it is clear that many a man would be compelled to surrender something of the power he now has—the power, where skill or chance makes the opening, to get "easy money;" the power to pick up some especially pleasant perquisite for himself. It can readily be said that men will not do this. But is not this very process the one which has been . . . [followed] by men in establishing all the safeguards they now enjoy in organized society? The members of a gang of bandits abandon their powers of preying on each other. In establishing a law against burglary or forgery, the men who establish it surrender many possibilities of easy acquisition, calculating that they are thus better off in the end. Predatory outrage, even without [outside] the statutory law, is [likely] to bring vengeance by mob or personal action. And in the same way, the present appropriative system is building up against itself a day of vengeance, which is vastly more dangerous than anything the worst of burglars or swindlers have to fear.

And so, we come again to the proposition that it is the deeper [economic and political] interests [of men] that must win over the lesser ones. And if the interests of men as consumers, imperiled by wastes, are knit together, the stage may easily be reached when the [middle-class and skilled-labor group] consumers will abandon some of their private powers of appropriation, because those very powers in the hands of the strongest appropriators [of big business and high finance] have been elaborated until they overshadow all our other [middle-class and skilled-labor class] interests.

Notes

1. "The right of revolution . . . [is] sacred and must not be interfered with" —President Wilson's statement of the attitude of every man at the [Versailles] peace conference table, in his address at [the Hotel Statler] St. Louis, September 5, 1919. [*New York Times*, September 6, 1919.] On George Washington and his policies, see the press report of an address by Professor Albert Bushnell Hart of Harvard University before the City Club of Chicago [*New York Times*, March 9, 1919].

2. Council of National Defense in . . . *An Analysis of the High Cost of Living Problem*, already discussed, made five recommendations, paragraphed and numbered. No. 2 was: "Some readjustment of income to the basis of higher price levels." Several newspapers [we] examined, agreed in mentioning four recommendations, omitting No. 2 altogether. This is a typical illustration, pointing apparently to the method of corruption of our information at its source.

The [1919–20] strike problem, it may be said, was especially prominent, and the would-be strikers were presumably especially in need of the editorial wet-blanket at that date. Another interesting illustration, one of the kind in which the pot calls the kettle black with great perspicuity, is to be found in an editorial in the *Chicago Tribune*, February 17, 1920, entitled "Perhaps Literary, but No Digest." Since the issue of news-perversion had to do with military preparedness, and not with industry or business questions, the *Tribune* was able to wield a trenchant pen.

3. "Whether viewed from an economic or financial standpoint the remedy for the situation is the same, namely to work and save: to work regularly and efficiently in order to produce and distribute the largest volume possible of commodities: and to exercise reasonable economies, etc., etc." Federal Reserve Board, Letter. [Date not given; cf., *New York Times*, January 9, and March 30, 1920.] Robert Smillie, the British labor leader, is reported to have said: "We could produce enough in less than a six hour day, if we were not producing to make millionaires." [Source not given. Cf., *New York Times*, March 11, 1920.]

XVIII

Confiscations and Compensation

If middle-class revolution is to direct itself at the heart of the appropriative process, it will soon find itself face to face with certain questions of confiscation, and with all the problems of rights and equities involved in them. No matter how deliberately and gradually such a revolution may proceed, no matter how strictly it may hold to established political and constitutional forms, no matter how fully and completely it may wish to give compensation to all who either need or deserve it, these questions will arise. If compromise and mercy in practice combined with clear and determined thorough-ness in purpose is to be the method of procedure, then we must have as great clarity here as elsewhere. So far as this work is concerned, it will present no program of confiscations directed against persons, and no program of confiscation of property. Its purpose is the direct opposite; namely, the prevention of all such confiscations. Nevertheless, fictions of property come early to question in every impending measure of politics, and with them fictitious rights to exercise unlimited power on the industrial highways. Therefore, now is the time to face these issues squarely.

Such questions are before Congress today [1920] in a preliminary form in connection with legislation on the meat packing industry. The Big Five assert in substance that their strategic position on the highways of industry is part of their property, and they argue their right, as against Congress and the people, to continue to main-tain these positions by all the methods and with the use of all the instruments they have enjoyed in the past. Their stockyards proper-ties and their use of them, though not the most prominent in dis-cussion, are at least central in the issue. Can the government take them over? What compensation shall be given, and on what basis? What privileges for further appropriative use by the packers of the compensation funds shall be admitted? What aspect have these questions, when generalized and applied to the totality of instruments of highway control used by the Big Five? What aspect [have they] when generalized still further, and applied to all similar autocratic [oligopolistic] domination of industry essential to public welfare?

The way to analyze these questions is in terms of the very industrial system that has produced them, not in terms of some fiction of argument or premise flaunted as governing them. We shall attempt this shortly, but it is first necessary to get the background, the industrial atmosphere in which the questions arise; or, in other words, to examine the everyday securities and insecurities, the everyday confiscations in the property-owning and property-using world around us. The subject needs a volume, but it can be given only the briefest sketch.

Is it not the literal truth today that everybody has a free field to confiscate as much of everybody else's property as he wants to, providing he can present to the other person some plausible argument or inducement which will lead to some act of initiative or assent by which the other man's property will slip into his hands? Is it not the literal truth that, over and above these special individual acts, great processes are at work by which wholesale confiscations of private property are carried out; with a comparatively small number of people . . . in protected positions, reaping the benefits—reaping, not indeed full benefits commensurate to the losses, but reaping what benefits there are over and above the colossal wastes? Is there any other field except that of commercial banking proper, in which the customer, the consumer, is adequately protected without being forever on his guard; without being, indeed, forever aggressively on his guard?

The widow and the orphan are [defenseless] types; and the inexperienced, the reckless, the happy-go-lucky [men] are in as bad case; in worse, even, to the extent that no appeal . . . [to] chivalry or sympathy protects them. The Chicago Association of Commerce, following the Council of National Defense, has publicly declared that $500 million is taken from the public annually by the sale of [false] oil and mining stocks, and similar worthless securities. Fraudulent advertising is the great agency of this work, and to fight its effects the Chicago Association has established a strong bureau. But our central and western states are plastered with "blue-sky" laws directed against this evil, and all to no avail.* The swindlers build up staffs of twenty-five, fifty, even a hundred salesmen, whom they carefully train to keep within the letter of the law, and often delude as to what they are really doing. They buy ground, or get it as a gift; build, for example, an automobile-tire factory, turn out a tire or two, and when the stock sales cease, take their profits, and leave the wreckage to the "suckers." "Sucker lists" are available for purchase by new adventurers in this field.

The "blue-sky" laws have been of no avail, and will continue to be of no avail, for the very reason that under our developed appropriative system of industry, no one can surely weed out the sheep from the wolves in sheep's clothing until after the event, and the wolf of the past is entitled to claim that he is an honest sheep in the present. Everyone is entitled, both by law and by dogma, to appropriate all of the income of the country he can; he is not supposed to be entitled to appropriate the capital, but capital is risked for income, and true capital is all tangled up with capitalized claims to income; legal and illegal methods are too much alike at [base], and the wolf continues to prosper.

To go back to the widow and the orphan, their optimistic next friend may lead them to a foolish speculation, or their unscrupulous pretended friend may prepare a deliberate pitfall. It is all in the game. Even with estates in trust-company hands, it is [in 1920] only too common for funds to be needlessly invested and reinvested for the sake of the commissions; and such funds have often been used to enable the trustee companies to take their participations in promotions, and, still less creditably, to tide over [their companies during] bad periods in promotions.

A list of everyday property confiscations would start with those now under the criminal ban: the burglaries, the forgeries, the adul-

* As noted in an earlier chapter, pervasive federal controls—in many instances more stringent, and generally more effective than the "blue-sky laws"—were enacted in the 1930's. It is true that concern persists, especially about companies not listed on the major national or regional exchanges, but the present situation (late 1960's) is without question far healthier than the period from 1910 to 1920.

terations, the short-weighting devices, the rate and price discriminations. Next might come border-line activities such as those
previously mentioned, and with them the great land-development
swindles, shipwrecks from the start, and the many forms of subsidiary and supply corporations which [unscrupulous corporation
directors and] officials use to milk the properties they have in trust.
The story of the founding of the Great Northern Railroad and the
fate of the Dutch bond-holders could be told.* The use by officials
of inside corporation information on the speculative market for
their personal profit is not an occasional thing but an established
custom, a reason for existence on the part of many masters of
corporate industry.

Pass to ordinary commercial operations, stock-waterings,[1] and
Wall Street manipulations and grain market manipulations of the
type the government Food and Grain Administrations have condemned. Add what has been secured by corrupt control of the various agencies of government; the land-grant frauds, the power-site
frauds, the tax discriminations and tax frauds, the acquisition of
franchises for public utilities.[2] Is there anyone who has not had his
property confiscated through some one or other of these methods?
Think of the fate of [the] private property that went into early organizations and reorganizations of railroads and other enterprises.

But there is also another range of confiscations, equal or perhaps
even greater, which is the doing not so much of personal confiscators
as of the whole industrial process. An investor . . . in long-term
bonds—which he chose twenty years ago for safety, for reality of
property interest—has seen prices drop to a point which, in case
of a sale, would leave him income-less during the whole time of his
holding. Bona fide investors in what seemed to be some of the
safest securities of public utility corporations are now [in 1920]
standing where their losses will be heavy, unless the public volun-
tarily places itself under obligations as to rates which will be, in
effect, merely the assuming of their burdens. Above all, the possessor
of a fixed income from invested dollars has seen his purchasing
power cut in half by the price changes of the last four years [1916–
20].

* Cf., J. G. Pyle, *The Life of James J. Hill*, 2 vols. (Garden City: Doubleday,
1917).

Such is confiscation as we have it [in the pre-New Deal period].

Alongside of all these, the recorded confiscations by direct action of governments are slight in importance. In this country we have had two direct cases; in the emancipation of slaves during the Civil War, and in the suppression of the liquor traffic [through Prohibition]. To add to them [there] are the effects of greenback issues, in departing from the gold standard during and after the Civil War; and the inflation elements rising out of war [World War I] bond issues in the present; also, some may say, the effects of rate and price regulations . . . [on the earnings of] public utilities. Other countries [e.g., in Europe after World War I] have wiped out seignorial rights over land, and [therefore] the income-value of privilege of rank and title, without compensation.

This much is clear, that confiscation is not the simple thing that [American] industrial dogma pretends it is when applied to probable future conditions and to acts of government. And this further should also be clear: that confiscation of property is one thing; and confiscation of powers masquerading as property is a very different thing. The commanding elements of our situation now seem to be that all private property and income is daily imperiled by small private raiders and by great, strategically fortified raiders; that [many corporation] capitalizations purporting to be property have been built up largely on the basis of past raids and confiscations of these kinds, and continue to hold their values on the basis of the possibilities of their future confiscating power; that all such values are, as a matter of fact, subject to a heavy discount today from the threat of proletariat revolution which their very creation has raised against them; and, finally, that most of them are subject to further discount from the fact that they exist solely because the public has withheld its authoritative hand in the past, and that they can continue to exist only while that same authoritative hand continues to be withheld.

Supposing, as a matter of established public policy, it should be decided to concentrate all the life-insurance business of this country into one organization under public control; what compensation would properly be given to [J. P.] Morgan or his successors for the $3 million that he paid for [502 shares] of stock in the Equitable [Life Assurance Society, originally valued, *circa* 1859, at $51,000] in order to gain the control of the assets of the company for a promoter's purposes?* The law would [should] give him the $51,000 [although Thomas Fortune Ryan, the banker from whom be bought these stocks, had paid $2.5 million for them in 1905]. His [J. P. Morgan's] only claim against the country for more would be that, since it had let him do what it did, it ought to pay for it. The country might kindly yield in one single instance. It clearly could not yield, even apart from discussion of the profits already won, if the instance were typical of many, for to yield would mean ruin.

Take now the case of the Chicago Stock Yards. The stock of the present [Chicago Stock Yards Company of] Maine corporation is in the form of bearer warrants. It has been proved that 19.6 per cent belongs to Armour; and it is suspected, though not proved, that Swift and Morris have heavy interests in [its] bonds, if not in the common stock. Suppose it decided that [the] public interest requires these stockyards to be owned and operated by the nation so that all packers may have equal business facilities.[3] What of compensation to Armour, and Swift, and Morris?

If the country takes its cue from these packers—if, to acquire from them what they hold, it uses the same methods that they used to acquire their holdings from the others—there would be no compensation. The story is fully told in Part III of the Federal Trade Commission's *Report on the Meat Packing Industry*. In 1892, by threatening to remove their business to Tolleston, Indiana, the three packers [Armour, Swift, and Morris] secured a gift of $3 million in bonds from the stockyards company—a bribe to them to stay where they were. Other bonuses followed when the first 15-year agreement expired. In 1910–11 a similar threat was used. Just what Swift and Morris secured has not been proved, but upon the basis of a complicated process of reorganizations and manipulation, a new company was established; the one in which Armour got his 19.4 per cent interest. Only $1 million of new cash was invested, but a "plan of organization" was drafted which, as a mere scrap of paper with a few signatures, was turned in for $7 million; and the value of the "control and surplus usufruct" of this cheerful enter-

---

* For the complexities of this transaction and the background history, see N. B. S. Gras and Henrietta M. Larson, *Casebook in American Business History* (New York: Crofts, 1939), pp. 528ff.

prise was placed two years later at $50 million according to the Federal Trade Commission. In six years it had paid over $2 million in dividends, and had surplus accumulations on its books, or in sight, of more than $15 million. Minor investors in underlying companies were cajoled or frightened away, glad to get their pittance and leave the wealth to their masters. The whole industrial technique of cunning, misrepresentation, and threat was used in handling them.

Following the models set [for] it, the [national] government could very easily use its power over interstate commerce so as to take much of the confiscated [inflated] values [watered stock] out of this property, leaving the honest values [original purchase cost], and preventing such confiscations in the future. It could move the packing industry itself to Tolleston [Indiana] or somewhere else, if it saw fit. This would overlook the question of compensation, just as the present titleholders overlooked it when they appropriated their titles.[4]

But now suppose the [national] government should shut its eyes to the precedents offered by the companies in the premises, and should say to them: "You have these dollar titles; we must take over the Yards and administer them for the public; but we are going to compensate you dollar for dollar." It would, of course, be placing upon the citizens burdens in dollar measure equivalent to the value of those it wiped out. It would indeed be burdening them [the citizens] twofold; once to pay the compensation, and again to undergo the sufferings which would be inflicted upon them by whatever new use of their cash these same gentlemen would decide upon. It would only be reasonable, therefore, for the government to add: "While we are going to pay you in full, we are going to attach a string to the payment; we are going to forbid your making any other appropriative investment with the proceeds on any part or parcel of the national highways of trade and industry."

What then would the gentlemen have for their compensation? A Barmecide's Feast. They could not invest the funds productively under their own directions, for they have too many enterprises in their hands already . . . [to which] they do not now give productive attention. No more could they personally spend the money in any way that would heighten their welfare or their desired measure of ostentation or exclusiveness. They have more income than they can spend in those ways already. It would seem that, under such a condition, compensation would merely mean investment in government bonds, coupon-clipping, and reinvestment in more bonds without end. In other words, in such a case the question of compensation would have perhaps academic importance, but certainly no practical importance; for no one outside of a lunatic asylum could long retain much real interest in such bond and coupon operations if there was never any question of spending the money or controlling its business application.*

Let us generalize this illustration. Let us assume that society decides to take into its control all of the great strategic positions on the highways, now tending towards centralization in [a] few hands, as rapidly as their public-utility characteristics manifest themselves. Suppose it lets men produce independently, and lets them use their capital under their own direction to produce, but takes into its own hands the ultimate control of output and prices—the so-called "financial function" of the corporations. Suppose it not only ends the present abuses, but takes definite precautions against [the appearance of] new ones of the same kind. . . . Is it not apparent that compensation might be given the present possessors in whatever dollar valuation they might choose to ask, no matter how high, and yet it would be a meaningless fiction to them? If they could not consume for lack of physical needs, if they could not reinvest productively for lack of capacity to stretch their time and attention further, if they were forbidden to invest appropriatively, their nine-figure or ten-figure or possibly eleven-figure dollar wealth would be nothing but a tinsel crown. Should they turn to investing in lands, they would so quickly absorb its titles and end its present limited quantum of free opportunity as to cause the nation to treat land also as a prohibited investment to them. Should they invest in government bonds, the rate of interest would quickly be forced down to the infinitesimal.†

* It is not clear why Bentley asserts that compensation paid to appropriators, with the restriction that it not be put back into appropriative investments, will be only of academic importance, even if the new investments would be only in government bonds or some other economically "powerless" area.
† It is not possible to say without qualification whether the moving of all compensation funds into the government bond markets would have drastic effects.

Thus, treating compensation as a matter of property rights rather than personal rights, and generalizing our cases, we find: first, that if society should do unto the appropriators as they have done unto others, there would be no need of paying compensation; and second, that if it should pay dollar compensation with regardless [heedless] liberality, accompanying it only with restrictions against further abuse, that compensation would quickly become a museum curiosity rather than a fact of real life.

But the real problem of compensation is not a problem of property, however much the shortsighted appropriators would at present like to treat it as such. The true ethical problem has to do with persons rather than with property. Middle-class revolution would certainly make it its rule (and in this, it would be in sharp contrast with convulsive, proletarian revolution) that no injustice should be done to individuals, either as regards their opportunities as producers or as regards their requirements as consumers. It would be inclined to stretch itself to the limit in protecting all rights that have genuine personal meaning and importance.

Consider the railroad stockholders. There are six hundred thousand of these, not to mention several million other people with small interests carried indirectly through savings banks and insurance companies. Their interests reach to something over half of the total value, and are directly convertible into terms of individual welfare in a way that the interests of the few thousand holders of the other half of the stock are not. Or take the United States Steel Corporation, with a thousand men holding almost three-quarters of the stock, while the other thirty-five thousand hold little over a quarter. Or take Armour and Company, in which one man holds 72 per cent of the common stock, with eight other members of his family holding the rest of it; but to whom there have been annexed of late a few thousand small holders of preferred shares, much as a Hun might send captive women and children into battle ahead of him to protect him. The two kinds of interest, in terms of persons rather than of property, are of very different nature and importance from the public viewpoint.

Since we are not considering these questions of confiscation and

---

In any case, interest rates presumably would not fall below some "floor," a level perhaps established by the cost of transactions in these bond markets.

compensation immediately and practically, but in the long range by way of thorough analysis, let us assume . . . that at some later stage of control the public decides that dollar compensation to property claims as such in the hands of the great appropriators is academic —a fiction, a joke—and that it will not bother with it, but will stand to the personal equities. The public then will clearly care to the full for these little people. Also, we may well believe, it will care to the full measure of real [earned?] personal position [acquisitions] for the greater [wealthier] people too—not on the level in dollars of the little people, but on their own personal property level, as opposed to their great appropriators' claims. Just as a possible supposition, it might protect all present incomes from the highways investments taken over, up to some figure like $5,000 or $10,000; it might say that of incomes of $50,000 or $100,000 it would protect a certain percentage, to a certain maximum; it might apply lesser percentages to still greater incomes, merely as a question of protecting the holders' acquired interests and habits as a consumer.

Beyond that—to the great appropriators who have productive capacity, or productive experience, or even who have a desire to develop it—society might readily allot them their holdings of plants and equipment, to whatever extent they might personally be able to administer [them], on a productive basis. It might be a matter of many millions. That would not matter, if the millions were productively used. One might speculate in various ways on the possibilities of personal equity as opposed to property equity, though the practical answer in the end would of course be some rough-and-ready standard, not any delicate unraveling of theories.

We have been arguing in the court of equity. Some disputant may, however, demand a change of venue to courts of law and morals. Any taking [of "property," or income, claims] by society, he may argue, is stealing; no matter how the present holder had acquired his title, or how he has developed or used it. We have already partly answered him in showing how the appropriative title, as it now exists, is subject always to the power of any stronger private appropriator to seize it; how, as in the Chicago Stock Yards case [discussed above], society could seize such a title without departing one step from the methods of its acquisition by its present holders; and how the very existence of these titles has always depended, and does now [in 1920] depend on the withholding by society of its authoritative hand. It remains to state more definitely these reserved and still valid powers of society resting in the government and in the people.

First is the power of taxation, and as Chief Justice Marshall has said, "The power to tax [involves] the power to destroy." A power which today [after the adoption of the Sixteenth Amendment in 1913] is constitutional in progressive taxation over both income and inheritance.

Next is the police power; [one] very specially developed by the United States in sanitation, in the control of public utilities, and in some of the flagrant minor trade abuses [defined as] "the power of the courts to interpret the concept property, and above all private property; and to establish its metes and bounds."⁵

Third is the power of potential public competition; the power of government or of citizens cooperatively to go into the field and give service of the kind they desire, even if, in the extreme case, they give it for less than cost and make up the deficit out of revenues from taxation. This power has its value despite the fact that, for the moment, with the present centralized appropriative strength [of Big Business], it is often little more effective than a goldfish in a school of sharks.

Fourth, we have the potentiality of the general strike by the Makers [the workers in the economy] and, finally, we have the potentiality of the general boycott by the Users [consumers].

The general strike may, indeed, be what [George] Sorel [the French syndicalist] has described it [as] (and the description is likewise true of the general boycott): a social myth, a wonderful dream, something rather in the nature of the millenium than of recorded or to-be-recorded history. But it has another quality than that. It is in its way a social sanction. It is the ultimate penalty of abuse. The general strike is the final appeal of the worker to his rights. And, by the same token, it is the justification of all lesser and more immediate appeals to these rights. Just so is the general boycott the final justification of all lesser and more immediate appeals by the consumer to his rights.

The most extreme dogma of the industrial government [Big Business] has never yet asserted that by nature's law we are bound to work for those who hold the title, and bound to consume what goods they may provide.[6] Industrial dogma has merely taken advantage of our long suffering, and assumed unexpressed its divine right in the premises. Yet without such natural law, such divine right, the titles and all their claims upon us are, and will remain, conditional upon our consent.

Under these sanctions, the middle classes can make forceful their present weak powers of potential competition; and [they] can extend the application of the police power. And, finally, with the power of taxation, they can trim the rough edges of the [wealth and income] structure, and give it such external adaptation to their needs as they may desire. Taxation, in so many periods of history the weapon of the appropriators, may become, if we will [so desire], the weapon against them in our future.*

The cause is the cause of property versus the [fictitious] claims [of appropriators] against property. The stake is the future income of the nation. With property itself but a trifling quantity measured in terms of our productive power, we have allowed the [unwarranted] claims against property to multiply and glorify themselves and assert their mastery over us. The remedy is in our own hands.

Notes

1. In comment on the conversion of [those] concerns capitalized at $10,500,000 into the $120,000,000 International Harvester Company by Morgan for a $3,000,000 commission, Justice Brandeis remarks that the early capitalizations were "strong evidence that in all the preceding years no investment banker had financed them." *Other Peoples' Money and How the Bankers Use It* (New York: The McClure Publications, 1913), p. 139.

2. A typical case is the Chicago gas supply, burdened permanently by the enterprises of the political Ogden Gas Co. [cf., Charles E. Merriam, *Chicago . . . Urban Politics* (New York: Macmillan, 1929)].

3. Written before the Palmer-Packer Compromise. [Acting after the appearance of the Federal Trade Commission Report, the U.S. Department of Justice attempted to prosecute the packers on grounds of likely monopoly. Although a federal grand jury failed to return indictments, these efforts resulted in a consent decree, concluded by the packers and Attorney General A. Mitchell Palmer (*U.S.A., petitioner,* v. *Swift and Company, et al.,* 37623 Equity, Washington: Government Printing Office, 1920). The decree provided, among other

* Cf., Sidney Ratner, *Taxation and Democracy in America* (Science Editions, New York: John Wiley and Sons, 1967).

things, that the major packers sell (a) all holdings in public stockyards; (b) all interests in stockyard railroads and terminals; and (c) all interests in market newspapers; to dispose of all interests in public cold-storage warehouses, except as necessary for their own products; and to disassociate themselves from such "unrelated lines" as wholesale groceries, fresh and canned fish, and other non-meat food products.] That the stockyards will really be divorced from the packers' control under the compromise is hardly to be assumed.

4. In [a detailed discussion] the problem of the Chicago Stock Yards, with its Maine and New Jersey and Illinois corporations, its three subsidiary railroad corporations, and its Central Manufacturing district property, would involve many questions of personal equities over and above the primary question of property equity above considered. These are not [considered in the text].

5. The definition is that of Professor Richard T. Ely, *Property and Contract in Their Relations to the Distribution of Wealth*, 2 vols. (New York: The Macmillan Company, 1914), Vol. 1, p. 206.

6. The obligation to work for the common welfare, whether in war or in peace, must not be confused with the obligation to work for other individuals.

XIX

Of Life and Liberty

Deeper than our interest in our property is our interest in the safeguarding of our liberty and in the free living of our lives. We do not indeed always feel this to be true. Liberty itself is concretely embodied in the winning and enjoyment of a competence. So long as we can earn and spend with reasonable equity, we feel that we possess the very substance of liberty. We take liberty for granted; we pay little attention to it as a special need in itself; and we leave its praises to the spread-eagle orator of Fourth of July while we laugh good-naturedly at his efforts.

But underneath there is grim reality. It is no frothing of words to proclaim that eternal vigilance is the price of liberty. Over and over in the history of the world has this been proved. Let some great appropriative power (founded on whatever instruments the technological development of the age may provide) get a foothold. This great power, as it develops, protects some of the lesser appropriators. It establishes its creed, and that creed identifies the protection it gives with liberty. It challenges all comers. But some day there is the awakening. Competence and liberty alike are gone. Then liberty indeed seems real in its own right, and the harsh struggle to regain it ensues.

Profiteering in the United States today, erected into a system, fortified at commanding positions on the highways, rapidly completing its centralizations of power, has its vehement creed. The "rights of property" and "law and order" are its sacred phrases; but by property it means its own profiteering; and by law and order it means its own established dominion; and, all the while, profiteering is destroying property; and the appeals to law and order, falsely and rapaciously used, are undermining liberty. We are at a critical point in this destructive development; critical, at least in the sense that now, at last clearly, the real meaning of the development opens to us, and that it is easier now to renew and re-establish our safeguards than it ever will be again.

The immediate issues are the issue of free speech, the issue of freedom of thought. If we lose . . . [these], we lose everything. We can lose only by our assent; and if we yield our assent, misled by whatever confusion of thought, whatever iniquity of propaganda, we shall become parties to a waste that out-tops all other wastes, to tyranny beyond all other tyrannies.

The great war has forced these issues, as it has forced the other issues of industry and politics, to more vivid realization. The espionage and sedition laws [of June 15, 1917, and May 16, 1918, respectively], in their practical enforcement, have shed a great light. It is indeed too early to decide how much of the war [World War I] hysteria in the enforcement will wear off, or how far its abuses will settle into habitual toleration among us. But it is not too early to recognize clearly what the tendency of these laws has been. The one flaming fact is that throughout, they have been used not so much against enemies of the political government—friends of Germany who did Germany's work in our land—as against enemies of the industrial [Big Business] government, who only incidentally and indirectly could be held to be harmfully affecting our war policies. The bitter proof is in the two-year sentences against enemy [Imperial German] agents, and the ten- and twenty-year sentences against [native American] industrial dissenters.

To trace even the outlines of the menace to thought and speech, and to all liberty, that has been developing in the last twenty years, and to show how it is not only the labor leader but every property-owning citizen who must be on his guard against it today, is hopeless within the limits of one chapter. The merest sketch in order to emphasize the danger, in order to locate it at its sources in the autocratic industrial government, must suffice.

The "privileges or immunities of citizens of the United States" as the Fourteenth Amendment to the Constitution describes them, are, for the most part, contained in the first six amendments, our "Bill of Rights," ratified by the states two years after the government under the Constitution was begun. They include freedom of speech and of the press; the right of peaceful assemblage; the right of security in persons, houses, papers, and effects; the right of trial by jury; and various other rights assuring fair treatment in the courts; and, under a later amendment [the Fourteenth], these privileges and immunities are all secured to us against aggression by the separate states as well as against [any by] the federal government. They are not mere matters of verbiage, no sop to the theorists, but hard-won possessions, the heritage of centuries of struggle.

We cannot hope to have a perfectly working government. We cannot hope that every citizen always will secure full and exact justice. We cannot hope that, practically, even his constitutional immunities will always be secured for him. We must expect occasional faults, occasional lapses. But we can hope, we can demand, that in the great averages these immunities shall be secured; above all, we can demand that no definite system for their overthrow exist, that there shall be no weakening of them as against the interests of one part of the people, and as in favor of the interests of another.

Before the war [World War I], in the thick of industrial conflicts there were such weakenings. Organized labor had its well-founded complaints of the use of the injunction against it. Its leaders found themselves punished as criminals under contempt proceedings, for acts committed outside of the presence of the judge, without the protection of a jury trial to which they were constitutionally entitled. Ruthlessly used, the [anti-labor] injunction could defeat them in their industrial contentions. In West Virginia in 1912, the writ of habeas corpus was suspended in direct violation of the constitution of the state. In Paterson, New Jersey, during the silk-workers' strike [of 1913] the right of peaceful assembly was most notoriously and continuously denied, and jury trials were refused. In Colorado, martial law was in effect ten times in twenty years to control industrial disputes; and in two counties in 1913, the Colorado Fuel and Iron Company substantially took over all local government into its own hands.[1] The maintenance of small standing armies by some corporations, with the permission of the state, has had at times much the same effect upon private rights. But despite all this abuse, and despite its many forms, we could still feel (unless, perhaps, indeed, we were closely identified with the party that was the victim of it) that the troubles were minor ones for the country as a whole, and that there was a solid strength in the Constitution and a solid, good sense among the people that would work out a restoration of all the rights that were violated and that seemed at times to be slipping away.

When this country entered into war, we had a situation in which different sections of the people varied greatly in their readiness for it. The central and prairie states were notably reluctant. Remote from the seaboard, remote from the commercial interests most immediately affected, they could easily convince themselves that it was not our war and that we could let it proceed without us. Similarly, there was industrial splitting. The administrators of business felt the compulsion much more urgently than did their workmen. Moreover, we had our pacifist groups, some religious, some humanitarian, some industrial (the last-named schooled in long argument that war was at bottom capitalistic and that it was for the internationalism of labor to save the world from its [capital's] grasp).

At the actual moment of the plunge, leaders in labor movements, leaders in farmers' movements, and leaders against profiteering (people whose thought was very closely centered on these problems), were a little in arrears in feeling that the true crisis was at hand. Their opponents jumped first, and even though their margin of aggressive loyalty might be only a matter of a week or a month, they capitalized [on] it to the full for their purposes. They identified themselves, including all their profiteering and autocratic elements, with the political government; and in substance they said: "Anyone who objects to our abuses is objecting with the same breath to all the good there is in the nation." Then, with the use of provocative agents, and with all the resources of political institutions (local, state and national, judicial and administrative) which they could control, they pushed their industrial fight. The espionage law [of June 1917] became their chief instrument.[2]

The most concrete illustration of this, the one on the largest scale, is that of the fight [against] the Non-Partisan League in Minnesota and the Dakotas, Colorado, Nebraska and other states.[3] The real race of loyalty was almost neck and neck, but the pretended issue of loyalty [to the United States during war], used as a cloak for political ruthlessness on an otherwise impossible scale, was kept steadily before the public; not only during the war, but after. At the 1916 elections the League had captured the government of North Dakota, root and branch, except for the holdover senators. In 1918 it seemed certain to complete its achievement and enter strongly other state governments as well. The stake was a big one, for the farmers' program proposed to eliminate, if it could, the profiteering of the millers, grain commission men, and bankers at Minneapolis that so injuriously affected them.[4]

Organization to fight the League was quickly enlarged. Mobs were equipped in almost every county seat of Minnesota and the Dakotas to drive out League representatives. Physical violence and destruction of property were common. Deaths directly resulted in some cases. Prosecutions under the state laws and under the federal espionage law came by the dozen. One old man, a veteran of the Civil War, was arrested and twice indicted for holding a political meeting with a few neighbors in his own yard, the charge against him being "failure to disperse" at the demand of the sheriff, just as though he were a riot himself. Former Governor John Lind of Minnesota, who resigned from the State Commission of Public Safety for reasons assumed to be connected with such abuses towards loyal citizens, defended this man. In another case, a soldier who had gone into the Army on the first draft after repeatedly trying to be accepted as a volunteer before that, was arrested on a charge of disloyalty when he came home on a furlough.

At the end of the war, the [Minnesota] Public Safety Board reported proudly that it had investigated 682 cases of sedition during the war and listed Non-Partisan League leaders as forming one of the three main classes of seditious persons with whom it had to deal. It failed to state, however, that not one of its League cases had finally held in the courts. A table prepared by League officials showed . . . only four federal cases and nineteen state indictments against it; with ten cases dismissed without trial, five jury acquittals, and eight pending cases.[5]

[Arthur C.] Townley, the chairman of the national executive committee of the League, with one of his associates, was finally brought to trial [under the Minnesota Espionage Act of 1917] in

July 1919, on a charge of teaching sedition in a county [Jackson County] in which he had never been, where League strength was at a minimum, and where all public officials were complaisant to [his] prosecution. He was denied the right to interpret the sentences of his speeches, complained of as criminal in the indictments, by producing their full context; he was denied the right to introduce most of his other writings and speeches; most of his witnesses were rejected; he was forbidden the right to address the jury in his own behalf after he had dismissed his counsel, so that the case went to decision without argument for the defense; and, finally, he was sentenced to jail without alternative of fine after a bitter arraignment by the judge. Disinterested witnesses of this trial unanimously report it [was] prejudiced and partisan to a degree almost incredible in a free government.

In the fall campaign of 1918, one-third of the counties of Minnesota were closed to League speakers by [state] administrative order. The governor of the state paid no attention to a joint petition from all League candidates begging for the right to address meetings. The League candidate for governor was himself arrested a few days before election, for trying to speak in behalf of his party in one of these counties. It is doubtful if Mexico [in 1918] could offer worse. [Nevertheless, the League candidate polled 111,948 votes against 166,515 votes for the Republican nominee. The League also elected 11 state senators and 26 members of the lower house.]

The way in which the espionage law is dangerous to liberty is not by any direct provisions, or by any direct applications of them, but by leaving the road wide open for interpretation by administrative officials and by judges as to what may conceivably, under any assumed circumstances, be the indirect effect of spoken or written words. These vicious characteristics became even worse in the several bills that were introduced into Congress after the [November, 1918] Armistice to replace the law that expires with the formal conclusion of peace. Officials who are themselves steeped in [Big Business] industrial dogma, consciously or unconsciously identifying profiteering with property and with government, have no difficulty in interpreting [labor, farmer, and small-business] industrial dissent as sedition; and their very prepossessions [preoccupations] hurl them into fearing the most frightful effects from any verbal attacks on their cherished confusions of thought.

Professor Zechariah Chafee, Jr., of the Law faculty of Harvard University has discussed this aspect of the espionage laws fully.[6] He shows that we already have legislation making criminal any scheme to overthrow the United States government, any levying of war against it, any conspiracy against it, and any conspiracy "to commit any offense against the United States." Such schemes and conspiracies are criminal even when unsuccessful. The courts have held that the federal government has full power to legislate for the special protection of the President and of judges and other officials. The government can also control to the last detail the sale and use of explosives.

Professor Chafee condemns the Espionage Act and the Overman Bill [providing punishment for advocating changes in the form of the United States government, encouraging disregard of the Constitution, and like acts] because "(1) they label opinions as objectionable and punish them for their own sake because of supposedly bad tendencies without any consideration of the probabilities of criminal acts; (2) they impose severe penalties for the advocacy of small offenses as much as for serious crimes; (3) they establish a practical censorship of the press *ex post facto*." Many writings of John Adams and Thomas Jefferson could no longer be published in this country under these laws without subjecting the publisher to criminal penalty. Books of the most theoretical nature on government would be in continual difficulty. One could not reprint anarchistic utterances [in order] to condemn them without committing a criminal offense. The anti-prohibitionist of enthusiastic utterance could hardly pass a day without liability to arrest.

Professor Ernst Freund, who has long been professor of jurisprudence and public law at the University of Chicago, has contrasted the crudities and dangers of our legislation with that of France and Germany.[7] France has found out through a hundred years [of] experience that it is not safe to punish speech or thought unless there is direct provocation to some definite and particular criminal act; and even then, if such provocation does not result in acts of crime, it only punishes it in connection with specific aggravated offenses. Germany's military imperialism went further with reference to incitement of military insubordination, but not nearly so far as we have gone. "The vagueness of definition that characterizes the espionage act," says Professor Freund, "finds, I believe, no parallel in modern foreign legislation."[8]

Return now to specific cases of abuse in this country in the interest of what we have called the [Big Business] industrial government, which is to say, of the established system of profiteering. We have no reliable figures of total convictions for all classes of offenders against the Espionage Act, the draft laws and other necessary war legislation; but the indications are that the vast majority of them were industrial [labor and farmer] dissenters. Except in the case of drafted men who were conscientious objectors, the pacifists and the religious objectors to war (as well as the selfishly short-sighted and ignorant objectors) came through with comparatively little trouble, save such as was made for them by the public opinion of their neighbors. It has been said that when the first group of offenders, numbering 52, were recommended for executive clemency, not a single one of them was of the industrial-dissenter type.

In this connection, we may pass over the [Eugene V.] Debs case, for while the zest of his prosecution was undoubtedly industrial, the zest in his defense was similar, and he joyously assumed full responsibility for all intent and purpose that anyone could desire to charge him with. But the [1918] trials of the five Socialists in Chicago, including Congressman [Victor L.] Berger [elected in November 1918 from the Fifth District of Wisconsin] were very different. Sympathy such as one may so readily feel for Debs' personality may be lacking entirely for these men; but it nevertheless remains true that they did show positively in certain cases that they had advised compliance with the draft act [Selective Service Act of May 18, 1917]; and it was not shown positively that any particular person was kept from military service by their attitude. The whole case against them was indirect, inferential; a matter not of probabilities but of possibilities, with their industrial [anti-capitalism] opinions the true storm center; and they were moderate Socialists, not [Communist] extremists, at that. And what were their penalties? Not the four years that [Karl] Liebknecht [Socialist and pacifist] got from military [Imperial] Germany in the midst of the war for a vastly more aggressive attitude, but twenty years apiece; and that four months after the [November 1918] Armistice had been signed.

Or take the case of the 112 IWW [members] sentenced in Chicago. Here we had not merely severe penalties, but the inclusion of the innocent with the constructively or inferentially guilty, and also the most arbitrary administrative interference with their efforts to defend themselves. Think of these property-less defendants trying to raise a defense fund by appeals for small subscriptions from the mass of their organization's membership; think of their mail being held in the Post Office, without notice to them and not being forwarded till after the trial was over; and then think of what the Constitution guarantees all of us in the way of impartial trials: ask then, if you will, whose turn may come next?[9]

In addition to the dangers of the law itself with respect to its possibilities of enforcement, we have witnessed a ruthlessness and, indeed, a ferocity of enforcement that greatly emphasizes the danger. Take the case of the five Russian boys and girls in New York, one beaten to death in jail, the others hurled [in]to prison for long terms by a judge who acted as though the fate of the world depended upon his violence [violation, savagery?] of court procedure. Take the case of [the noted Anarchists] Emma Goldman and Alexander Berkman—undoubtedly offenders—but their offices raided, their papers destroyed, their rights of counsel and fair trial swept away, because of what they wrote in an issue of their paper prepared before the law was passed under which they were sentenced. Take the case of the Socialist lecturer, Kate [Richards] O'Hare, who made the same [anti-war] address in a North Dakota town that she had made sixty or seventy times in the preceding year; but who paid a visit to the postmaster's wife in that town, which resulted in the postmaster's political enemies initiating her prosecution as a phase of their campaign to get him out of office. Judge Wade, in sentencing her to five years in prison, after hearsay evidence of her remarks which she denied and which did not correspond with the written text of her memorized speech, read with evident pleasure a letter from an agent of the Department of Justice who had written him: "We have been unable to obtain anything specific on her that would be a violation of the federal law. Nothing would please this office more than to hear that she got life."

Ferocities in the infliction of punishment have also been only too common. Alcatraz prison is getting a reputation comparable to the Spanish Inquisition. The fact that the Secretary of War [Newton

D. Baker] had to issue an order commanding that certain tortures cease is significant enough. Offenders of the kind we have been describing are political prisoners, if that term has any meaning whatever. And yet this country is so far below even the standard of Tsarist Russia in recognizing them as such, and in allowing them certain privileges over ordinary criminals, that it has gone to the other extreme and even seems to single them out for abuse.

To what the courts and jailers have done we must add a long list of administrative abuses, all motivated in the same way and having the same meaning; political on the surface, industrial [economic] underneath. Aliens, and even citizens who cannot prove their native birth, are subject to deportation because of their opinions—and this upon administrative decree—with the Commissioner of Immigration, or some assistant, sitting as prosecuting attorney, judge, court reporter, and executioner, all at once.[10]

The Postmaster General [Albert S. Burleson] has exercised unlimited powers of censorship and exclusion from the mails, often not tempered by a glimmering of intelligence.[11] An issue of *The Nation* [dated September 14, 1918] was excluded from the mails during the war because it spoke slightingly of Samuel Gompers.[12] A book of Thorstein Veblen's on Germany [*Imperial Germany and the Industrial Revolution*] written [in 1915] before the war, was excluded at the very time George Creel's Bureau of Public Information was recommending its use for patriotic educational purposes. Similarly, in Nebraska (though this [by] chance was overlooked by Mr. Burleson) a Non-Partisan League folder consisting exclusively of quotations from President Wilson's writing was barred from circulation by the State Council of Defense.[13]

The mayor of Toledo [Ohio] prohibits public meetings at which anyone of . . . radical tendencies is expected to speak. The chief of police of Philadelphia forbids any meeting at which any pamphlet is offered for sale written by a man convicted by court—that would include the words of Jesus, the writings of Thoreau, and *Pilgrim's Progress*. The burgesses of Pennsylvania towns in the steel districts unanimously forbid any meeting addressed by union labor organizers, and arrest their speakers.[14] In Bisbee, Arizona in [July] 1917, [1200] men, American citizens who were [IWW] strikers, were deported into the desert—shelterless, moneyless, wagonless, no matter what property they were forced to leave behind—much as the Turks drove out the Armenians. Finally, we come to the case of a Memphis editor who wrote an editorial comdemning boss rule, just as such boss rule has for decades been condemned by papers all over the land, though without any specific application to any particular case, and who was haled into court and sent to jail for contempt by a boss-loving judge. The Memphis editor [case] provides us a little middle-class snapper to the long and heavy labor whip.

The case of [Tom] Mooney, as set out in federal reports, is perhaps as bad as any in our history, though not involving the question of free speech. There was a vicious bomb explosion during a [preparedness-day] parade [in July, 1916] in San Francisco. Mooney was a labor leader hated by the industrial powers, and by their tools in office. He was on a roof watching the parade a mile and a quarter away. Opposite him was a street clock, and by chance a YMCA man on another roof took a photograph showing both Mooney and the clock with its hands pointing to the time. Mooney was indicted and charged with being in a taxi-cab from which the bomb was thrown. The prosecution secured the photograph first, and touched it up to obliterate the clock hands. [In February, 1917] Mooney was convicted and sentenced to hang. The only "credible" witness against him was later confronted with written proof of his perjury.[15] The trial judge appealed to the governor [of California] who alone could act to take steps granting a new trial. President Wilson, for war reasons, appealed twice. The governor finally commuted the sentence to life imprisonment. There Mooney stays [pardoned only in 1939], one of the strongest challenges to revolutionary violence this country contains, a challenger not in his own purposes, but by act of industrial [Big Business] government controlling political forms and overriding the Constitution.[16]

The connections between industrial dogma, between "direct action" on the part of the industrial [Big Business] government, and between the overriding of our constitutional privileges and immunities are only too clear.[17] A few more facts of scattered nature will exhibit them. The Rockefeller and Carnegie institutions [Foundations] have annual revenues twice as great as the appropriations of the federal government for social and educational purposes, which they administer without public control and which, it has been proved [as of 1916], they use at times for insidious propaganda; misrepresenting facts for the benefit of special interests.[18] The Commonwealth Fund, the administrator of which is [Professor] Max Farrand, is mysteriously used on a very large scale and, it is believed, solely for this purpose. The Big Five packers maintain a "joint fund" on regular-scaled percentages for purposes stated by the Federal Trade Commission[19] as being:

"To employ lobbyists and pay their unaudited expenses;

To influence legislative bodies;

To elect candidates who would wink at violations of law, and defeat those pledged to fair enforcements;

To control tax officials and hereby evade just taxation;

To secure modifications of governmental rules and regulations by devious and improper methods;

To bias public opinion by the control of editorial policy through advertising, loans and subsidies, and by the publication and distribution at large expense of false and misleading statements."

A university professor prepares a scientific study of taxation in Montana, at the direction of the university. Not by any radical purpose or program, but by mere statement of facts, this work displeases the copper-mining interests. When he insists on publishing it personally after the university has refused to publish it, he is discharged.[20] Justice [Louis D.] Brandeis of the [United States] Supreme Court, before his nomination [in January 1916, by President Wilson], fearlessly investigates and reveals the financial abuses of the New Haven Railroad, and publishes his positive views about the misuse by investment bankers of "Other People's Money"; his enemies, upon his judicial nomination, force two volumes of the most scurrilous charges upon a Senate investigating committee, leading, however, we may happily say [on June 1, 1916], to his most complete vindication.* The American Bar Association annually adopts [as of 1917–20] resolutions characterized by dogmatic ignorance in order to show that no industrial heresy [critical of capitalism] affects it.[21] A state investigating committee [Lusk

---

* Cf., Alpheus T. Mason, *Brandeis: A Free Man's Life* (New York: Viking Press, 1946), pp. 465–508.

Committee] in New York raids colleges and newspapers of a radical type and lies about the contents of papers it seized.

And so we come down the line to May Day Socialist parades, in which there is always disorder, and in which the disorder is usually started deliberately by enemies;[22] but with the public always hearing the stories the other way 'round, and believing them because of the great [mass-media] propaganda of selfish misinformation with which profiteering [business groups] has befogged us for its defense. We come to the "fake" bombs and bomb plots, so stupidly prepared by the *agents provocateurs* of industrial government that not even the most befuddled reader can believe in them if he reads the facts twice. We come [down] to some President [John Henry] Kirby of a National Lumbermen's [Lumber Manufacturers'] association, advocating a Ku Klux Klan of employers against laborers; or some Mayor Ole Hanson of Seattle, proclaiming over the land heroic resistance to violence following a [general] strike [early in 1919], which was most significant and indeed most ominous because of [the] very absence of violence.*

We come finally to the assault in the name of industrial dogma upon representative government itself; an assault in which unblushing bigotry makes open denial of the very agencies by which liberty and self-government are secured.† The case of [Victor L.] Berger, twice excluded [in 1919 and 1920] from Congress (the second time after an overwhelming re-election) is only slightly and disputatiously the case of a convict unwelcome to Congress. Essentially, it is the case of a congressional district [in Wisconsin] denied its right to represent itself in accordance with its own political views. The case of the [five] Socialist assemblymen in New York, they themselves, like Berger, members of the right wing of socialism—political socialists rather than revolutionaries—is frankly this, and nothing more. As representatives of a true political party, with political principles and political methods for realizing them, these Socialists [Claessens, Solomon, Waldman, DeWitt, and Orr] were hateful to the Janus-faced Republican-Democratic orga-

---

* Cf., Robert K. Murray, *Red Scare, A Study in National Hysteria, 1919–1920* (Minneapolis: University of Minnesota Press, 1955), pp. 67–121.
† Cf., Chafee, *Free Speech in the United States*, pp. 247–69.

nization. Hence, they were . . . [considered qualified], not for constitutional opposition, but for unconstitutional expulsion; and their constituents with them. Met with violence [forced from their seats by the Sergeant-at-Arms] at their first appearance [on January 7, 1920]; driven from their seats [officially expelled April 1, 1920]; refused the simple rights which the New York [City] Bar [Association] committee, led by Charles Evans Hughes, requested for them; forced to a costly defense of themselves and their constituencies; their cases are writ large on the sky of the future, not as enemies of our form of government, but as victims of the usurpation of our government.*

To such end and in such purpose has our knowledge been corrupted, have our views been perverted. Thus have we been brought to tolerate the denial of free thought and free speech, and to face the overthrow of representative, republican institutions. The blow at a few socialists of today [1920] may be the blow at all liberals, at all hopeful reformers of society, at all free voters, tomorrow.

The purposes of this corruption by [anti-liberal, anti-radical] propaganda, the purpose of the suppression [even of peaceful critics of capitalism] by government agency is the same. It is maintenance of that wasteful system of appropriating the wealth of the land which has grown so powerful among us. If we lose our right to think, our power to speak freely and fully as we will, what hope has anyone against the master appropriator except in the ultimate resort to violence? What hope have those who, at all costs, would prevent such violence, [of] really succeeding in their aim?

Notes

1. For the abuse of the injunction, and for many illustrations of other abuses similar to those mentioned in the above paragraph, see the *Final Report of the Commission on Industrial Relations* (Washington, 1916), pp. 38–61, 228–30; and the testimony referred to therein. Attorney General [Frederick] Farrar of Colorado and former United States Senator [Thomas H.] Patterson testified to the political control of the Colorado Fuel and Iron Company in Las Animas and Huerfiano counties; and State Senator [Helen Ring] Robinson said of these counties: "While they are geographically a part of Colorado, yet industrially and politically they

* *Ibid.*, pp. 269–72.

are a barony or a principality of the Colorado Fuel and Iron Co." For the whole story, see George P. West, *Labor Conditions in Colorado*, prepared for the Commission on Industrial Relations.

2. The writer is able to speak frankly on this subject, for he himself had a highly developed case of war hysteria, dating not merely from April 1917, but from August 1914; and during the entire period of our participation in the war, he could hardly have done more, so far as the volunteering of his time and energy to such war work as offered itself was concerned. But what is permissible and necessary during war is one thing, and what is permissible during peace is another. Nor is the after-effect of war hysteria our main trouble today, for that will wear off. It is the abuse of the war spirit and war power for private and class interests that counts most heavily during war and after. This will not wear off so readily, if at all; for the massed interests of those who benefit by the abuse, and who have control of the means, both of stimulating it and applying it, [are] concentrated to maintain it. There lies our grave peril.

3. See Chapter XII: The Memorial to Congress by the Non-Partisan League, 1918, 120 pp.; A. K. Horwill, "The Nonpartisan League," *The New Republic*, Vol. XIX, No. 231 (April 5, 1919), p. 304; "Due Process of Law," *The Nation*, Vol. CVIII, No. 2817 (June 28, 1919), p. 999.

4. The war fortunes of grain dealers are well known. For millers' profiteering, see Federal Trade Commission, *Report on Flour Milling and Jobbing* (Washington, D.C.: Government Printing Office, April, 1918).

5. [As of] March 1919. [Cf., Zechariah Chafee, Jr., *Free Speech in the United States* (Cambridge, Mass.: Harvard University Press, 1941), pp. 70–71, 100–103.]

6. Zechariah Chafee, "Legislation Against Anarchy," *The New Republic*, Vol. XIX (July 23, 1919), pp. 379–85.

7. Ernst Freund, "The Debs Case and Freedom of Speech," *The New Republic*, Vol. XIX, No. 235 (May 3, 1919), p. 13.

8. [*Ibid.*] See also address by Senator [Joseph I.] France of Maryland: *Congressional Record*, 65th Cong., 3rd Sess. (January 9, 1919), Vol. 57, Pt. 2, p. 1159.

9. Captain Alexander Sidney Lanier, of the Military Intelligence Division, General Staff, USA, prepared for the Army a summary of the 40,000 pages of evidence and testimony in this case. After the war and after his resignation, he addressed an open letter to President Wilson on the case—published in *The New Republic*, Vol. XVIII, No. 233 (April 19, 1919), p. 383)—in which he asserted: first—as fact—on the basis of precedents, that the indictments were defective in not giving the defendants the information on the nature of the charges against them to which they were entitled under the Constitution; . . . second—as his opinion—that the evidence was insufficient to prove a conspiracy; and third, that there could be no question of the absolute innocence of three of the convicted men—Ashleigh, Laukie, and St. John. Mr. Lanier is a conservative, fundamentally and in every detail hostile to the program of the IWW, but he believes that "they were convicted contrary to the law and evidence solely because they were leaders of a revolutionary organization against which public opinion was justly incensed; and that the verdict rendered was a foregone conclusion from the beginning."

10. For later stages of these deportations, after [the] novelty had worn off and "deportation trains" were no longer featured by the newspapers, see: two articles in *The Dial;* Phillips Russell, "Deportation and Political Policy," and Sailendra nath Ghose, "Deportation of Hindu Politicals," *The Dial*, Vol. LXVII, No. 797 (August 23, 1919), pp. 147–49, 145–47, respectively.

11. See articles by William Hard, "Mr. Burleson, Espionagent," *The New Republic*, Vol. XIX, No. 236 (May 10, 1919), pp. 42–46; and "Mr. Burleson,

Section 481 1–2B," *The New Republic,* Vol. XIX, No. 237 (May 17, 1919), pp. 76–78.

12. It wrote: "The opinion of a Cornish miner or a Lancaster overlooker would help us more to an understanding of British labor than any number of observations by Mr. Gompers."

13. For similar stupidities in Colorado see article by Judge Ben B. Lindsey, "Our National Faith Cure," *Cosmopolitan,* Vol. LXVI, No. 5 (April 1919), pp. 30–33, continued pp. 123–126. Professor S. H. Clark, a Red Cross speaker sent out on behalf of its war fund campaigns by the national organization, was not permitted to continue to speak in that state because in one of his talks he said that the entire amount needed was only a fraction of the yearly dividends of one corporation, [in] the Steel Trust [U.S. Steel Corporation]. Doctor Charles Zueblin, lecturing before grade school teachers at Colorado Springs, spoke of the unequal distribution of wealth and the need of industrial reforms. He was accused of being pro-German, despite his undoubted loyalty and long record of public service, and [was] hounded off the lecture platform.

14. See articles by Basil M. Manly, "Steel Companies Discharging Men for Joining Unions," and Charles E. Russell, "Mr. Russell Gives Some Inside Facts About the Paris Peace Conference," *Reconstruction,* Vol. I (May, 1919), pp. 132–34 and 141–43, respectively.

15. Mooney's companions indicted with him, who were not placed on trial till the proof of this perjury had been secured, were all acquitted. Federal officials, by the use of a dictaphone, recorded conversations among the [California] prosecutors which clearly proved their conspiracy against Mooney and their unscrupulousness.

16. See J. B. Densmore's report to Secretary of Labor Wilson; Address of Rabbi J. L. Magnes at the Madison Square Garden, New York, May 1, 1919, printed as "The Mooney Trial," *The New Republic,* Vol. XIX, No. 236 (May 10, 1919), pp. 52–53; "Justice and Labor in the Mooney Case," published by the Industrial Workers Defense League, 1919.

17. The extent of the power of this propaganda is best appreciated by those who try in any detail to fight it. Senator Borah is quoted by Lincoln Colcord in "A Receivership for Civilization," *The Nation,* Vol. CVIII, No. 2817 (June 28, 1919), p. 1010, as saying in connection with his fight against the League of Nations: "We stand a chance unless the international bankers can buy us out. The country doesn't want the League of Nations that they have arranged—I know that—and if we could get the truth out to the country, it would want the League still less. But they have a perfectly inconceivable control of leadership and opinion. The country imagines that it is thinking its own thoughts, and doesn't dream that it is being bamboozled. So the pressure will be brought to bear in the Senate, and a lot of men will change their minds."

18. *Final Report by the Commission on Industrial Relations* (1916), Vol. I, pp. 82–84.

19. [Federal Trade Commission,] *Report on the Meat Packing Industry,* p. 37.

20. Professor Louis Levine. See William MacDonald, "The New United States," *The Nation,* Vol. CVIII, No. 2809 (May 3, 1919), pp. 691–92. So much unfavorable comment from all parts of the country was heard that the university later restored Professor Levine to his position.

21. In September 1919 it distinguished itself especially by fathering the stories of the nationalization of women in Russia, which our own State Department has officially stamped as untrue, and, further, by applying these stories to American industrial reformers as the certain goal they were aiming at.

22. As in Cleveland [in] 1919, where Army lieutenants in two places deliberately forced rioting.

XX

The Deeper Structure

In the rapid transformations of the times, we are all of us perforce involved. The fight on the [mass-media] surface is between rival claims. The claims of the masters of [American] industry are expressed in their system of capitalizations, their titles to the future income of the nation, their titles to their strategic highway positions. The claims of revolutionary proletarians are expressed in their creed of labor (labor as the source of all wealth and its rightful master). For each side, the world is its jam-pot. Capital and Labor are the slogans. The range of transformation is from industrial autocracy to convulsive revolution, alike unstable.

But underneath these claims lie the essential realities of the nation at work: the people, with all their technical information and skill and methods of workmanship; with all their physical possessions and permanent modifications of the face of the earth; with all their adaptations of man-to-man and [of] community-to-community in the industrial organization, which has arisen in the new harnessing of nature in the last century, to the supply of our many needs. Here also there are transformations going on in which we are all of us involved. But here, under proper guidance, the transformations may work themselves out without tyranny, without convulsion, and with the hope of stability of results.

If the struggle of industrial autocracy and proletarian revolution runs its course, the middle classes will become the trampled battleground of the opposing forces. And if these classes accept the formulas and slogans of the two sides as covering the truth, or if they potter with trivial symptoms and trivial remedies, this will be their fate. But if they turn to the essential realities beneath, if they envisage the work and income of the future as going hand-in-hand; if, well-informed, they aim constructively at the essential national good and strike forcefully at the roots of evil, they can dominate.

We have now to consider the material with which a radical political program of the middle classes must work; the transformations of the essential things in the life and labor and workmanship of the people which are now under way, and which, under such guidance and such clearing of the way to freedom as may be necessary, will furnish the structure of a stable industrial and political future. The first of these transforming things of our generation (and of the generation that preceded it, and of that [which] is to follow) is the very organized structure of the nation at work: the bigness and the many ramifications of that structure, understood not as the system of titles and claims, but as the relations of man with man, and of community with community in national industry. The second is the experience government has already acquired and is still acquiring, and is bound still more to acquire, in controlling the policies of industry from the point of view of public needs and especially in the experience of war-time. The third is the new range of cooperative tendencies and possibilities among our people, rising to meet and join hands with government guidance. The fourth is to be found in new characteristics of workmanship and leadership, showing themselves in specialized forms among various elements of the population, ready to meet the demands that may be made for such services as they can offer.

We all know that any man who looks back longingly towards such conditions of industrial enterprise in industry as once existed, or seemed to exist, is dreaming and trifling so far as any practical results that he may expect are concerned. The big structure of the present must be reckoned with as it is. We cannot throw it away or replace it; we must evolve with it. How then must this structure be described, if it cannot be described primarily as a system of titles to property? The answer in [the] last analysis must be in terms of coal and oil, of steam and gas engines, and of electricity. It must be [described] in terms of the knowledge and skill which has given us control of these powers of nature, which now determine the kinds of work we do, the localities in which we live in largest numbers, the way our various kinds of work are fitted together, and, to [a] great extent, even the kinds of products we consume. These are the determining elements of our industrial organizations, understood as the essential reality of the national industry, rather than as a superficial, and probably transitory, form of [economic oligopoly or] dictatorship.

There are, it is true, still deeper-lying characteristics of workmanship and of the control of nature than these—such as we have in agriculture and all raw food production, and in the use of rivers and harbors—but they are not the special determining factors of the present, though they underlie and persist through the others like the cowpaths and lanes that now are city streets. New York [City] rests on a harbor, and we shall not lose it [as a business center]; for it has woven into itself and knotted together thousands of threads of the new organizing powers.

Coal deposits, iron ore, and water-power sites are localized, but their employment, by the aid of transportation (still mainly [as of 1920] that of steam), is universalized. Oil is more freely distributed, and the gas[oline] engine which it brings into being promises a more elastic transportation system, and forecasts perhaps shorter hauls between agricultural regions and centers of manufacture. But to date, despite all the pipelines, oil in the hands of Standard [Oil] Companies is still tied in with the steam transportation system, and its utilization is governed by the profits that can be made with reference to the facilities of that other system, not the broadening of service that we might have from it.

Upon this basis has arisen an integration [vertical] of manufacturing in certain lines, as, for example, in steel; which reaches from the raw products (iron ore and coal) through the intermediate products (coke, pig iron, and merchant bars) into commodities ready for direct use such as rails, pipe, [and] wire; all under one centralized control [as in U.S. Steel Corporation]. In other lines, such as meat, where the manufacturing and distributing processes go hand-in-hand, the [oligopoly corporate] organization has spread sideways [or developed a horizontal integration]; covering by combination and community of interests the greater part of the industry, and, by indirect authority, all of it. Again, organization has spread out from one line over other [allied or related] lines, as the meat industry is now spreading over the wholesale grocery trade. In retail trade, a few great enterprises do a tenth of the country's business; one of them with 4,000 separate stores, another with 20,000 wagon routes, another with 6 million mail-order customers who buy with some regularity.[1] These, too, have their agencies reaching back through jobbing fields to manufacturing. Had the government not dissolved the Tobacco Trust [see *U.S. v. American Tobacco Co.*, 221 U.S. 106 (1911)], that industry, from first process of manufacture to last retail sale, would now have been largely in one [corporate] organization. Practically all of the commercial banking of the country is done under a system [called the "Money Trust" by the Pujo Committee] which provides, in the most vital matters of judgment, a control from one central point [Wall Street]. Above all [the banks] there is integration well on its way to accomplishment.

Now, all of this organization is played over by appropriative forces (to say nothing, for the present, of the participation of the political government) which show themselves in two ways; here constructive and productive in their results, and there destructive and wasteful. The great productive integration, which is the residuum of the appropriative process up to the present time, is that which corresponds to the newly known forces of nature brought by our technique of workmanship to our service. But however much, historically, the campaigns of the great appropriators have been knit in with this productive [technological] integration, it is this very phase to which they, as the masters of industry, now give the least attention.[2] They demand certain results; they turn the problems of getting these results over to men [technologists] whom they hire for a price; and they concern themselves with the manipulation of [the differential between costs and sale prices, and the possible consequent] wastes, in such [a] way as to secure financial rewards for themselves which turn into new social wastes as fast as they secure them. Their own work, their own interest, their own attention [as appropriators] is consistently of the destructive type—both in immediate purpose and direct result.

It is the constructive residuum of organization, therefore, that is the first transforming thing which any stabilizing political program must recognize and with which it must deal. It includes all this bigness, this broad typing together of functions, this managing and engineering capacity, this productive service corresponding to the interrelations of the various sections of the land and classes of the population under our existing type of workmanship with nature. Elements in it that we now have may indeed require rejection, but it will be by tests of productivity and efficiency. Where centralization of slaughtering and packing has produced inefficiency, there the field will open to greater service by independents; but should, . . . refrigerator-car routes, warehouses, and branch houses give greater efficiency in handling groceries along with meats, there we would have a permanent part of our centralized organization once the abuses of appropriative control are removed. Take off, in short, the appropriative control, and the full constructive organization will quickly reveal itself in all its details.

For our second element underlying a radical political program, we have named [selected] the experience [that] government has already acquired in controlling the policies of industry. This experience covers notably the control of the banking and credit systems, the control of the railroads, the development of information service, and, above all, the war [World War I] experience in direct adjustment of output and prices for national needs. Needless to say, none of this experience shows fully the possibilities of government action. Only in the one field of credit has government control of this type been able to work in accord with appropriative powers; in all the others it has secured what it has . . . only through bitter conflict, and its results have been subject from that source to heavy discount of their true productive possibilities. And even in credit legislation the success, while seemingly positive, is very limited compared with what would clearly be possible under a credit organization designed for the fullest possible benefit of all of the citizens; a credit system motivated primarily by the needs of the whole population, envisaged as consumers as well as producers.

In the preceding pages in which were sketched the facts of bigness and ramification of underlying industrial structure, the investment and promotional banking system was not included; nor was mention made of the financial functions of the corporations, the control of output and prices, so far as this still lies in individual corporation hands outside of the investment-banking nexus. This was for the very reason that all of these functions have come to be purely appropriative, differentiated as such, and therefore outside of the material [the economic reconstruction] of the future, forming rather the superimposed elements which must be stripped off. That these functions have indeed arrived at a state of failure and collapse has been previously shown,[3] the proof [as of 1920] lying in the discouragement of meat production; in the confusion and uncertainties with reference to grain production; in the restricted production of shoes at the very times [that] the warehouses were full of the leather of the profiteers and the people were [in] need of footwear;[4] in short, in the whole postwar era of profiteering, distorted industry, and high cost of living.

This is the field in which [national] government experience in the control of the policies of industry, imperfect as it still is, must be accepted as a hopeful fact of the future. Here it was that government had its successes, under the exceptional conditions of war, in its Food Administration and its [War Industries and] Trade Boards. It is here that it must take similar control in peace, if we are to save ourselves from ruin as a nation of makers and users. We will consider this aspect of government experience first, and we shall find that this alone is enough to make it clear that the burden of proof under the actual conditions of today is no longer upon the people and upon the government, but upon the industrial masters—whose functions are in collapse so far as [lies] any claim to genuine public service they render.

The government War [Industries and] Trade Boards [and the Food and Fuel Administrations] were absolutely essential to winning the war. They did much to check profiteering, but it was not because there was any settled objection, either theoretical or practical, to the making of great profits. The reason was that the direct result of the profiteering system under the spectacular war conditions [of 1917–18] was to throw production more than ever out of balance, and make it a mere gamble whether the Army's needs for food and supplies would be provided.

These boards [and other war agencies] took account of the nation's stock of supplies, and they took account of its possible product. They took account, at least so far as they could in their haste, of wastes. Wastes in dollars to be made good in the future were of trifling importance, compared with wastes in real labor and materials for the use of the moment. Under the cogency of their advice and commands, the people shifted and limited their consumption, changed their programs of production, adapted themselves in many cases to prices that were ordered for them, and did vastly more and better productive work than they had been capable of doing for a long time under the throttling hand of the established industrial control.*

To procure more wheat, the [national] government guaranteed a price to the producer, or rather to the trader; and it did something to eliminate the wastes between the grower and the miller, and between the miller and the consumer; it made it possible to figure the costs very closely, and to compute the excess parts of them which were wastes, barring the inequities of grading and transportation.† To procure more manufactured products for war uses, the government guaranteed prices, and also guaranteed reimbursement for such special investment in plants and equipment as [was] necessary for producing them. To get quick action, it employed contractors on that most expensive basis possible—cost plus a fixed [percentage of] profit—a basis that meant to the contractor that the more costly he could make the work to the government, the more profit he would get for himself. In all this, the guiding thoughts were economy of available resources, efficiency of work, and maximum output in the present, no matter at what extravagant reckoning to be settled in the future. The policy was of course the right policy for war; it was the policy that enabled us to gain victory.‡

Eliminate now from this record the special war extravagances (the dollar wastes, including the compromises with appropriators and the bribes given them) and we have left a solid achievement in price regulation and in control of output. But these functions are the very, so-called, financial functions of the corporations and of the investment bankers which are now [1920] in collapse in the profiteering of peace. The government has, therefore, given us proof that it can accomplish just what we need to have ac-

* Cf., Grosvenor B. Clarkson, *Industrial America in the World War* (Boston: Houghton Mifflin Company, 1923).
† Cf., William C. Mullendore, *History of the United States Food Administration, 1917–1919* (Stanford: Stanford University Press, 1941).
‡ Charles Hardy, *Wartime Control of Prices* (Washington: Brookings Institution, 1940).

complished: the provision of that wise direction and oversight which will enable the engineers and administrators of industry and trade to do their work efficiently and productively, to stimulate output instead of limiting output, to remove wastes, and to assure us fairly adjusted prices instead of excessively profiteering prices. After the Armistice [of November 11, 1918], the government at once dropped the greatest part of its system of control, threw industry back on its old methods, and let it whirl us into disastrous profiteering; and within the year we were desperately hunting for means to check the riot—means that Washington hoped to find by this little trifle of palliative measure or that little trifle, but means which cannot be found except by constructively developing all the vital lines of control [that] experience has proved practicable.[5]

Chief among other contributions of government experience are its information services. For [competition with] the private information systems and guesses which are the reliance of the speculator and financier, the government has been successfully making the beginnings of providing public information, the lack of which has so often been the ruin of the isolated producer. It has long had its surveys, geographical and geological; its weather service; its highly developed patent office, records, and judgments; its census investigations of agriculture, mining and manufacturing; and its permanent statistical services of the Departments of Agriculture, Labor, and Commerce. With these no private enterprises can compete; they are the reliance of the nation, and all they now need is further development ever more fully in the interest of real wealth production and efficiency. To them have more recently been added the market reports of the Bureau of Markets in the Department of Agriculture, issued daily during the producing seasons for the benefit of the producers of the principal crops of fruits and vegetables.*

The last of these lines of government experience which we may list has to do with the railroads. Here we may be said to be in a debatable field; but it is a debatable field only if discussion starts out with confusion of thought as to what is really essential in railroad control, and if the essential is subordinated to the inessential.

---

* Cf., George Soule, *Prosperity Decade, From War to Depression: 1917–1929* (New York and Toronto: Rinehart, 1947), pp. 336ff.

If the essential thing for the nation is the best utilization of resources so [as] to get the greatest amount of service out of them with the least cost, and if this requires the elimination of duplications and frictions, then the government . . . [can give] it to us [in peacetime as it did] through its wartime unification. If the essential thing is to establish equity in the use of the services between . . . users (producer with producer, industry with industry, locality with locality), then government . . . [has been giving] it to us, or at least much of what we need of it, through the Interstate Commerce Commission. And, in neither case could we have gotten it under the appropriative mastery, except through government action. [During World War I] rates were stabilized and given certain qualities of reasonableness and equity. Routings were made economical. Duplications of offices and stations were wiped out. "Business capturing" employees [salesmen] were eliminated.

Just as in the case of the War [Industries, Labor, and] Trade Boards, the government had to secure these results at a great cost to itself: the cost of recognizing and guaranteeing excessive income claims, the cost of surrendering outright to the wage demands of employees. [Today] . . . the absolute necessity of such control as it was recognized in war remains to be recognized in peace, when solutions may be worked out with less need of yielding to profiteering demands or meeting them half-way.

If, on the other hand, the discussion of the relations of the government with the railroads is concerned with inessentials, if all of the fundamental equities and wastes are ignored, if the present imperfections are contrasted—not with what we would have had without government control, but with some assured state of perfection—then, of course, any conclusion can be drawn by any arguer which will best satisfy his own personal interests. The government took charge in war when the roads were burdened with their fictitious capitalizations and with their incubus of financiering; when past public regulation had been allowed by their [the railroads'] masters to cut into their physical conditions, rather than into the profiteering charges upon them; when a harvest of trouble was due to be reaped as the result of past misdeeds; when a period of excessive high prices and excessive costs was approaching, and with it further effects in a resulting period of diminished production and hence diminished railroad revenues. Of course deficits resulted; of course the railroads so burdened could only be carried by the sustaining hand of public favor. But that is not an argument against government administration. This very government administration has been, indeed, in the main, only a direction of policy, and that of economical and profitable policy. The actual management of the roads was throughout in the hands of trained railroad men inherited from the private regime. And so, to treat the present evils as the results of government operation is doubly an error.*

Of direct government operation in any and all lines, the arguments pro and con have indeed little basis to rest on. The Post Office can only be adjudged in contrast with what mail service would be, as a whole, in private hands; either scattered or centralized, or profiteering. The parcel post can only be judged in contrast with the express companies. The Panama Canal construction is perhaps the best available case of what government operation is or might be, for it, almost alone, has been free from complications with the appropriators and from undermining by them.

Having considered, first, the productive industrial system in its ramifications as it stands; and second, the [World War I] experience of government in the control of industry; there remain now, of the [various] transforming conditions which were named at the beginning of this chapter as the material with which political programs had to work, two more. (1) The cooperative tendencies and possibilities of the population, and (2) certain personal characteristics which are showing themselves in differentiated form among the occupied [employed] population. These both might indeed be treated as phases of the structure of our existing working population, our nation at work, but they have certain aspects which justify their detachment for special consideration.

So far as actual cooperative experience among consumers and small producers in the United States in the past is concerned, there is little to offer which would give a reliable guide to future developments. Nevertheless, there are clear possibilities of large development in this respect in the near future.[6] Not only are enterprises of a great variety making substantial gains, but the massive achieve-

---

* Walter D. Hines, *War History of American Railroads* (New Haven: Yale University Press, 1928).

ments of certain other countries—especially England and Denmark, and Siberia under war conditions—seem to be showing a stimulating influence. There is no reason to think that, when conditions are ripe, what has happened in these other countries will not show itself here; moreover, the very organization-systems of chain stores and mail-order houses which has been so successful, is ready at hand for cooperation adaption. The British cooperatives have a wholesale business of half a billion dollars a year and a retail business of [one] billion. Siberia has 18 million cooperators carrying on a large part of the trading of the land, and several societies have recently joined in extensive headquarters for American buying in New York City. In Denmark, a large part of the small-scale agricultural production is knit together by cooperative distributing and selling agencies, some under state supervision and some not. Australia and New Zealand also have their marked successes to show.

In the United States today [as of 1920], so far as consumers' buying agencies—cooperative stores—are concerned there are probably now between 3,000 and 4,000. There are already six Cooperative Wholesale Societies (and these are in process of federating into a National Cooperative Wholesale), headquarters of which have already opened in Chicago. Minnesota is one field of success under the Rochdale plan. The Finns, where they have settled in communities in the Northwest [of the United States] are very successful cooperators. Illinois miners, emerging from a past history of company stores, are getting their trade widely organized in this new way. North Dakota is trying a plan under the auspices of the Non-Partisan League which provides, not for the Rochdale system of patronage dividends, but for a fixed 10 per cent mark-up on its goods. Seattle cooperators already have a large investment.

On the side of producers' cooperation in marketing, the California Fruit Growers Exchange is well known for its success over many years in handling the orange trade and preventing the ruinous conditions that formerly existed. Most of the fancy apple trade of the far Northwest is handled by cooperative packing and selling societies. There are several thousand cooperative grain growers' associations owning their own elevators, and cooperative livestock marketing is increasing. Milk producers' associations have been successful on a considerable scale; so successful indeed, that the one in the territory around Chicago has had to defend itself in the courts from charges that would make it out to be a vicious combination on the analogy of those against which the antitrust laws were directed.

Another type of cooperation is shown in a dozen or more large farmers' associations which have central buying agencies distributing goods to the members in carload lots, or to stores maintained by members, and which also sometimes conduct selling agencies for grain and livestock. The Farmers Union in Nebraska, for example, has 40,000 adult male members, with about 150 affiliated grain elevators shipping to it $50 million of grain a year; a livestock commission department which has passed $50 million in sales a year and has saved shippers half the usual commission charges; and a warehouse at Omaha which distributes to the members about $3 million of goods a year. The local branches of the several farmers' organizations combined number about 12,000.

A more recent development is that of certain railroad unions which in 1919 began to experiment in the use of their idle funds, often amounting to millions of dollars, as capital with which to secure cheaper supplies of goods to their members. The maintenance and right-of-way workers, especially, have had success in this venture.[7] First buying goods at wholesale, they soon began to buy direct . . . [from] factories, then to contract for the entire output of factories, and finally to establish factories [of consumer goods] of their own. . . .

The most recent development has been a movement to bring together for common action the various farmers' organizations, consumers' cooperatives and labor unions.[8] Initiated in the fall of 1919 by the Farmers National Council at a preliminary conference in Chicago, this movement resulted in the All-American Farmer-Labor Cooperative Congress in Chicago, held in February 1920. A new national organization of cooperative interests was formed and steps taken toward several new ventures, the most important of which is a series of cooperative banks; to be founded in the larger cities under state and federal laws, affiliated with the national reserve system, and introducing their cooperative features through their bylaws. To these it is hoped to attach minor local banks or credit organizations. Railroad union funds were offered for pre-liminary capitalization, but with the intention of wide stock dis-tribution as early as practicable, and with precautions against the domination of any one interest and against business incentives for excessive earnings to stockholders.

Such success as cooperative associations have had in this country, has been wrested out of a milieu of cut-throat appropriative struggle in which all contestants have joined to overthrow the cooperators as their common enemies. They cannot get their rep-resentatives upon grain exchanges, their applications being rejected because, to the exchange members, cooperative profit-sharing is a violation of the first principle of their business, which is fixed rates of commission and no rebates. Wholesalers often refuse to sell to them. Their trade is lured away by the suggestive, trade-compelling advertising of ordinary business. They are not free to venture as most businessmen do, expecting to recoup their losses in some fields by bigger gains in others, but must run carefully to form at every point without gambling adventures. Moreover, in the last few years, since the demand for cooperation has arisen to its present strength, the country is filled with promoters of the most vicious type who use the cooperative cloak in order to start enterprises out of which they can get commissions, and which they know will collapse as soon as they have taken their profits and moved on. The gain that has been made [by the genuine cooperatives] has been in the face of all these and other difficulties placed in the way by the many agencies of profiteering.

Although we still allow the mastery of our industry to rest in the hands of men who are motived throughout by the prospect of what they can capture, not what they can produce and earn, we have in our land a world of capable men whose services [in the cooperative movement] would be available for true productive control; and we have had already a development of these men, a specialization of them for that purpose. The very withdrawal of the masters to the financial problems of the directorates, the executive committees, and the banking houses, has left the industries themselves in the hands of efficient managers. To replace the present type of control by such control as the government could give would free these men for much more efficient service than they have ever before given.

They include all of the real industrial organizers and administrators, and the engineers and industrial experts of many kinds. A [George Washington] Goethals was readily available for the [engineering work on the] Panama Canal, and men of his capacity are at hand in every line; awaiting fuller opportunities of service than they now can hope for.

Everyone knows how much of the best work in winning the war was done by men picked out of the ranks to handle it. The problem arose, and the man appeared to . . . [cope with] it. Clerks from the departments [in] Washington often showed powers [abilities] when sent abroad that might never otherwise have been discovered. After the Civil War, the young veterans found the chance to utilize their training and spirit in opening up the new West. After the great World War—in which we have been fortunate among the nations of the world in having [most of] our young men saved for us and not destroyed—those very powers of initiative and discipline that have been developed are brought back to us to settle into the machine of industry; there to be exploited with the right hand and with the left, first as wage-earners and then as consumers, if the present regime of profiteering continues. One of the early fears when fighting ended was that these men on their return might, through mere spirit of adventure and unrest, cast in their lot for revolution. But no matter how much destruction they may conceivably produce under some industrial circumstances, they are available in just as great strength for the new constructive and productive uses of industry. Here is unlimited manpower [for] the country's use if it will provide the opportunities.*

And, finally, we may consider the new spirit of labor. That spirit is not the spirit of sabotage, no matter how much sabotage we find in fact to offset the sabotage and exploitation of capital. Its demand is for participation in the control of industry. That such participation will be secured by labor in some form is more and more recognized. Given its participation, not as an ally of profiteering powers, but in the constructive administration of industry, its possibilities of development are unlimited. "Scientific management" has studied the method of producing more; it has made the worker conscious of

* For some later developments see Horace M. Kallen, *The Decline and Rise of the Consumer* (New York: Appleton-Century, 1936).

how to produce more; and, no matter what its net results have been under existing conditions, it is an element in workmen's equipment for the future which, in their own hands for real productive purposes, has the greatest possibilities.

Notes

1. The Atlantic and Pacific Tea Company; the Jewel Tea Company; and Sears, Roebuck and Company, respectively.

2. See the essays of Thorstein Veblen, "The Modern Point of View and the New Order," *The Dial*, Vol. LXV (1918), Vol. LXVI (1919) already quoted.

3. Cf., Steinmetz' analysis quoted in Chapter III.

4. See U.S. Council of National Defense, *An Analysis of the High Cost of Living Problem* (Washington: Government Printing Office, 1919).

5. For a broad-minded discussion, see Chapter XII, "An Employer's Vision," in Frank A. Vanderlip, *What Happened to Europe* (New York: The Macmillan Company, 1919). [Cf., Paul A. Samuelson and Everett E. Hagen, *After the War— 1918–1920* (Washington: National Resources Planning Board, 1943).]

6. Of the possibilities of cooperation, the National Catholic War Council says: "Our superior energy, initiative and commercial capacity will enable us, once we set about the task earnestly, even to surpass what has been done in England and Scotland." [John A. Ryan, *Social Reconstruction* (New York: Macmillan, 1920), p. 229.]

7. The Gleaners and the Maintenance of Way employees, for example, propose to exchange products at cost plus a definite margin of product, each giving the other the right to audit its books. The Gleaners not only distribute the fruit and vegetables grown by their members, but operate canneries. The railroad union has clothing to exchange for the most part.

8. For some of the methods of attack on cooperation see E. P. Harris, *Cooperation, The Hope of the Consumer* (New York: The Macmillan Company, 1918), pp. 128ff; and testimony of C. H. Gustafson, president of the Farmers Union of Nebraska, House *Hearings on Government Control of the Meat Packing Industry*, House Committee on Interstate and Foreign Commerce, 65th Cong., 3rd Sess., January, 1919, p. 295. Also, L. D. H. Weld, *The Marketing of Farm Products* (New York: Macmillan, 1916), p. 424. The latest descriptive work on cooperation is that of Albert Sonnichsen, *Consumers' Cooperation* (New York: The Macmillan Company, 1919), which has a chapter [XII] on developments in the United States.

XXI

Political Programs

It goes without saying that all [American] middle-class action will be political. It will use political forms, and will use them honestly and democratically. It will neither undermine and distort them in the way of autocratic industrial revolution, nor will it strive to destroy them and advance over their destruction in the way of proletarian industrial revolution [as in Soviet Russia under Lenin]. There remains to consider the political programs that the middle classes may form, the political strength that they may conceivably develop, and the political methods that they may use.

The general goal of middle-class counter-revolution, set for it by its true interests in industrial life [the economic system], will be to rehabilitate [restore] property [to the middle classes] in its ownership, enjoyment, and productive use, and to liquidate those claims upon the future income of the nation which depend upon the appropriative control of property [by Big Business and High Finance] through the occupation of strategic positions on the industrial highways.

This may be elaborated in two ways: first, from the point of view of that true productive industrial structure which underlies the superficial appearance of our industry; and second, from the point of view of the citizen working in the organization.

In terms of the underlying productive structure, the goal will involve an effort:

1. To eliminate (a) its appropriative control, (b) its wasteful costs, (c) its incentives to restriction of production, (d) such part of its capitalizations as are arbitrary confiscations of future national income;

238

2. Better to utilize the available natural resources of the land;

3. Better to employ the engineering and administrative ability of our true industrial experts.

In terms of the position of the individual, it will involve:

1. Fostering the productive use of private property in the hands of individuals or cooperative groups, and assuring them true profits as the rewards of their efficiency.

2. Protecting the savings of individuals from confiscation at the hands of appropriators; to the end that the earners and savers may secure from their ability, self-denial, and foresight, protection against illness and the incapacity of old age, and the assured enjoyment of the comforts and pleasures which they have chosen to defer to the future.

3. Developing through government agencies such services of information, advice, and control as will guarantee that the common technological possession of the nation, and knowledge of the necessary facts as to its needs and resources, shall be freely and fully at the service of all makers and users.

4. Overthrowing that arbitrary power which through a propaganda of deceit, and through abuses of instrumentalities of government, now threatens the liberty of all citizens in the interest of their appropriative masters.

5. And we may well add, in the words of the preamble to the Constitution: Maintaining a firm purpose to "establish justice, insure domestic tranquility, provide for the common defense, promote the general welfare, and secure the blessings of liberty to ourselves and our posterity," interpreting these clauses by common consent to include a decent provision of income for the health and well-being of all of our workers according to their capacity, both in political and in industrial government; and the maximum addition to the general welfare out of the general income, not merely in the form of public buildings and parks and limited educational facilities, but in the widest educational facilities, the greatest funds of freely available information, and the widest distribution of all surpluses which growing control over the powers of nature may place at our disposal.

Fortunately we do not require a political program of the day that will attempt all this at once. What we do need (what we cannot avoid if we are to hope for political success) is to hold this goal, this central issue of property against profiteering power over property, clearly in mind; and then attend to our immediate political affairs of the day in such manner as best to conform to our ultimate purpose. We must cultivate our garden, but if we are well-advised, we will keep a close eye on the kind of crop we are raising. It is not, indeed, any meticulously precise logical definition of the distinction between the consumers' and producers' uses of property on the one hand, and the appropriators' uses on the other, which we need to guide us. We are concerned with the great differentiated appropriative abuses of the present day. We must strike at the worst of them first, and then at the worst that are left, and we can proceed in this way until common sense tells us when to stop. But we must strike at the heart of each one in turn, and not politely beg its pardon while we trim a little scrap off of one claw. We have always our practical, common-sense judgment of what is freedom of opportunity and what is not to keep us from going wrong.

Some people require a full plan of social reform, a blueprint of the society of the future, ready in advance and properly authenticated and approved, before they are willing to proceed. But society is not like a bridge or a steel building in which an error in computing the structural strength of one member may lead to the collapse of the whole. Society is forever changing. We watch what happens, and we help or hinder the process here and there by putting in this element of guidance or taking out that other. We must trust to our own ability to carry through our plans, and we can better trust to that ability in action than trust it to form a satisfactory plan complete in all details in advance of action. The nation sets the problem, and the people of the nation must do the work. It is not the tinkering with government and industry that fails, but blind tinkering; the tinkering that deals with incidental evil while it lets the essential evil raise new harvests of harm.

It is indeed unfortunate that we are not able to apply more systematically a process of invention and experiment to our institutions. Helen Marot has suggested, for example, that the Post Office might be run much more efficiently if instead of being under bureaucratic control, it could be turned over to a chartered post office association—with each local postmaster and each local clerk responsible to his peers, and the rewards of all dependent in some part on their mutual efficiency.[1] Some may applaud, and some jeer at the suggestion, but under existing conditions the tendency for all is to generalize it and talk of it primarily as a problem of universal application, or of no application at all. But inventors in mechanical fields do not [achieve] their successes in this way; they do not make one great plan and stand or fall by it; their first plans merely state to them their problems; their experiments test and develop them.

How much better off we would be if we could take such a suggestion as this about the Post Office, apply it systematically in some one branch of work or some one district—or even some one local office—give it favorable opportunities to show what was in it, and be guided by such results as showed themselves when we had given it its best possible chance on a small scale. Could we do things of this kind, our problems of political reform would be much simplified. But, as it is, all appropriative forces are keen to fight suggestions or experiments of improvement as bitterly as complete programs, and what they cannot defeat as proposal, they combine to defeat in application. Such reactionary forces must be battered down before improvement can be secured, and so long as they exist in full strength as determining and controlling factors, they must be battered down each time, over and over, as improvement shows its necessity and is demanded.

In what is now to be said in detail of possible political programs of the present, we may pass provisionally the question of constitutionality, since the amendment of the Constitution is as much a right of the people as is ordinary legislation, no matter how bitterly [monopoly or oligopoly] industrial dogma hates the thought.[2] We may perhaps best group projects of legislation under the following heads, regarded not as logically distinct, but as fields of attention, with results in each bringing aid to progress in the others:

1. The opening up of the main industrial highways, by the destruction of the strongly maintained strategic positions which have been established upon them.

2. Clearing the field for free development of cooperative enterprises.

3. Opening the land to greater productive use by independent farmers.

4. The development of government control of prices and output, with attached services of information and advice, and, to a minor extent and provisionally, of certain marketing agencies.

5. The adaptation of the credit system to productive, rather than appropriative, enterprise.

6. Specific applications of inheritance and income taxation in aid of the preceding measures.

And, we may add, outside of the general legislative field,

7. Coordination of individual and community efforts and government agencies into one system, to handle on a basis of service such parts of our trade as are, through the preceding reforms, in increasing measure set free to avail themselves of opportunity.

If, in the above, none of the great measures of the day for the protection of labor are included, it is not because of lack of recognition of the necessity of such measures, as the case now stands. The minimum wage, industrial pensions and insurance, child-labor laws, laws for the protection of women workers, maternity protection [benefits], and unemployment protection, are all demanded in ever-increasing scope—given the continuation of the appropriative control of wealth and industry that now exists. They are omitted here because in their very nature they recognize and assume the continued existence of that appropriative power. They are bulwarks against it for great classes of the people, and by that very token, they do not belong in a legislative program directed against the continued existence of that type of power. To such a program they appear rather as temporary expedients, with the need for them diminishing in direct proportion as the program itself advances towards success.

Much the same comment may be made of public ownership as a program of reform. Public ownership—understood to include operation—derives its strongest advocacy not from a love of having the government take over industry, but from a deep purpose to keep autocratic industry from finally taking over the government. As such, it may be a bulwark against certain great evils, but it inherits so many other evils that it is far from stimulating the hope that wastes and sabotages can be eliminated by it. Let us regard it, therefore, as a provisional weapon to the great struggle, not as part of our goal itself. With public ownership understood, not as business management by the government, but as a provision of capital and credit for citizens, individually or in groups, working towards productive efficiency, the case is different, as it is also with the provision of agencies on the analogy of the parcel post or municipal markets through which the products of ordinary enterprise may more readily pass.

Taking up briefly these seven classes of measures in order, we have:

I. *The opening up of the main industrial highways by the destruction of the strongly maintained strategic positions which have been established upon them:* Here we at once meet many projects of public ownership and see the reason for evaluating them as necessary fighting measures, rather than as parts of the real goal we should set up. Typical are the Federal Trade Commission's recommendations as to the meat industry, the program of the Non-Partisan League in the Northwest, and the various plans for public ownership of the railroads, culminating in the [Glenn F.] Plumb Plan [of 1919], where already they have transformed themselves into something very different from bureaucratic government enterprise.

The Federal Trade Commission's recommendations, based on its thorough studies, proposed that the [national] government acquire, through the Railroad Administration (the railroads then being in government hands), all cars [used] for the transportation of meat animals and all privately owned refrigerator cars and equipment, and hold them as a government monopoly; further, that the government acquire the principal and necessary stockyards of the country, to be treated as freight depots, and that it establish such further yards as are necessary from time to time; finally, that the government acquire "such of the branch houses, cold-storage plants, and warehouses as are necessary to provide facilities for the competitive marketing and storage of food products in the principal centers of distribution and consumption."[3]

In every one of these recommendations, the emphasis was upon the opening up of the highways. The fact that it was suggested that the government, through the Railroad Administration, take the ownership of cars and stockyards, is incidental. That was merely the method towards gaining the end. The most radical thing in these recommendations was the extension of the highway concept over the warehouses and cold-storage plants and, above all, over the branch distributing houses. Just as it is necessary to give free highway facilities to the independent packers if we are to benefit by their admittedly greater productive efficiency, so it is necessary to give facilities to wholesale grocers corresponding to those the packers enjoy, if we do not wish to see the grocers reduced to the present position of the independent packers.[4] And this national need is not merely a matter of packers and grocers, but runs back to farmers and livestock growers, who must have freer markets and fairer prices as encouragement to produce what the country needs from them. . . .

Turning to the case of the North Dakota farmers led by the Non-Partisan League, we find them seeking the same ends, but forced by the situation to different methods. Acting for the grain and livestock industries of one state involved in the great nexus of interstate trade, they have seen no way of assuring their success except by going further than the Federal Trade Commission in the way of public ownership. They have established, through constitutional amendment, a state industrial commission with power to build and operate a state terminal elevator, a state flour mill, and a state slaughterhouse, and to create a state bank to give the necessary credit backing to these enterprises.

A visit to North Dakota for purposes of firsthand study while these laws were being enacted showed hardly a trace among the farmers of a desire for state ownership. On the contrary, one heard them commonly express the hope that they could secure the fair treatment they demanded merely through their power to establish these enterprises without actually having to establish them all, and they showed their spirit practically by many measures on other lines to promote individual enterprise in the state. Their method has led their enemies to call them Socialists, but their purpose is the very opposite of that bureaucratic system of industry which state socialism presumably stands for. They knew that they would be hampered by grave difficulties in the operation of state industries, and would be burdened with heavy costs arising out of the very necessity of conflict with the appropriative enterprises of other states, but they saw no other course open to them.

Finally, in proposals for public ownership of railroads, we find the [Glenn E.] Plumb Plan [proposed in 1919]—backed by all the great railroad labor unions—appearing to people who judge it with preconceived bias, and with attention only to certain of its aspects, as the crowning enormity of the assault on private industry. And yet, in fact it is far different. Far from proposing to set up a great bureaucratic government organization, its purpose is to restore initiative, enterprise, and ability to railroad management by stripping off the rewards of thievery and substituting rewards for efficiency. It would make all railroad workers, from lowest section laborers to highest managers and presidents, directly interested in production and its results. This is indeed obscured to view, and quite naturally, by the very fact that the plan is presented by the railroad unions, and that these (though not belonging to the American Federation of Labor) are under the taint of the [Samuel] Gompers [American Federation of Labor] policy of "More;" the policy of seizure of all that by main strength can be seized out of the existing fund of earnings [in] the hands of the owners and manipulators of the property. But the truth, nevertheless, remains that the Plumb Plan is a fruit, not of the old spirit of labor, but of that new spirit mentioned in the preceding chapter. Its emphasis is on a "more" of efficiency, not a "more" of seizure. It is a great program of cooperation in service and in the rewards of service, and is as truly representative of the needs of the general public as it is of those of railroad workers.

As a matter of government ownership, the Plumb Plan involves only the acquisition of the [railroads'] physical property by the government; through purchase, after court adjudication of values, by the issue of government securities [bonds]. But so far as that alone goes, such a purchase is not so much a matter of government ownership (understanding government in the limited sense of the differentiated official functions) as of the common ownership by the people. It would put the railroad right-of-ways and equipment and terminals where the public roads and highways now are, [and make them] a common possession which we, the people, all think of not as belonging to our government, but as belonging to ourselves. [The railroads would be managed by a corporation with directors representing equally the government, the operating officials, and the employees. The net profits would be split between the government and labor.] The actual operation would be in the hands of trained experts and technicians, with the employees working with them in one common spirit and not as now, for the most part suspiciously and hostilely.

Given such a situation, where would the government stand under the Plumb Plan or under some method of railroad operation developed out of it, apart from its functions of overseeing payments, debt amortizations, and surplus accumulations? It would then be doing, in a perfected and positive way, what the Interstate Commerce Commission now tries to do in an imperfect, negative way against the enormous resistances of all the profiteering elements surrounding the roads. It would be looking after the public interest. And this public interest would present itself as the adjustment of railroad business with other business in the country on terms fair to all. It would mean seeing that the output of transportation service was great enough for our needs, seeing that rates were adjusted so as to bring compensation for this service on a par with compensation for other productive services in the country; with that compensation not regarded merely as a matter of wages, but of earnings including the rewards for personal efficiency. In short, it would occupy the very field of the "financial function of corporation," in the special matter of transportation, which our program proposes it should enter for all industry.

There are many other fields beside those of which we have spoken, in which strategic positions on the highways need to be demolished for the benefit of free producers; notably those of [the] grain and produce exchanges. The long-proclaimed and much-boasted function of speculation has broken down, and the speculators now are increasing the spread of prices between producer and consumer rather than decreasing it. The abuses of dockage and grading resist reform. The Government Grain Corporation, following the work of the Food Administration, has uncovered the grossest evils and has repeatedly had to issue orders requiring decency in business methods in fields in which now nothing but the most thorough reform, designed to destroy the possibilities of such methods, will suffice.

II. *Clearing the field for free development of cooperative enter-*

prises: Cooperators (and . . . independent individual enterprises as well) need certain classes of central agencies—terminal grain warehouses, public markets, slaughterhouses, cold-storage warehouses, stockyards, and commission agencies—which the government can provide; either directly if it must, or indirectly, through strict provisions as to their administration on terms that give freedom of opportunity to all producers. They also need special information services to offset the advantages which the great appropriators now enjoy. The [1919] Kenyon-Anderson [Meat-Packing License] Bill is suggestive in this respect. [It especially] . . . has one set of admirable provisions which might be copied with great elaboration in other fields.

It provides, for the benefit of cooperative and other small packers, that the Secretary of Agriculture shall furnish them (free of charge): standardized plans and specifications for plants, and reports "embodying existing knowledge" concerning all technical processes and improvements in the arts of cold-storage, freezing, cooking, and dehydration; that he shall detail experts from his department for advice and consultation on such subjects; that he shall cooperate in securing them adequate service from common carriers, furnish them all available information as to "supplies of foodstuffs" and "the location and movement and transportation costs of such foodstuffs"; and shall furnish them inspections and certificates of inspection guaranteeing quality. Comment need hardly be made as to how such services from the [national] government would shift the emphasis of the great packers, as well as the small, to true productive efficiency, and how consumers and producers alike would profit from it.[5]

Cooperators need laws to prevent discriminations against them, both in selling their products and in buying supplies.[6] They need assurances of credit facilities, such as North Dakota is attempting [in 1919–20] by its difficult and dangerous state bank, and such as cooperators in many other countries have had to fight for. They need legislation, such as Illinois recently adopted, to protect them from prosecution under the old anti-trust laws which were primarily directed against monopolies, but which are now being enforced against small producers who combine to fight off the evils of such monopolies.[7]

III. *Opening the land to greater productive use by independent farmers:* Here a mere reference to the copious recent discussions rising out of reconstruction problems must suffice.[8] Every project in this field is fought by the profiteer, and, where practicable, distorted to a greater or lesser degree to serve his interests. The federal farm loan system [created by the Federal Farm Loan Act in 1916] has been helpful, but, unfortunately, almost as helpful to the farmer-speculator as to the farmer-producer. The joint-stock land banks under federal law have had their main result in rich profits to their stockholders. The North Dakota land loan system is more directly adapted to true producers' needs. The Durham colony [for settling home-owning farmers] in California [established under the 1917 California Land Settlement Act] points the way.[9] New government irrigation and development projects should be definitely framed to the advantage of small settlers on some such model.

The more completely the [economic] highways are cleared of their profiteers, the more rapidly the small producers will take advantage of such openings, and the result cannot fail to be that consumers and producers alike, all along the line, will get more goods for their efforts, as weighed in prices. The retention by the government of its coal, oil, and ore deposits, and of its power sites; the acquisition on a fair basis of such deposits and sites as are now [in 1920] in private hands; and the requirement that mining output be handled for the benefit of the nation at work, are proposals the importance of which needs no argument.

IV. *The development of government control of prices and output, with attached services of information and advice; and, to a minor extent and provisionally, of certain marketing agencies:* Here is the heart of the whole program, and, nevertheless, the part about which one must be least specific. Least specific, because it concerns the function which must gradually develop and find itself in exercise. Must the government take over the "financial function" of the great corporations, the control of output, and the fixing of prices? The answer is that it most certainly must, if any other reform is to avail. For the needs of war, the answer was overwhelming. Any other action would have visibly meant ruin. The half-way action of war saved the country, but still with by-products of loss and waste that are now coming to be admitted and reckoned on every hand. The complete collapse of these financial functions in time of peace, by any test of public weal, is, however, just as apparent in post-war profiteering as it was in war necessity. Here now the nation must intervene, or else say in the spirit of the grand monarch [Louis XIV]: "After this little moment of splendor, the deluge."

The problem is to adjust output in the main line of our needs; stimulating it instead of restricting it as now, and yet give every incentive to producers, individually or in any form of combination, to work with all of their powers to the limit of their abilities, and with full advantage of the common possession of the technological knowledge and skill of the nation. This adjustment must be partly by direct advice or command, based upon studies of fact, and it must be partly through relative price determinations. It is not a new field to be entered by government.

As a field of activity, it has been forced on the country through the growth of coordinated industries. It has been seized and occupied, and scandalously abused for private advantage by the great corporations. It must now be taken over and developed by the people through their highest servants. We have already noted such a [public ownership and operation] function as offering its appearance in one phase [of the economy] in the Plumb Plan. We have spoken of it again in discussing the fostering of cooperation generally. It is the function which the IWW and other syndicalists would ravish in the interests of labor as it has already been ravished by capital. It is a function clearly described by the English Guild Socialists, which they hope to see occupied by joint deliberations and compromises of a dozen or more national producing guilds, supplanting in their development, in fact, the government itself in its most important aspects. But it is a function which we can better still assign to government as we may have it, the agency of all of the people, all of the consumers, of the nation. It is a function which can grow and succeed in government just to the extent that profiteering is driven out and productive profit-making supplants it; and [conversely], it must be the main technical method of such progress.

Such a control by government might probably involve the licensing of all corporations, a suggestion which was a pleasing makeshift of reform (unobjectionable to corporations when made in the

Garfield report on the meat industry [J. R. Garfield, *Report of the Commissioner of Corporations on the Beef Industry,* March 3, 1905] with public comprehension so little developed as it was at that time), but which would give at least the potentiality of complete government oversight, if enacted and enforced under the terms of the [1919] Kenyon-Anderson [Meat-Packing License] Bill. It would include requirements of absolute honesty of accounting by the corporations, something the government with all its efforts during war [in 1917–18] could not force on them even in the essential food industries. It would include information services which would be very costly from the point of view of present budgets, but [which would be] a trifle as compared with the wastes and extortions that come to the people through lack of it. And surely, if Swift can afford to spend close to two million [dollars] a year for a misinformation service to fortify his industrial position, the government would come off cheap at five hundred times that—a billion dollars —to get real information to all the people about all lines of industry.

President Wilson made several . . . suggestions along similar lines in his address to Congress on the high cost of living, August 8, 1919. Cold-storage products should, he urged, be stamped with date of entry and market price at that date; package goods should be marked with producers' selling price; corporations should be licensed under conditions that would give maximum publicity; their security issues should be controlled; and the government food control established during the war, should be extended in time and scope. Finally, there would be needed minor marketing agencies, perhaps temporary, perhaps permanent, adaptable to conditions as they exist from time to time; but these are touched on under other headings.

V. *The adaptation of the credit system to productive rather than to appropriative enterprises:* Into credit reform we shall not venture here with suggestions, further than to say that the structure that we have must be most carefully safeguarded through all transition stages. That structure is now controlled for appropriative rather than for productive purposes. The investment and promotion bankers dominate commercial banking. The greater city banks have passed through a stage of trust and savings bank company annexes, to a further stage of investment company annexes. The speculator always has credit for his operations, and the great highway master has credit, when the small producer is buried in difficulties. It is but natural. The highway master is sure to succeed; the speculator is reasonably sure, and he has his warehouse receipts for collateral. But the little producer is not at all so sure of his fate, and the banks inevitably tie their credit to the certainties of income, rather than the uncertainties. What is now sound as credit inside of the appropriative field is the heart of unsoundness for the producing nation.

Of the developments and transformations possible to credit, of the great economies its socialized use might produce for the nation, under such transformations of industry to the benefit of the maker and user as we have been discussing, it is venturesome to speak at this day. They lead into fields that have proved their unsoundness in the past when the despoiler had a free hand, but which under new conditions might show the very essence of soundness. "In pre-war times" says the Council of National Defense, in discussing currency and credit in relation to prices, "every dollar finding its way to market was supposedly the counterpart of some commodity or part of a commodity also appearing in the market."[10] One has but to take this as a text and develop it with an eye primarily to product and public service, to reach conclusions of a most momentous nature.

VI. *Specific applications of inheritance and income taxation in aid of the preceding measures:* These are weapons of control which are constitutional in [their] progressive [tax] forms. The power to tax is the power to destroy. If in the past it has too often been used to destroy prosperity, it can in the future be used with equal facility to destroy the enemies of prosperity. The excess-profits tax, which under the manipulation of profiteering is merely passed on to the consumer in the form of higher prices, is (apart from minor inequities) simply a way of taxing the consumer and deceiving him into thinking that someone else is paying the bill. The consumer has only to look at the income statements of the great corporations, which do not figure or report their profits till after the taxes have been paid or provided for, to know which end of the burden he himself carries. To hope to use this power of taxation directly to solve the problems of the age of profiteering is as futile as to attempt it by direct limitation of the rate of profit, without distinguishing between appropriative profit and productive profit.*

Nevertheless, the progressive tax on incomes and inheritances may so be used as to take away, in time, the possibilities of further great encroachments on the highways of trade by the holders of the present huge fortunes. It may be the simplest method of clinching the work that is done by other forms of legislation. It may be the best way to settle the problem of compensation to persons dispossessed of their present strategic positions, without entering into the intricacies of the equity as between man and man in such compensation. What is given as compensation legally, but inequitably, can be taken back both legally and equitably. If so, this power must be used with very positive purpose in that respect.†

VII. *The coordinating of individual and community efforts and government agencies into one system to handle, on a basis of service, such parts of our trade as, through the preceding reforms, are in increasing measure set free to avail themselves of opportunity:* Here is not a question of specific legislation, but of action (individual, cooperative, municipal, state, or national) for realizing the gains in welfare that are possible. A simple illustration, thoroughly practicable even today should the profiteering resistance to it be restrained, will suffice. The secretary of the National Wool Growers Association offers detailed figures to show that in 1919 the Idaho wool grower received $4.50 for enough wool to make a $50 suit of men's clothes.[11] In the summer of that year, Indiana wool growers were receiving about 50 cents a pound from local buyers. Through a city dealer, who was induced to make a specialty of direct trade from growers, they got about 11 or 12 cents more. In organized groups by communities where they made the effort, they realized 4 to 5 cents more than this. But they had to spend time getting their information and they had to take unnecessary trade risks. Further

---

* Bentley's views on the shifting of excess-profits taxes are dogmatic. For a balanced discussion of the burden of different forms of taxation, including the excess-profits tax, see Joseph A. Pechman, *Federal Tax Policy* (Washington, D.C.: Brookings Institution, 1966).

† Cf., Sidney Ratner, *Taxation and Democracy in the United States* (Science Editions, New York: John Wiley and Sons, 1967).

than that, ignorance of how to handle their wool decreased their receipts, and there was no one to set them right.

Suppose the state, through any of its branches, provided them simple warehousing facilities, with a corresponding information service, carrying their wool directly to the manufacturers who used the raw materials; how great the gain would certainly have been. Suppose beyond that, it contributed credit facilities, which could as simply and as safely be provided direct as through the long intermediation of the banks; again, what a saving. But beyond that, is this very certain fact: The wool supply of the year [1919] was reasonably definite, and the needs of the year were definite at given price ranges. Price-fixing could easily have been achieved that would give greater rewards to the producers, stimulate production as far as desirable, give the manufacturer certainty as to his future, and through publicity of material cost, go a long way to discourage profiteering in its later stages. Not the difficulties of fact, but the resistances of profiteers are in the way of such action. It is enough to state it.

The present profiteering control of industry is full of weak points. At any one of many points its bubble could be pricked, and it would burst. It is easy to speculate upon them, but not exceedingly profitable, for the pricks will not be given unless the clearly formed purpose is arrived at: to get rid of profiteering. Then they all become details of the program; possible weapons to be used, not for their relative hurtfulness on the way, but for their relative hurtlessness in accomplishing the necessary restorative work.

One such weak point is advertising. Suppose it should be forbidden, the types of it, at least, which stimulate wasteful expenditure; which maintain merely this aggression against the consumer; or that . . . do not, in reality, promote trade as a whole at all (though, indeed, there is little other advertising now that is not of such types). What would happen? Trade could go on. There would not be the slightest necessary interference with the buying of goods by consumers, or the production of goods, or the knowledge necessary to produce, distribute, and consume. But the inflated costly enterprises, built upon advertising, would collapse. The wind would be out of their sails. They would have to proceed upon merit,

and they know not of it. While there would be no necessary interference with trade, structurally speaking, there would of course be
a tremendous temporary interference due to these collapses; but
they would all lead straight back in responsibility to the over-
capitalizations, and to the dictatorship of industry by the beneficiaries of such over-capitalizations. And the blame for these
interferences would clearly lie not with the producers or consumers,
but with the usurping masters.*

The elimination of profiteering may indeed require a trenchant
blow against the profiteers at some stage; a blow that will teach
the usurpers once [and] for all that they are usurpers and that their
true master, the public, has reinstated itself. It may need to come
in a rigorous insistence towards the railroads that their literal
franchise rights be adhered to in valuing their properties, and that
their legal position as occupants of the highways of the nation in a
national service be enforced. It may have to come in dealing with
such an institution as the Chicago Stock Yards, [which has] become
so enormously valuable through the vicious control it has attained
over food. Such a blow, if it does become necessary, will only become necessary because otherwise the truth of power and right cannot be driven home. It can be, it should be, tempered with mercy
to the small investor, the innocent bystander, and, if it is not, the
fault will lie only with the great profiteer who stands in the way of
equity. And at its worst such a blow will be insignificant, compared
with all of those confiscations which we have always with us under
the reign of things as they have been.

Notes

1. Helen Marot, "Labor Control of Government Industries," *The Dial,* Vol.
LXVI, No. 788 (April 19, 1919), pp. 411–13.

* Some economists, e.g., Thorstein Veblen and Stuart Chase, strongly support
Bentley's critique of advertising. Others justify it, in part, at least. Cf., Neil
Borden, *Economic Effects of Advertising* (Homewood, Ill.: Richard D. Irwin,
1942); Martin Mayer, *Madison Avenue, U.S.A.* (New York, Harper & Row,
1958); David M. Potter, *People of Plenty* (Chicago: University of Chicago Press,
1954). On advertising in relation to monopoly as well as consumer welfare, see
Fritz Machlup, *The Political Economy of Monopoly* (Baltimore: Johns Hopkins,
1952), pp. 10, 124–26, 160.

2. This attitude has finally reached its full expression in the arguments before the [United States] Supreme Court about the power of the people to amend the Constitution: in the Prohibition Amendment cases [*Rhode Island v. Palmer*, 253 U.S. 350 (1920)].

3. Federal Trade Commission, *Report on the Meat-Packing Industry: Letter to the President*, Vol. I, pp. 25–26.

4. Written before the [Attorney-General] Palmer compromise with the packers; but in substance not affected by that compromise, which is one of surface appearance, not of substantial fact. [The consent decree was recorded in the Supreme Court of the District of Columbia on February 27, 1920.]

5. "The United States is the only nation in which private slaughtering is permitted, with the possible exception of Great Britain and Turkey." Frederic C. Howe, *The High Cost of Living* (New York: Scribner's, 1917), p. 145. The context limits the reference to Europe.

6. Compare as to such discrimination in packing and grain selling the testimony of Charles H. May, manager of the Farmers' Cooperative Packing Company, quoted, Federal Trade Commission, *Report on the Meat Packing Industry*, Vol. II, p. 116; and the testimony of C. H. Gustafson, House *Hearings on Government Control of the Meat-Packers Industry*, pp. 295ff.

7. One of the latest and most suggestive writers on cooperation, Albert Sonnichsen, has insisted that the only true field of cooperative endeavor is that of consumers' cooperation, and that it will be fatal to attempt to harmonize producers' cooperatives with consumers' cooperatives, because a split of interest over prices will inevitably appear. His ideal pattern of a developing society is that of consumers' cooperatives entering the field of production until they finally control it, never with producers conflicting interests in mind, but always with consumers' ultimate interests. He seems not to solve, but rather to evade the conflict of interests, and above that to lose sight of the need of appeal to productive stimulus in all our work. The view taken here is the opposed one: that these deeper conflicts of interest will always exist; that they must be encouraged on their productive side and suppressed on their appropriative side; that the solution of the conflicts, the adjustment of interest to interest on an equitable basis, is the function of government; that to that end government should enter, for public benefit, the field of financial control of output and prices now usurped by the greater corporations for private benefit; and that specially, as an incident to the whole development, it should encourage both producers' and consumers' cooperative organizations by every means in its power. [See Albert Sonnichsen, *Consumers' Cooperation* (New York: The Macmillan Company, 1919).]

8. Cf., Frederic C. Howe, *The High Cost of Living*. [Cf., E. S. Sparks, *History and Theory of Agricultural Credit in the United States* (New York, Crowell, 1932); B. Henderson, "State Policies in Agricultural Settlement," *Journal of Land and Public Utility Economics*, Vol. II, No. 3 (July, 1926), pp. 284–96.]

9. Howe, *op. cit.*, p. 257 [and see Paul Vandereike, "Planning Land Settlement," *American Cooperative Journal*, Vol. 15 (January, 1920), pp. 6–7].

10. U.S. Council of National Defense, *An Analysis of the High Cost of Living Problem* (August, 1919), p. 10.

11. *Indianapolis News*, September 14, 1919. At the meeting of the National Association of Retail Clothiers in Chicago in January 1920, a Chicago Tribune reporter showed a telegram from the secretary of the National Wool Growers Association placing the wool value in a suit of $60- to $75-clothes at $5.25, and asked an official of the Amalgamated Clothing Workers of America who was present to state what the labor cost in such a suit of clothes was. The answer he received was: "I have the information, of course, but it is confidential between the garment workers and the manufacturers."

XXII

Political Strength and Methods

The questions next arise as to how large a middle-class following is probable for such political programs; what methods will be used; and what will be the chances of success against existing predatory forces which, however [much] smaller in numbers, always have advantages in the narrow concentration of their purpose, their power of initiative, and their ruthlessness in execution.

Political parties are presumably the agencies through which voters will advance, but it has long been recognized that the two established American political parties, the Democratic and Republican, are not really parties in the sense of [the usually accepted] definition; they are not groups of persons "who favor or are united to promote certain views or opinions";[1] rather they are semi-formalized institutions of government, more in the nature of administrative agencies than of free groupings of voters. As such, they are often less agencies by which the people accomplish things than they are hindrances to accomplishment. As a result, the real parties must often be sought behind the formal parties, and especially in non-partisan associations or leagues of citizen voters for the accomplishment of specific political objects.

The two established political parties operate on a foundation of their "hide-bound" straight vote, their 25 per cent or more of the voters who rarely question and never change their party affiliation, who, through their apathy or stupidity or lack of contact with the facts and arguments on which policies are based, stay always where they are put. The party programs do not initiate, but strive to avoid real issues; the platform planks, even where aggressively framed, are universally understood to be taken with a grain of salt; the candidates must be men against whom no positive objections can be brought rather than men for whom positive purposes or achievements can be urged. The parties stand, not as proponents of political changes, but somewhat as shock absorbers against rapid change; and they have indeed distorted even this function until now they seem to absorb the minor shocks of gradual transformation, as well as the great ones, with the result of heaping up [problems for] a day of wrath for the future. Under such conditions, it has been well said that Democrats and Republicans are not so much rival parties as one party in two sections; the Northern or Republican, and the Southern or Democratic.[2]

Given such a situation, the possibilities for the development of a third party, meeting them on their chosen ground and with similar methods, is insignificant except under catastrophic conditions. It took the Slavery issue preceding the Civil War to produce the last successful party of our established type. Since then, a dozen or more minor parties have nominated national candidates, but not one has won success; and, indeed, all have now vanished, saving only the Socialist irreconcilables, whose dual parties are rather evidences of interest than anticipations of political achievement. Catastrophic conditions are indeed again at hand, and the time may soon be ripe for the appearance of a new party which will sweep away the two existing parties or drive them into consolidation. But such an event is not for this year or next. And in the meantime, the political struggle continues on the old basis. Let us examine, therefore, what results have in recent years been achieved by the method of non-partisan organization operating behind the formal parties, in order to learn what such a method may accomplish in the coming issues and what kind of political organization may be developed by its use.

One of the earliest successes of this method on a notable scale was secured by the Municipal Voters League of Chicago. This League [in the early Twentieth Century] was formed to fight the Yerkes control of the street railways of Chicago, which was threatening to turn itself into a perpetual control of the streets themselves; and which had already established a bipartisan corrupt control of the [Chicago] City Council, and was well on the way towards equally thorough control of the [Illinois] state legislature. The

League announced its principles, kept full records of each alderman's votes and connections, published summaries of these records before each election, and endorsed or condemned candidates on the one test of public interest in the streets. It saved the streets to the city, made Chicago unattractive as a field for such exploitation, and, in the end, unloaded Yerkes upon London. So far it was a brilliant success. But when its issue disappeared, when it continued as a self-constituted leader of public opinion with no clear understanding of what kind of opinion it led, it lost all its prestige and became almost as insignificant as the Chicago newspapers in guiding the action of voters at the polls.

Another great success, and on a much larger scale, was that of the Anti-Saloon League. The Prohibition Party had early reached the limit of its direct party methods, but the new league—taking the stress off of drink and placing it on the saloon as an institution, nominating no candidates of its own, but rallying its supporters in both parties to vote for whatever candidates in either [party] supported its program—became a power in the nation, and won through to success, first in the states, and then with the [Eighteenth] Prohibition Amendment to the national Constitution.

It should be noted that this method is fundamentally not so different from that of the old lobby and machine, working in the interests of the industrial government. Omit the bribery, substitute an open following with avowed purposes for a hidden backing with secret purposes, and there is left the underlying similarity of an organization of voters with a political purpose, playing upon both established parties and working through both with one aim. Repeatedly it has happened in large cities under the boss system that two party bosses, apparently fighting each other, have had behind them a secret higher boss ruling both. The method of the American Federation of Labor, with its headquarters in Washington and its stress on lobbying, also represents to some extent the same type of effort [as the Anti-Saloon League].

By all means the most highly developed organization and the most brilliant success of this method [in 1920] has been achieved by the National Non-Partisan League, dominant in North Dakota, strong in Minnesota and in three or four other states, and full of possibilities in perhaps a dozen states of the Northwest. The farmers of North Dakota wanted certain legislation; they secured its endorsement in party platforms; they elected legislators who were supposed to favor it; they even voted heavily for it on referendum; but they failed to get it under established party methods. They were told to "go home and slop the hogs." They retorted that they would continue to slop the hogs, but that it was the other fellow who would go home and stay there. They proceeded to organize for results. To the bipartisan combination which had cheated them of success year after year, they opposed their own non-partisan organization. They paid $8 a year apiece for expenses; developed a thorough system of endorsing candidates;[3] voted for the men they endorsed; controlled the entire state government, except for the holdover senators at their first election; and at their second election completed the job, and put through their program as they wanted it, constitutional amendments and all.

They clinched their reforms by an unparalleled showing at the referendum on the constitutional amendments in July 1919, when nine-tenths as many voters turned out on question of policy alone as had gone to the polls at the preceding presidential election. In this work in North Dakota, the League organization used the Republican Party primarily because that party was heavily in the majority, and it even succeeded in making one of its national executive committee members the chairman of the Republican State Committee. But it kept itself free to use the Democratic Party in the same way in other states, and it is possible that in some future national contest, the League may swing its membership from both parties in support of the same presidential candidate.[4]

So much for the non-partisan method as it has actually shown its powers in issues of very different kinds appealing to different classes of people. We are now, however, on the eve of a great elaboration of it, whereby not merely single groups can use it for single issues, but whereby widely different groups with different ranges of issues can use it to join forces for action on such fundamental parts of their programs as are common to all. This is already forecasted [in 1920] in Minnesota by the understanding arrived at by the farmer and labor groups for joint action. But before discussing this let us review the elements of the population that may combine for its use.

We have already identified to [a] considerable degree the middle-class interest of the country with the consumers' interest. The argument rests on the high cost of living, not merely in its superficial but in its fundamental aspects; on the small portion of the cost in retail prices that goes to the producers of raw material (compare the 10 per cent for the wool in a suit of clothes); on the small part of that cost that goes to labor (compare the 10 per cent [for] wages in a pair of shoes); and on the centralization in comparatively few hands of the income that survives the atrocious wastes in the distribution of the lion's share of the product. We have seen that the rewards of the minor profiteer and waster in the trading system are held low by the very system of fixed prices that seems to safeguard them; for as fast as total retail profits in a community are big enough to permit it, new traders appear to share the trade by wasteful multiplication of establishments.

Now this very consumers' interest is identical, as we find it among wage-laborers and among farmers, with what it is among those members of the middle classes in towns and cities who cannot be identified with either of the other two groups. The farmers may be described as middle-class by the further test that they earn their livings by the use of personal property; and while this test will not apply directly to wage-earners, the following considerations do apply to them. Every advance towards profit-sharing, towards participation in business management, towards distribution of preferred-stock shares among them, gives the wage-earners something of this property interest.

The rapid rise of retail prices has turned their attention towards the spending of their wages rather than towards the actual increase in the dollar amount of them. [This has been] notably witnessed by the statement of the railway unions in midsummer 1919, that they must either strike for higher wages or have the cost of living reduced; coupled with the statement that they preferred the reduction in cost of living to the increase in wages; again, in the action of certain of these unions in using their strike-benefit reserves deliberately to undertake trading and even manufacturing operations by which to secure for their members cheaper and better supplies. Above all is the fact that, in the last analysis and under the severest strain, it is income, and not property, which is the final reality and test of position. Let us see in more detail how this works out for the three groups.

If we take the Non-Partisan League program as typifying developed farmers' opinion, not in its details, but in its underlying purposes (and we are here taking a case which is at the extreme distance from the usual conception of middle-class attitude), we, nevertheless, find all the typical elements of middle-class interests. The League is not in any way identified with convulsive revolutionary agitators, nor is it in any way sympathetic to them, any more than it is a party of class conscious wage-workers. It is a party of men using their own capital and planning deliberately to clear the ways for freer use of private capital in free individual enterprises. It is giving almost as much thought to consumers' welfare through cooperation as it is to political programs to help producers. Its state enterprises are not primarily its desire, but its necessity. The denunciations of it as anarchist, socialist, and Bolshevik have at the outside the 6-cent valuation which the Henry Ford jury saw in such terms as applied to him by the wanton writers of the *Chicago Tribune*. Its program is to foster production, to eliminate waste, and to eliminate profiteering.

Omitting now the special planks and projects applicable primarily to [the] farming business, this program is far from being in opposition to the programs of the newly formed [local and state] labor parties in this country. It is indeed in very close sympathy with them in most fundamental matters. The labor parties likewise strive for the elimination of profiteering and waste, and for the increase in production. The labor party platforms contain, it is true, more planks primarily of interest to wage-earners and they stress these planks more heavily; but they also include an ample supply of fundamental policies that match those of the farmers.

These labor parties were formed in the early months of 1919 in many cities and counties, and rapidly developed state organizations in eight or ten states. They combined for national purposes in August [1919], and held a national convention in December. In making their call for this convention, they opened their ranks to all hand- and brain-workers,[5] and named as their test of party allegiance the support of three demands: first, for the "restoration of all civil liberties"; second, for "the national ownership and

democratic management of the means of transportation and communication, mines, finance, and all other monopolies and natural
resources"; and third, for "the abolition of excessive land-ownership
and of the holding land out of use for speculative purposes." It
might appear that in this last demand they would come in conflict
with the farmers' programs, but such is not the case. The North
Dakota farmers are favorable to measures such as their mortgage-
loan system that bring more farmers into the state, and they are
favorable to taxes that bear with special weight on land value as
distinct from improvement. One large representative national group
of farmers, the Farmers National Council, shows similar interest; it
maintains a single-tax department in the *Farmers Open Forum*
which it publishes, and its reconstruction program is very close in
all respects to these labor party demands.

The [National] Labor Party, it is true, does not start with the
non-partisan method. It adopts the party method and the Labor
standard as the best means of rallying its chosen following, even
though this name and method will eliminate directly many people
whom it would gladly welcome into its ranks. It is anything [but]
. . . a "class-conscious" labor organization in the narrow and aggressive sense of that term, however. It has no use for revolutionists,
and they have no use for it. The policies it supports are of the
step-by-step kind. It definitely welcomes all cooperative organizations into affiliation with it, and the many labor cooperatives were
specially invited to send their own delegates to its convention.[6] Out
of twenty-four planks in the 1919 platform of the Illinois state
party, ten were primarily labor planks; six related to political reforms, none of which were essentially or primarily advocated by
labor; two concerned profiteering and cooperation; two were general declarations in favor of the restoration of civil liberties and the
democratization of industry; and the other four proposed legislation
concerning education, income taxation, public ownership, and state
aid to home-building. Even its labor planks were of a broad type
that are getting ever wider support outside of labor circles. So by
all these tests, the Illinois party [Labor] may be said, despite its
"Labor" name, to be in fact what it claims to be: a party, not only
of hand-workers, but of all workers, a party for all citizens except
parasites and deliberate profiteers.

Another evidence of the middle-class quality of the new labor parties lies in the very fact that they are almost as sharply condemned by the out-and-out union labor organizers as they are by the class-conscious wage-earner revolutionists. Reference has already been made to the opposition of the dominant Gompers machine (in the American Federation of Labor) to this development. At the annual convention of the Federation in 1919, a resolution disapproving of these parties was passed, and this opposition has become increasingly bitter. The old attitude of union labor has been that its work is forcefully to appropriate a part of the earnings of the great capitalistic appropriators, and its established political tools have been lobbying, dickering, and log-rolling after approved methods for the legislation it desires. The new spirit, as shown by these parties, is to approach the deeper problems from the point of view of all citizenship.

Political organization of the farmers is in a less advanced stage [than] that [of] the labor parties, except in the one case of the Non-Partisan League, which has already gone much further, both in organization and in political success. The League has limitations, however, in its economic background and in its type of problems which will doubtless prevent its successfully entering, on its present footing, [into] states in which [the] type and conditions of farming are radically different. The great farmer-organizations of social, business and lobbying types have been the Grange, the Equity, the Union, and the Gleaners; and all of these except the latter are today split through the middle by issues of liberalism and of political reform. They have all maintained, independently or in combinations, legislative bureaus at Washington; and among these, the Farmers National Council which represents the Liberals, is coming more and more to be the nucleus of a new national organization—comprising in varying degrees of affiliation all of the Western and Northwestern Granges, the whole of the Gleaners' organization, the greater part of the Equity, and the strongest of the state farmers unions, though not the majority of those unions.[7]

Latest in the field, among farmers' organizations, is the [American] Farm Bureau Federation, a development of [November] 1919 which bids fair to become one of the greatest national farmer associations, and the active rival of the newly forming consolidation of

liberal farmers' associations. Its organization is definitely terri-
torial by states, counties, and townships; one of its main functions
in some states is the support of the county agent system, and it has
close connections with the state agricultural colleges and extension
departments. Even in this organization, which received much of its
initiative from non-farming leadership of a reactionary business
nature, the tendency to split on questions of the day with varying
degrees of liberalism is showing itself, and the forceful surge of
awkward problems from the ranks of the membership is being felt.[8]

If the farmers and wage-earners have made very considerable
strides towards organization for political purposes, what can we say
of the vaguer elements of the middle classes, the city and town res-
idents with moderate incomes gained largely by personal efforts,
exclusive of wage-earners, of successful profiteers and their minions,
and of parasites? It is not a question of arguing here their true
interest, for that theme has already been given much attention. The
question concerns the actual development of their viewpoint based
on these interests, and the beginnings of organization of it for political purposes.

A nucleus here, possibly for party organization and certainly for
non-partisan organization, will be furnished by a large element of
the rank-and-file of the old [1912] Progressive Party (those who
voted for its candidates because of its reform program); and to these
there may be accessions from the moderate socialists who split from
their party on war issues and are left permanently outside its breast-
works. The single-tax advocates will furnish accessions, for they
are already recognizing that the same types of conditions which
they have fought in land tenure must now be fought in other reaches
of the industrial system. The National Party, formed in 1917 [by
Progressives, Prohibitionists, Single-Taxers, Social Democrats, and
Independents] which gathers a considerable strength in some localities, but not enough to ensure its survival, may also contribute
men and women who have taken the first steps in such organization
and are looking for a more promising opportunity on a greater scale.
The societies in behalf of civil liberties and the freeing of political
prisoners are also to be reckoned [with].

All these are mentioned merely as organizations in the nature
of forerunners to that which may soon be expected. The people to

whom the appeal will reach will include clerks and salespeople, public school teachers, members of the artisan trades, and small shopkeepers. The typical shrewd tradesman must be counted out as hostile, but men of this type are probably not nearly so numerous as census and other figures, which estimate all the storekeepers and include among them their employees, would at first sight seem to indicate. The engineers and the organizers and administrators of Big Business, who have command of materials and men, but are shut out of all share in control of output and prices, are in a position to reflect deeply on what is happening, and may be expected in time to furnish a very substantial strength. The housewives, newly possessed of the ballot [through the Nineteenth Amendment in 1920]—the purchasers of perhaps 90 per cent of all goods sold over the counters of retail stores, and natural enemies of excessive prices—have here a chance to express their interests, and conceivably may do so with heavy weight.[9]

Of the general expressions of interest from such classes, without any direct political intention, we have had interesting illustrations in the last two or three years from the churches. The Social Reconstruction program of the National Catholic War Council is the most thorough in its study and conclusions. It names three evils in our present system and insists they must be remedied: "enormous inefficiency and waste in the production and distribution of commodities; insufficient incomes for the great majority of wage earners; and unnecessarily large income for a small minority of privileged capitalists." It favors strongly the development of cooperative selling and cooperative marketing. In producing establishments, it insists that "the majority must somehow become owners, or at least in part, of the instruments of production." It demands "prevention of monopolistic control of commodities, adequate government regulation of such public service monopolies as will remain under private operation, and heavy taxation of incomes, excess profits and inheritances.[10]

The Central Conference of American Rabbis, at their Chicago conference, adopted a declaration of principles with fourteen planks, all liberal towards labor.[11] The General Assembly of the Presbyterian Church has advocated a number of industrial reforms tending towards a more equitable division of wealth; and the social service division of the Presbyterian New Era movement has gone further into detail in urging its members to interest themselves actively in such reforms. The Board of Bishops of the Methodist-Episcopal Church has declared in favor of giving an equitable wage for labor, "the right of way over rent, interest, and profits," in favor of "collective bargaining and the advance of the workers themselves through profit-sharing and through positions on the boards of directorship." A commission of the American Unitarian Association has issued a statement on the social duty of the churches. The Federal Council of Churches, representing a membership of 23 million, has gone on record as favoring industrial councils and shop committees and the making of a living wage "the first charge upon industry before dividends are considered."[12]

The above are but the signs of developing middle-class opinion. Of definite political organizations following the Progressive Party, there came first the National Party; largely dominated by the pro-war Socialists, inaugurated at a most unpropitious time, and abandoned after a few slight local successes. This has been followed by the Committee of Forty-eight and the National Peoples League; the former an attempt at national organization of liberal thought preliminary to political action, the latter a northwestern organization sympathetic to the Non-Partisan League and allied with the Public Ownership League of America.

The Committee of Forty-eight, taking its name from the forty-eight states of the nation, began as an organization of liberal thinkers, writers, speakers, educators and other professional people, and has proceeded to organize the country into districts through which its educational work can be carried on. When it had about 3,000 members, a referendum showed these to be about 80 per cent in favor of government ownership of railroads (with half of this 80 per cent favoring the Plumb Plan); 94 per cent in favor of the Labor Party program in general; 94 per cent in favor of limiting the power of the courts in declaring laws unconstitutional; 96 per cent in favor of the Non-Partisan League; 90 per cent against the espionage laws, 99 per cent in favor of free speech; and 88 per cent in favor of progressive transfer of real-estate taxes from improvements to land values. The Committee [of Forty-Eight] has confined itself to generalities thus far, both in its program and in its propaganda. It has made the essentially defensive measure of public ownership its main plank, and it has sought adherents on an argumentative basis rather than in direct analysis of the various groups of the middle classes and direct appeal to their interests in national welfare.[13] What power it may secure through this method, or what further developments there will be in its methods, remains to be seen. There should certainly be a great possibility of combining many local non-partisan leagues, consumers' leagues, housewives' unions, and even local political parties, into a unity of purpose.

So far as actual alliances have gone among these three groups, the progress is not great but it is nevertheless significant. Fraternal delegates have gone from [their own conventions] to the conventions of the others, beginning with the visit of Governor [Lyn J.] Frazier of North Dakota to the nominating convention of the Chicago Labor Party in the spring of 1919. The Minnesota alliance between the Non-Partisan League and the state labor party bids fair to produce results at the fall election of 1920, which will greatly stimulate such alliance. The national convention of the [National] Labor Party in November 1919 did not go so far as its leaders, or . . . the Minnesota delegates, desired in this respect. The constitution it adopted opened the way to all working alliances with "any organized farmers group" or "other progressive organization or party"; but only in case such groups "shall endorse the principles and platform of the Labor Party," which would make them annexes to it rather than allied bodies.

Alliance proper cannot come until the various groups combine for the big essentials of their programs which are common to all, and leave each other free in the planks peculiar to the needs of each.[14] At present [early in 1920], the Committee of Forty-eight is still seeking a following, rather than actually representing one; the Labor parties have not yet shown that they can overcome the resistance of the old-line union labor politicians; and the Non-Partisan League is distinctly a sectional organization. The progress that has been shown elsewhere towards an economic understanding between the farmer and labor groups is a more important signpost than the actual accomplishments in political alliance.

The enemies of the political programs of farmers and laborers have, of course, done their utmost to make the two groups quarrel with one another. They have insidiously emphasized the old assumed conflict of interest between them. They have tried to make the laborer believe that the farmer was responsible for high prices of food; and to make the farmer believe that the laborer with his short hours was making manufacturing costs high, and with his strikes was destroying the market for produce. As against the organizations we have been discussing, this effort has not made the slightest headway. These organizations have seen clearly where the costs and wastes lie, and are a unit in fighting them there.

But in some states, especially in the central west, "back-fire" organizations of farmers, as they are called, have sprung rapidly into existence. Sometimes they have been created out of whole cloth by men who are far from being farmers themselves or [far from] representing farming interests; at other times, existing organizations have been used, or sometimes seized and twisted for the purpose. State agricultural colleges and county agricultural agents have been mobilized. One has no difficulty in recognizing associations of this type. Their speakers harp endlessly on the wickedness of union labor. Their officers have a disposition to hold lunch-table conferences with the Big Five packers at Chicago hotels, and to oppose all projects . . . [towards] legislation for the control of the packing industry. They are very free to denounce minor evils in stockyards, or special losses in grain-handling, but they have no sympathy with any effort to pry into the heart of the trouble.

All of this development was transitional, and some of these organizations have disappeared while others have merged into the Farm Bureau Federation, into which they have dragged their outside interests (at such value as they can maintain for them there) against rising opposition from the membership. In Indiana, for example, where the origin of the state federation was not in farm bureaus, . . . but in county farmers' associations interested in marketing problems, and where the control of the federation was snatched from these associations by machine methods of a highly ruthless type . . . some of the worst elements of this external domination have already been stripped off.

If the immediate future is one mainly of non-partisan methods for working upon both established political parties to get results, it is not difficult to believe that the day is not far off when a true second party may appear which will force the fight and compel consolidation of the Democratic and Republican parties, making one body as well as one spirit out of the twain. Under catastrophic conditions, it has been said, and under such conditions only, can this come to pass. And such conditions are well advanced in their development.

What would be the issue, the slogan, of such a new party, combining these various elements of the citizenry in self-defense? Would it not be the issue of property against all profiteering, the issue of safe property and fair income against the centralized powers of appropriation?

Might it not, even under the name of a National Property Rights party, undertake this task in defense of income and of property and of their enjoyment by all of the people?

Might it not find its spearhead of attack in insistence on two amendments to the Constitution as the basis of its reconstruction?

The first:

The privileges and immunities of citizens of the United States under the Constitution and the amendments thereto are reaffirmed. It shall be treason against the people of the United States for any individual or association or for any officials of the United States, legislative, executive or judicial, or of any state, to deny or abridge them. The Congress shall enforce the provisions of this article by appropriate legislation.

The second:

The immunities of citizens of the United States with respect to their property shall extend to all land and commodities and instruments of production in their possession, use, and enjoyment by individuals and by associations of makers or of users. This shall not be construed to include claims upon the future income of the people arising and exercised apart from the participation of the owner in productive service; but the enjoyment of claims arising from the productive service of the owner, by hand or by brain, and their privilege of sale or exchange, shall not be impaired. The Congress shall have power to enforce the provisions of this article by appropriate legislation.

Notes

1. The *Century Dictionary* definition: "A company or number of persons ranged on one side, or united in opinion or design, in opposition to others in the community; those who favor or are united to promote certain views or opinions: as the Liberal party; the Democratic party; the party of moral ideas."

2. Allen McCurdy, "Wanted—A Ballot Box," *The Nation*, Vol. 109, No. 2818 (July 5, 1919), pp. 8-10. Indeed, Senator Thomas was quoted as saying, when the Sims Bill embodying the Plumb plan of railroad control had its first hearings in committee, that so radical and dangerous was this plan that the two parties might have to combine to "save the Republic."

3. The primary system of the League consists in gathering all members in local districts, townships or other, placing on a blackboard the names of all candidates for each office in that district, and balloting with the elimination each time of the low name. By the same method, a district representative is sent to the county convention or legislative district convention. There the same process is gone through, both as to candidates and as to choosing a representative to the state convention. The present governor of North Dakota was nominated under the blackboard method without his own knowledge or presence.

4. The League has maintained an educational department that has been very efficient and has supplied books at low cost, sometimes having special editions of standard works printed for its purposes. Woodrow Wilson's *New Freedom* (New York and Garden City: Doubleday, Page & Company, 1913); Frederic C. Howe's *High Cost of Living*, and Emerson P. Harris' *Cooperation, The Hope of the Consumer* have been widely circulated.

5. In this they are at one with the British Labor Party. In the tentative program of that party prepared in 1918 it was said "the interests of the clerk, the teacher, the doctor, the minister of religions, the average retail store keeper and all the mass of those living on small incomes are identical with those of the artisan," and it was estimated that these classes composed four-fifths of the population.

6. The number of union labor cooperative stores is increasing rapidly, and some of the ablest union labor leaders are very active in this work. Duncan MacDonald, former president of the Illinois State Federation of Labor is a member of the executive committee of the National Wholesale Cooperatives.

7. The Grange has about 600,000 members (counting both men and women) of which about 85,000 are in the Liberal movement. The Union has about 125,000 members of which the Nebraska Union, which is at the very front of the Liberal movement, alone has 40,000.

8. Immediately after the Senate and House hearings on the bills to control the meat-packing industry in January 1919, representatives of the Big Five packers became active to promote "cooperation" between packers and livestock growers. A conference in Chicago appointed a committee of 23 to consider it, see "Packers and Producers Plan Cooperation," *National Provisioner*, Vol. 60 (March 22, 1919), p. 15. Thomas E. Wilson, of Wilson and Company, made addresses advocating it in several states immediately, in connection with the appearance of the new state farmers federations. Harvey J. Sconce, first president of the Illinois Agricultural Association, delivered an address at its first convention in which he advocated legislation authorizing price-fixing by a commission consisting of packers, members of his Agricultural association and consumers. (See *Prairie*

Farmer, February 8, 1919.) Mr. Sconce and other leaders of this movement later became active Lowden campaign workers [Frank O. Lowden, candidate for President, Republican Party], some of them resigning and some not resigning their official connections with the farm organizations. One cannot help harking back to the packers' confidential memorandum on the Bourland Resolution: "Get something cooperative started which cannot be finished for some time," and "Would we favor a permanent marketing committee of the livestock men and packers?" This lion-and-lamb proposition continues to be pushed by farmers' associations of the kind described in the text. J. Ogden Armour said at the Senate hearings "The tendency of the natural individual is to be selfish; and I claim that . . . there could be some arrangement that would take the livestock man into our confidence . . ." (Senate Committee on Agriculture and Forestry, *Hearings on Government Control of the Meat Packing Industry,* 65th Cong., 3rd Sess. (1919), p. 681.) The Illinois association, in connection with some incidental dispute, has inspired members of the Chicago Board of Trade to give interviews saying that the association seemed to be acting directly in the interest of the packers.

9. Very significant indeed was the fresh and joyous intelligence with which the delegates to the 1920 convention of the Woman's Suffrage Alliance at Chicago greeted the appearance of Swift's ex-professor and present commercial research manager, L. D. H. Weld, and his attempts to prove to them that the Big Five packers were their best friends.

10. [See the program printed in John A. Ryan, *Social Reconstruction,* pp. 235–36.] Other expressions are "The man who utilizes his ability to produce cheaper than his competitors for the purpose of exacting from the public as high a price for his product as is necessary for the least efficient business man, is a menace rather than a benefit to industry and society." "The employer has a right to get a reasonable living out of his business, but he has no right to interest on his investment until his employees have obtained at least living wages. This is the human and Christian in contrast to the purely commercial and pagan ethics of industry."

11. See *Nation,* Vol. 109, No. 2818 (July 5, 1919), p. 20.

12. See "The Voice of the Churches," *Nation,* Vol. 109, No. 2842 (Dec. 20, 1919), pp. 788–89; [for] correspondence between Ralph M. Lasley and William Fellowes Morgan concerning the Every Name Movement of the Episcopal Church, and two other Episcopal movements, the Church League for Social and Industrial Democracy and the Church Socialist League [see "Business and the Church,"] *Nation,* Vol. 109, No. 2829 (September 20, 1919), pp. 393–94.

13. Its tentative platform adopted at its national conference at St. Louis in December 1919 is as follows: "1. Public ownership of transportation, including stockyards, large abattoirs, grain elevators, terminal warehouses, pipe lines and tanks. Public ownership of other public utilities and of the principal natural resources, such as coal, oil, natural gas, mineral deposits, large water powers, and large commercial timber tracts. 2. No land (including natural resources) and no patents be held out of use for speculation to aid monopoly. We favor taxes to force idle land into use. 3. Equal economic, political, and legal rights for all, irrespective of sex or color. The immediate and absolute restoration of free speech, free press, peaceable assembly, and all civil rights guaranteed by the Constitution. We demand the abolition of injunctions in labor cases. We endorse the effort of labor to share in the management of industry and labor's right to organize and bargain collectively through representative of its own choosing." [See Lincoln Colcord, "The Committee of Forty-Eight," *The Nation,* Vol. 109, No. 2843 (December 27, 1919), pp. 821–22. These three planks, differing only in elaboration and emphasis, are the same as those set forth in the preliminary call for the convention of the National Labor Party, [cf., *New York Times,* December 11 and 12, 1919].

14. In Minnesota, each group drafts its own platform, and then each appoints a small harmonizing committee to bring the two into agreement where verbal expression or minor details of program are in conflict. Thus far there has been no difficulty with this, since leaders on both sides agree that their general aims are the same. The Labor Party will nominate its own candidates in such districts as it hopes to control, and the League will support them. Where direct labor candidates are not named, the Labor Party will follow the League recommendations.

XXIII

Productive Property in the Future

Would such a program of changes as has been advocated in the preceding chapters make a striking difference in the ordinary everyday business and manufacturing relations of man to man? Would it require men to reorganize their practical points of approach to one another in their business of getting a living? Would it make them feel themselves in a strange world to which they were unadapted? I believe it would not. On the contrary, I believe such changes would be less striking in this respect than many of the changes to which we have recently submitted ourselves. They would require less adaptation from us as individuals than was required by the conditions under which we lived in wartime [World War I], and which we found not at all so startling in practice as it seemed they would be when their necessity was first proclaimed. Rather, they would be our salvation from the extreme changes in our personal lives to which we will perforce submit, should our future involve either autocratic industrial dictatorship or convulsive proletarian revolution [like that of the Bolshevik Revolution of October 1917].

Even should we think in terms of the position of the wage-laborer rather than of the businessman, the changes would be restorative and assimilative rather than something involving the development of a new type of person. What the hand-worker has gone through in the development of the factory system and in the development of his fighting [trade-union] organization to increase his income and [to] improve his working conditions has searched his nature deeper than what, we may hope, he will go through in the years to come. Moreover, the changes in the position of wage-labor are upon us, entirely regardless of any program one may consider.

273

We have not presumed here to speak for the man under the wage-system. We have noted what is happening. The growth, on the one side, of the rigid [socially] protective measures such as the minimum wage and unemployment insurance; and the trend, on the other, towards participation of labor in industrial management, whether by small grant or by great seizure. We have recognized the apparent inevitability of some assimilation of the workers' position to that of the other owning and producing men; and we have sympathized with a change which will put him on a plane with these other men through his acquirement of [a] property interest and management interest in business. Such a change we may call restorative and assimilative for this very reason, that it breaks down the growing class differentiation in the nation based on the two existing, two radically different, connections with the great business of getting a living: those of labor and of capital.

Revolutionary the program we have suggested must be for all citizens; revolutionary in its attitude towards industrial dogma; revolutionary in seeking the heart of the trouble instead of trifling with symptoms; revolutionary as a substitute for the other impending revolutions (those of [business] autocracy and of [labor] convulsion); revolutionary also, we may hope, in the great heightening it would mean for the common weal. But not revolutionary in what it requires in character and habits of the citizen-maker and the citizen-user.

Consider the future from the point of view of "man, the adventurer." We are most of us adventurers in life; and those of us who are not are unhappy because we cannot break through to adventure. Vitality, the spirit of adventure, progress, are all terms pointing at the same fact. History records the results of adventure. Man, we may almost say, is man because of his unquenched curiosity, initiative, adventurousness. A society cutting out our adventuring possibilities will never be attractive, will never, perhaps, even be stable.

But just because the great adventures of the last generation have been those of the appropriators, that is no reason for thinking that their peculiar type of adventure holds any essential [inevitable] place in the nature of things; no more than it is necessary to think that cleverness in seeing appropriative opportunities and ruthlessness in pursuing them is the highest type of intellect and ability; nor that [a] society organized with appropriative [Big Business] leadership and mastery, is the best of all possible societies.

Had it not been for our adventurers in exploration, our adventurers in science, our adventurers in engineering, where would our adventurers in appropriation now stand? Certainly not far advanced on the paths they so glorify with their self-praise.

The spirit of adventure may put three war crosses on the breast of a boy, and later, through unhappy surroundings and opportunities, lead the same boy to the penitentiary or to the gallows. It may find for us America, the Oregon Trail, the North Pole. It may develop the highest explosives, start a cooperative enterprise or a social settlement, build a political career, give life to the IWW, or lead in a revolution. It may do all of these things, and a thousand others, giving us all of the best of our welfare, just as well as it may lead to an appropriative [Big Business] mastery of industry and to the accumulation of fortunes swollen far beyond the capacity of the owners to enjoy or to administer wisely and productively.

And, even if the appropriative [business-profiteering] adventure were the great adventure for man, it has the fatal defect in its various developments of destroying itself. At one end it involves an anarchy of rapine, and, at the other, an anarchy of centralized power, both alike fatal to all the mass of merry adventurers of life. So strongly has the privilege of such adventure today been concentrated, that opportunities to succeed become ever fewer to the many: the costs win out over the rewards. To cut off the most vicious appropriative opportunities, to work back from them to the less vicious, and so . . . towards some point of practical, every-day balance, will not destroy initiative and adventure but will open scope to them. The engineer, the administrator, the inventor—now at the service of the entrenched [Big Business] appropriator to whom they must sell themselves—will find openings to get rewards dependent, in truer measure, on the productiveness of their services. The greatest adventures of all will be theirs; those that set all men free to more adventure, and ever more.

But "man, the adventurer" is not [a] mere adventurer, . . . [clinging] ever to the end of some rainbow of promise. He is also "man, the established citizen," "man, the sharer in the common weal," "man, the property-holder." Changes which will increase the stability and security of the property which he can acquire by his own ability and efforts will surely not overthrow the traditional position [that] the individual holds in society, and to which education and experience have adapted him. Rather, they will be a guarantee against such subversive changes being convulsively brought about. "Private property" now has a range of meaning running all the way from actual commodities and tools to the sheerest [most tenuous] of claims set up to a part of the future national income. The value of these claims is established by the strategic power to realize on them. Given such positional and strategic power, no claim is too . . . [steep], too brazen, too voracious, to be incapable of conversion into ownership of the actual commodities and tools of the future. Given this power, no property of the present is safe in the future.

If the United States Steel Corporation makes $891 million in five years; if it successfully establishes (1) its resolute policy of never permitting an employee, or group of employees, to deal with it through outside representatives,[1] and (2) its further policy of never keeping an employee on its payroll who acts as a representative for other employees; if the Standard Oil Company interests are greater [than those of U.S. Steel] and equally resolute, and if these are both but agencies of a close-knit band of industrial masters; if the consumers of the country are bearing the burden under this system of autocratic [monopolistic or oligopolistic] control of output and prices, of high costs and profiteering; then, indeed, the private property of today has little hope of remaining safely and surely private property in the future.

And it is not only property, it is men, that are thus controlled and mastered. The free man of today has little assurance of being the free man of the future. It is the nation at work—the tools and the men together—that are imperiled. And so, in reality, the possibility of violent changes in the relations of man to man in society is involved—not in such programs as are here suggested, but in the lack of them; in the slothful permission on our part for the present tendencies to work themselves through to either of their alternative disasters.

After man, the adventurer, and man, the property-owner, we have to consider man, the worker, in his relation to his tools and to the use of them along with his fellow workers. What will the changes be? In some branches of industry the necessary tools are not so elaborate but what one man, or one small group of men, can hold and use a full equipment of them; but in other branches of industry the equipment must be perforce so enormous that this is impossible. The large or small farm managed by its owner, the normal-sized store, the blacksmith shop, the small factory, are types of the first class; while the second class is typified by our railroad system which is already, for the whole nation and from its general point of view, one consolidated equipment, one huge tool-complex. Such huge equipments require their many owners and their million or more coordinated workers.

So far as farming is concerned, nothing has been here advanced which would alter the industrial position of the farmer in what concerns his personal attitude towards work and reward. Through prices stabilized under government direction, instead of fluctuating under monopolistic [or oligopolistic] control, he would be set free to receive reward more certainly apportioned to his ability. He would be assured of reward as a farmer, even though he was deprived of it in his capacity of a land speculator. His land appreciations have been all, or almost all, that have saved him in the past; in the future he would not need such speculative aid. The field would be open for many more farmers independently operating with land of their own. The stimulus to production would be greater. The supply of labor to assist the independent farmer would come, as now [1920] from boys and young men getting a start, from small landholders not yet having full-sized farms of their own, and from older men working, perhaps, only a part of their time. The hopeless tenant-class, which we have in some sections, and the fixed adult agricultural labor-class would be, if not eliminated, at least given every opportunity to eliminate itself. Nothing would prevent the retired farmer holding the farm he had long owned, while some young man working to establish himself, farmed it with him. Nothing would prevent him from ending his days in comfort on the income from his past savings, still invested, should he so wish, in the very property in the use of which he had spent his active years.

Or take a small factory, which a man could establish and enlarge through his productive ability. His labor force would come to him in much the same way as to the farmer, from apprentices, from men getting their start in life, from men satisfied to work along in harness. Through whatever methods of profit-sharing or of participation of labor in factory management, the productive note would be emphasized. The owner's appropriative powers, whether against labor or against the consumer, would be trimmed down—that is all; his productive abilities would be freed.

Through the transitional stage of the large factory, or group of factories, with its intermediate array of problems, we pass to the nation-wide industry like the railroads. Railway workers under the Plumb Plan [for national ownership of railroads] would indeed have a radically different relation to life and to their fellows from what they have had under the extreme evils of the wage-labor system; or from what they have had as organized [trade-] union appropriators fighting capitalistic appropriators; but they would approach vastly nearer to the type of the working relations of farmer, tradesman, or small manufacturer than they now are or have been for many decades. Enough has been said of the possibilities in this field. The practical veto power which railroad unions now exercise on railroad [corporation] control, resting on a fighting [trade union] organization, would be replaced by a constructive interest, just as the present veto power of the Interstate Commerce Commission [when it is] representing the public would develop into a constructive direction [of] and harmonization with, other industries for [the] public benefit.

Something of the same nature seems to be inevitable—barring, of course, autocratic government or proletarian revolution—in the other great nation-wide industries, such as meat. Prices must be controlled, and output studied and stimulated, or otherwise regulated, by the [national] government in the public interest. Given a field for efficient management, next arises the need for efficient labor, [with] a stimulus to production rather than a stimulus to sabotage, and the answer is forecast. It is here, as elsewhere, an answer in terms of the man with his tools; and it is not essentially different so far as human relations go, whether it is a case in which one man has his tools and his equipment for himself and his associated helpers, or whether it is a case of a great organization of men handling a great tool-complex as their productive property in joint ownership.

As for trade, both wholesale and retail, the possibilities, have also been previously discussed, with special attention to the initiative and the stimulus for efficiency on the part of the business manager after his appropriative grasp has been loosened. By whatever development of cooperation among the people, and by whatever facilities of information and warehousing provided by the government, these qualities of enterprise can be retained. One can imagine further possibilities in which plant and equipment are owned by cooperators or by individual tradesmen, while government credit provides for the commodities passing over the shelves. Here also, the enterprise of efficiency would receive its proportionate productive reward. Whether as private entrepreneur or as profit-sharing manager, the head of such an establishment would receive rewards of similar type, rewards of productive profit, not of profiteering; and with him, or perhaps even all of his associated workers.

Of man as a self-respecting person, perhaps another word might be added. No suggestion has been here advanced for any direct attack on our evils of advertising, though the possibility of such a direct attack has been mentioned. Whether flagrantly dishonest or verbally truthful, whether innovating or iterating, whether commercial or "educational," whether suggestive or compelling, our present advertising is the tyrant of consumers' minds as well as a mainstay of profiteering. It may be that direct attack will be possible, or even necessary, but it seems more probable that the way that this Old Man of the Sea will be thrown off will be by cutting out the inducements that he has for his present stranglehold. Assume that we do thus get rid of the worst of our advertising burden, then surely consumers will again draw free breaths as human beings, become less victims of commercial hypnotism, less like flocks of sheep "tolled" by their butcher.

Notes

1. [Testimony of] Elbert H. Gary, October 2, 1919, before the Senate Committee on Education and Labor. [*Investigation of Strike in Steel Industries. Hearings,* 66th Cong., 1st Sess. (Washington, D.C.: Government Printing Office, 1919), I, p. 208. Cf., David Brody, *Labor in Crisis: The Steel Strike of 1919* (Philadelphia, New York: Lippincott, 1965).]

XXIV

Utopia

"Human nature" is the last refuge of the man who resists change. "Human nature," he will tell you, has always striven for profit, the greatest possible profit, and always will. "You can't help it," he will insist, "and if you expect anything else, you are a dreamer, you are [a] Utopian."

But how if the question at issue has to do, not with profit-making, but with a special excresence of profit-making, with profiteering? Slavery was once a form of profiteering; and whole structures of society, government and industry alike, were founded upon it. It has passed away. Serfdom, the bond[age] of man to the soil, and the feudal system erected upon it, have passed. Brigandage and privateering, and many other forceful methods of gaining a living which once were common enough, have likewise gone under the ban, and still we have not reached Utopia. Perhaps, after all, it may not be so utopian to expel the industrial profiteers of our land from their strongholds.

Which, indeed, is more utopian by the test of human nature: to look forward to some such change, or to hope that the present system of profiteering can maintain itself? The crux of the present system is production. (Was it not also the crux with slavery and with feudalism?) "Produce more" is the daily exhortation. But it is an exhortation directed at the working man. Is it human nature for these working men, given the amount of information and energy they now have, to continue to produce more for the benefit of other people? Their answer is already apparent. Human nature is expressing itself in sabotage, the twin brother of profiteering.

How simple is the problem in terms of human nature!

Is it good to have property to use and enjoy? Yes.

Is it bad to have your property and income at the peril of organized powers wastefully seizing it for their gain? Yes.

What chance has everyman's profit in the age of centralized profiteering? Little now, and ever less.

What becomes of civil liberties in eras of centralized profiteering? They vanish.

Is it American human nature to submit? Americans will not submit.

"It is their right, it is their duty, to throw off such a government and to provide new guards for their security."

They may do it swiftly, and thoroughly, and peacefully, through the use of their political powers [as] ordained and established by them and for them in their Constitution.

Index

283

California Fruit Growers Exchange, 233
California Land Settlement Act, 248
Canada, 181
Capital, 49, 50, 64, 91, 163–65, 170n10, 261;
industrial capitalization procedures, 14, 21,
29n13, 38, 54–55, 56, 57, 61, 74, 75, 81–82,
126–27, 141, 144, 145, 160–61, 179, 196,
205n1, 231, 238, 254; labor union, 234, 235
Carnegie, Andrew, 31, 160–61
Carnegie Foundation, 134, 217
Carnegie Steel Co., 160–61
Census of Wealth (1912), 12
Central Conference of American Rabbis, 265
Chafee, Zechariah, Jr., 213
Chamberlin, Edward H., *xvii, xviii, xix*
Chamber of Commerce, 103–104, 105, 108,
195–96
Chandler, Alfred D., Jr., *xx*
Chase National Bank, 124n
Chicago, Illinois, *x–xi, xii,* 130, 142, 233, 257–
58; labor conventions, 182n7, 265, 267,
270n8; prices in, 144, 234
Chicago, University of, *x, xix,* 213
Chicago Association of Commerce, 195–96
Chicago Stock Yards Co. of Maine, 199, 203,
205n3, 206n4, 254
Chicago Board of Trade, 113n6
Chicago Street Railway Employees, 26
Chicago Tribune, 261
Children, 26, 27, 89; labor of 25, 38, 44, 69,
242
Civil liberties, *xxv,* 8, 192, 207–22, 239, 282;
of assembly, 209, 211, 216–17; of due pro-
cess, 42, 58, 59; political means toward, *xxi,
xxiv,* 38, 261, 262, 264, 266, 271n13; of
speech, *xv,* 5, 6, 41, 167, 177–78, 187, 208–
17, 218, 219, 266, 271n13; voting, 7, 37, 38–
39, 40, 265
Civil War, *xv, xxi,* 44, 46n4, 96n21, 198, 236,
267
Clark, John Bates, *x*
Clark, John M., quoted, 27n, 166n
Clark, S. H., 222n13
Clayton Act, 29n11, 71n1
Cleveland, Ohio, 222n22
Coal, 21, 98, 99, 127n2, 224; land use, 11, 225,
248; strikes, *xxii,* 85
Cochran, Thomas, *xx*
Colorado, 209, 210, 220n1, 222n13
Colorado Fuel & Iron Co., 209, 220n1
Colver, William B., cited, 140
Committee of Forty-eight, 266–67, 271n13
Commodities, 1–2, 12, 13, 27, 74–76, 127n2,
160; as property, 48, 49, 50, 55, 57; shoddy,
89–93; standardization of, *xvii–xviii,* 76, 82–
83, 94n9, 145–46, 149n8
Commons, John R., *xv,* 107
Commonwealth Fund, 218
Communist Party, 174, 182n7
Competition, *see* Monopoly
"Condition of the Western Farmer as Illus-

trated by the History of a Western Nebraska
Town" (Bentley), *x*
Consumers, *xxiv,* 5–6, 127n2, 190–91, 200–201,
204, 265; crises and, 162, 172, 173, 229;
fixed price costs to, 109, 110, 111, 143;
industrial management and, *xx,* 33, 36, 39–
40, 43, 45, 46n8, 84–85, 115, 251; property
rights of, 12, 48, 49, 50, 51; waste and,
xvii–xviii, 73, 74–76, 77, 78, 80, 141, 150–58,
193, 260
Coolidge, Calvin, *xxiii*
Cooperatives, *xxiv,* 49, 83, 127n2, 139, 232–33,
262, 265, 270n6; British, 35, 56, 80, 82,
94n7, 111, 123, 147, 233, 237n6; farm, 103,
104–105, 233, 234, 237n7; government and,
45, 111, 224, 241, 246–47, 255n7; industry
and, 46n8, 80, 125, 235
Cooperative Wholesale Societies Limited of
England, 80–81, 94n7, 111
Cost of living, *xv,* 18, 56, 170n8, 187; wages
and, 24–25, 26–27, 179, 193n2, 260, 265;
waste and, 89–93, 150–58, 166–67, 179–80,
189, 191–92, 250, 265
Costs, *see* Prices; Production, costs
Cox, James M., *xiv*
Credit, *see* Banking
Creel, George, 216
Cudahy Packing Co., 114
Currency, 1, 12, 73; inflation, 150–53, 155,
170n11; issue, 83, 123, 127, 198

Dartmouth College case, 58
Debs, Eugene V., *xiv,* 214
Democracy, 4, 31, 59–60, 192, 238, 282; indus-
trial autocracy *versus, xv, xxi,* 38, 39–40, 44,
45, 68, 87, 137, 185–86, 219, 262, 276–77
Democratic Party, *xiv, xxii, xxiii,* 124, 219,
256–57, 259, 269
Denmark, 233
Denver, University of, *x*
Dewey, John, *x, xiii*
Dictatorship, *xi, xxi, xxiii,* 31. *See also* Indus-
try, autocracy of
Distribution: of goods, 79–83, 97–113, 115–18,
140–49, 152, 154, 180, 225, 233–34, 239, 243–
44, 252–53, 260, 265; of wealth, 14, 15–18,
28n6, 239, 260, 265

Edison, Thomas A., quoted, 146–47
Education, *ix–x, xxii,* 37, 89, 239, 262, 270n4;
agricultural, 264, 268; costs, 26; industrial,
86–87, 99, 100, 133–34, 137–38
Einstein, Albert, *xii*
Elgin Butter Board, 110
Ely, Richard, *x, xv*
England, 41, 55, 87, 95n11, 148n2, 165, 249,
270n5; cooperatives in, 35, 56, 80, 82, 94n7,
111, 125, 147, 233, 237n6; crises and, 168,
171n13, 172, 187; health in, 96n22; waste in,
78, 86–87
English Guild Socialists, 249